STRESEMANN AND THE GREATER GERMANY
1914-1918

STRESEMANN

and the *Greater Germany*

1914-1918

by Marvin L. Edwards

BOOKMAN ASSOCIATES, INC.

New York 3

To MARGA and AUDRAY

PREFACE

This study became possible when the unpublished papers of Dr. Stresemann came into the possession of the Allied governments as part of a vast collection of captured German documents and were opened up to research. Acknowledgment is therefore due to the recently dissolved German Documents section of the U. S. Department of State for its part in making these documents, in microfilm form, available to scholars at the National Archives in Washington. The author is also indebted to the Columbia University Libraries for making them even more conveniently accessible to him in New York. To Professor John H. Wuorinen a special obligation is recognized for kind support in many ways, all contributing to the completion of this book. Both Professor Wuorinen and Professor Fritz Stern read and criticized the completed manuscript and gave generously of their advice. Thanks are also due to Professor Peter Gay, the late Professor Walter Dorn, and to Dr. Hans Trefousse for many useful suggestions. Finally, I should like to express my appreciation to my wife, Marga Schuhmann Edwards, for assistance at all stages of the work.

M.L.E.

Glenside, Pennsylvania
June, 1962

CONTENTS

PART ONE:
STRESEMANN THE ANNEXATIONIST

PART TWO:
THE STRUGGLE FOR THE GREATER GERMANY

INTRODUCTION

The frequent newspaper headlines concerning Germany in the post-World War II era—early headlines regarding control of the Saar and a "new Locarno"; later, about German rearmament and entry into the North Atlantic Treaty Organization; and, more recently, about Germany's growing economic strength and her role between East and West—remind one of a previous encounter with similar problems in an already vague though not-too-distant past. They remind us, too, in spite of preoccupation with an East-West struggle of which a beleaguered Berlin in a divided Germany is the major battleground, that the addition of the complicating reality of Soviet power cannot obscure the fact that Germany must be dealt with not only as an element in a larger struggle but as a problem in itself, one which, even though we may not care to follow the skeins of its history back to the Investiture Conflict or the Golden Bull of Charles IV, must certainly be retraced to the first World War, its immediate background, and its settlement.

Gustav Stresemann, the subject of this study, provides a link to this earlier period. His life span (1878-1929) extended from the time of enthusiastic German expansion following the creation of Bismarck's Empire to the eve of dissolution of the Weimar Republic into Hitler's Third Reich. Stresemann was active in the political life of the Wilhelmine era as a member of the Reichstag both before and during the war. As Chancellor in the critical year 1923 and in each succeeding Cabinet until his death Germany's Foreign Minister, he seems to have become an embodiment of the Weimar Republic—evaluations of what one might call the political morality of both the man and the nation he represented have become indissolubly fused. Stresemann's role after the war in bringing Germany, the pariah among the nations, back into the world community of states comes easily to mind when we observe Germany's recent emergence from the chaos of military defeat and the removal of the stigma of Nazism under the leadership of Konrad Adenauer. Comparisons of Stresemann and Adenauer—of personalities, tasks, and techniques—have not been lacking.[1] The "European outlook" of the later Chancellor has no doubt been accepted or questioned in some cases contingent upon the view held as to the attributed European or non-European outlook of his predecessor.[2]

Stresemann has not been neglected in the growing historical literature of the post-war era. Since the late Twenties numerous Stresemann biographies have appeared; [3] the amount of material directly or indirectly concerned with the late German statesman has reached the point where a bibliography, published in 1953, listing in addition to his own writings more than one hundred books and articles about him, is already out of date.[4]

The problem is not that too little has been written about Stresemann, but rather that this material gives neither a complete nor a balanced picture of the man. The writers of the Twenties and early Thirties lacked the pertinent materials and stood too close for proper historical perspective, and Stresemann has not been spared the later attempts to read and write Hitler, "the barbarian on the Rhine," into almost every German action since the capture of Varus's eagles in the Teutoburger Wald.[5]

The result has been that Stresemann was caught up early in a whirlwind of extremist views and a veritable "Stresemann problem" has been created.[6] Hailed as a "good European," he has also been branded as a Machiavellian nationalist. Considered by some to have been a great champion of European pacification working incessantly to bridge the gulf between Germany and France, he has been branded by others as a "successful hypocrite" who merely "finessed" while Germany was regaining her military strength.[7]

Even a cursory examination of recent historical literature discloses the striking divergence of views regarding Stresemann. A closer inspection permits several observations: it is patent that the controversy concerns primarily the question of motivation, for charges of opportunism, lack of sincerity, duplicity, and ulterior motives have arisen in every quarter and have been met with counterclaims supporting Stresemann's motives and actions in shaping Germany's foreign policy.[8] It is apparent also that in this controversy the basic source material used has been the Stresemann *Vermaechtnis*,[9] the publication of which, despite the good intentions of its editor, has probably raised more questions than it has settled.[10]

Finally, it must be noted that in this rapidly growing Stresemann literature attention has been paid primarily to the period from 1923 to 1929 (once hailed as the Era of Fulfillment), which was marked by the termination of the Ruhr conflict, the settling of the reparations problem through the Dawes and Young Plans, the signing of the Locarno Pacts, and the agreement for the evacuation of the Rhineland. The disputants over Stresemann, concerned with his activities as Chancellor and Foreign Minister, have touched hardly at all upon his many years of public life prior to 1923, and when they have it has generally been only to state briefly that during the war Stresemann had been an ardent nationalist and annexationist, that he had supported the unrestricted submarine warfare, and had believed in Germany's ultimate victory. They emphasize either that a metamorphosis took place sometime between the end of the World War and Stresemann's assumption of ministerial office under the Weimar Republic or just as emphatically assert that such a fundamental change never did occur.[11]

In view of the fact that Stresemann lived forty of his fifty-one years under the Empire, there can be no doubt as to the importance of the Wilhelmine era in the shaping of the man, his character, thoughts, and aspirations. The pre-Weimar period cannot be dismissed with a few paragraphs before turning to Stresemann's later career, for, even though one might emphasize his activities as Foreign Minister from 1923 to 1929, to comprehend fully the post-war epoch in which he played such an important role or to understand the role which he then played would be impossible without prior study and understanding of this earlier period. Merely to ask, "What did Stresemann plan to do for Germany after clearing away the wreckage of the lost war?" is to bring home the realization that death truncated this culminating phase of Stresemann's career before he was able to complete his tasks or even to lay down completely, so far as the materials now available tell us, exactly what he thought those tasks to be.

The period of the Great War of 1914-1918 represents, in fact, the central panel in the triptych which made up Gustav Stresemann's life. From this key period one may look backward into the era in which William II sought leadership for Germany with his "new course," in which Bülow through insouciance and Bethmann-Hollweg through maladroitness let Germany drift toward the catastrophe of war.[12] It was then that Stresemann, son of a lower middle-class purveyor of Berlin *Weissbier,* moved from the university as a Doctor of Philosophy in political economy into industry and thence into politics.[13] It was then, as a member of the National Liberal Party's Reichstag delegation, sharing the enthusiasm of German *Bürgertum* for the "world policy" best exemplified by the expansion of the fleet (which contained so little of the *Realpolitik* it purported to follow) that Stresemann began his rise to a position of political prominence.[14]

One may also look forward beyond the war when, with the collapse of the Empire, the third phase of Stresemann's life began, that which gave him the task of ameliorating the disaster of the defeat and of leading Germany back to a position of equality among the nations. The war epoch, consequent of the first period, determinant of the last, holds together and gives meaning to Stresemann's life. It is with his relationship to the issues and events of the Great War that this study is primarily concerned.

The acquisition by the National Archives in Washington of Stresemann's personal papers, the so-called *Nachlass,* recovered from the mass of captured enemy documents at the close of the second World War and now available in microfilm form,[15] has made possible a new approach to the subject, and that portion of the *Nachlass* pertaining to the period 1923 to 1929 has already attracted historians.[16] It may be pointed out, however, that more than half of the microfilmed material is concerned with the earlier part of Stresemann's life, particularly with the war years, and this portion of the *Nachlass,* which serves as the principal source for the present study, has not previously been made use of.[17]

What, we may ask, was Stresemann trying to accomplish during these eventful years? What were the delimiting factors of his own nature and of his environment? Can we find anything here which will help us to appraise better the motives and actions of this controversial figure? Stresemann himself, in testifying in 1927 before a Reichstag committee concerned with determining the causes of the German collapse in 1918, discussed his war-time activities under three general headings: the aims and conduct of the war; the domestic and constitutional questions; and the problems of the period of collapse.[18] His differentiation has suggested the approach to these matters in the pages that follow.

PART: ONE

STRESEMANN THE ANNEXATIONIST

Chapter I

WAR ORIGINS

The crisis which followed the assassination at Sarajevo found Germany clinging in desperation to Austria, her only ally, who was now plunging Europe into a "limited" war. The German people were in the main unaware of the tortured diplomacy which had alienated both England and Russia and destroyed the authoritative position achieved under Bismarck. Alive only to the danger to their country they were convinced that theirs was a defensive war.[1] Germans from all parties, having heard the solemn words of Emperor and Chancellor calling for support against the enemies of the Fatherland, responded patriotically to the war declarations.[2] The Reichstag acknowledged the Emperor's statement that he knew "no more parties, only Germans," by proclaiming a political truce *(Burgfrieden)* which was to submerge all party differences for the duration of the war, while the Government announced a state of siege which imposed a rigorous censorship on the discussion both of military operations and of the war aims of the Government.[3] With these tasks accomplished and war credits voted, the Reichstag adjourned leaving the conduct of affairs to the Emperor and his Chancellor, thus abandoning at the outset of the conflict what little power it had to those whose inept policy had brought Germany into its present critical situation.[4]

If in this awesome moment in Germany's history there was passivity in the patriotism of the Reichstag, the response of the Imperial military establishment was completely active, for no time was lost in launching the German war machine in gigantic operations on both Western and Eastern fronts.[5]

The rapid advance through Belgium, the occupation of
Rheims, and the rollback of a French offensive in Lorraine,
together with the brilliant successes in the East against over-
whelming Russian odds—successes which made the reputa-
tions of Hindenburg and Ludendorff—hid from the German
people the truth of the Marne, the failure to bring the war
quickly to a triumphant end, which for German arms was
not only a tradition but a strategic necessity.[6]

1. August 1914

The outbreak of the war which was to play such an important role in his life seems to have taken Gustav Stresemann completely by surprise. He learned of the assassination
of Archduke Francis Ferdinand while attending the Kiel re-
gatta in company with Ernst Bassermann, leader of the National Liberal Party. While his brief diary notations record
his shock at the news, they reflect no presentiment of the
war which was to follow.[7]

Stresemann had been out of political office since 1912 following the defeat in his race for re-election to the Reichstag
in that year.[8] In the ensuing period he was more attentive to
domestic issues than to questions of foreign policy, with regard to which he seemed more concerned about the timidity
of those who directed Germany's diplomacy than with the
possibility of repercussions to a more aggressive German attitude.[9] He keenly desired to regain his seat in the parliament,
and his correspondence reveals a preoccupation with the
practical side of local politics—finding a district where his
electoral victory would be assured and getting the promise
of full support from the party leadership for the campaign.
By May of 1914 Stresemann had obtained both a constituency and the pledge of party backing and became busy with
fund raising and other preparations for the coming election
campaign.[10]

Organizational work in business, from which he had originally entered into politics and to which he had returned following his defeat in 1912, also occupied Stresemann's close attention in the immediate pre-war period.[11] As an expert in this field his talents were much in demand.[12] However, neither in this area nor as a commentator on world economic matters did he manifest any uneasiness concerning world peace. On the contrary, in typical economic articles written in the late spring and early summer of 1914, he pointed optimistically to the pending trade agreement between Germany and Russia as a vital measure in strengthening world peace, which he regarded as dependent upon the preservation of the economic interests of the Great Powers.[13] In order to strengthen the *Deutsch-Amerikanischer Wirtschaftsverband*, which he had helped to create, he had in the summer of 1914 made tentative arrangements for a business trip to the United States, and in the event that his plans for re-election to the Reichstag did not materialize he was prepared to sail for New York in September.[14] The events of the summer, however, were decisive: the election campaign was an abbreviated one, in fact a mere formality, and when the Reichstag reconvened in December Stresemann was once again a member of that body, beginning a new phase of his public career, this time in a nation at war.[15]

2. The War Guilt Question

Stresemann made clear his position concerning the origins of the war at the outset in speeches and published articles as well as in his personal correspondence. He shared fully the popular view that the Germans were fighting in defense of the Reich and were not morally responsible for having caused the war; this was the theme of a series of speeches culminating in the widely publicized addresses at Dresden and Aurich in December, 1914, which brought to a close his campaign for re-election to the Reichstag.[16] Stresemann supported this stand in an early pamphlet concerned with the economic aspects of the war by pointing out that Germany had made huge agricultural exports as late as July, 1914, much going to countries soon to be at war with Germany, a fact, he noted, which "even more than all the White Books of the Government" proved that Germany did not, "as Sir Edward Grey asserted, seek the war and for a long time prepare for it." [17] The newly elected Deputy also rejected the attempt of the British Foreign Secretary to fasten the responsibility for mobilization upon Germany by the "conjurer's trick" of citing—as Grey had done—the premature announcement of Russian mobilization made by the *Berliner Lokal Anzeiger*.[18]

"There is no doubt," declared Stresemann before the Finance Committee of the Reichstag, "that it was right to answer the Russian mobilization with our own." [19]

Stresemann did not believe it necessary, however, to reply to all such charges of German war guilt for he was convinced that the entire past history of the Empire proved that Germany's desire for peace could not rightfully be impugned. He pointed to what he termed Germany's policy of "political resignation" in world affairs which Germany had pursued for decades "for the sake of peace," a policy which had not attempted to capitalize on the difficulties in which other Great Powers had found themselves from time to time, as when England fought against the Boers. He recounted how Germany "had looked on" while "all North Africa was being divided"; how Germany had kept the peace while others had forcibly built colonial empires or carved out spheres of influence—the world could always depend upon "the love of peace of the Emperor and the German nation." [20]

The war guilt issue tended to become submerged as attention turned from origins to the unfolding spectacle of the war itself; [21] but whenever it arose Stresemann took a clearcut stand in keeping with his views indicated above. In framing the war aims petition of the Great Economic Organizations, he wrote of the war which had been "forced upon" Germany.[22] When the Entente rejected the German peace offer of December, 1916, and called instead for restitution and compensation, he was indignant that "the states guilty of bringing about the war" had made such demands of Germany.[23] At the same time he angrily attacked the Chancellor, Bethmann-Hollweg, for his words spoken in August, 1914, concerning "the wrong to Belgium," which had given grounds for the charges of Germany's enemies of German responsibility.[24] In January, 1918, when Prince Lichnowsky, the former German Ambassador to England, published a brochure attributing to Germany the guilt for the outbreak of the war, Stresemann objected strongly in the Main Committee of the Reichstag and pressed the Foreign Office to take action to put a stop to the former diplomat's activities.[25]

It was not until the war had ended in German defeat that the war guilt question *(Kriegsschuldfrage)* arose as a formidable "moral and political issue" in the field of German diplomacy and in domestic politics as well.[26] Even before the peace treaty was submitted to the German delegation in 1919, however, Stresemann, in an address delivered at Jena to his newly organized German People's Party, upbraided the Social Democrats for indulging in the "political masochism" of self-accusation of war guilt when Germany "should be struggling to build up its foreign policy and world position anew." He acknowledged an "instability" and "clumsiness" of German diplomacy if compared with that of the other Powers in the last weeks before the war, even admitted the political inadequacy of German diplomacy of the prewar era, but denied that this implied a "moral guilt before the world." [27]

There was no change in Stresemann's outlook in the years which followed. "I do not wish to leave any doubts with you about my position in this [war guilt] question," he wrote to an American acquaintance, Phelan Beale, who, in 1921, had queried him on several points concerning the war. "You may be sure that no people has been done more injustice by the public opinion of the world than the German people in this war, and if there exists a right and a claim for restitution the German people . . . are the first which could make such a claim." That the United States saw the Germans as "guilty of the whole misfortune of the war" he attributed to the failure of German propaganda and the cleverness of the English in this field, but he pointed out that even Lloyd George, "who more than any other man led world opinion against Germany," had in a recent speech retracted the claim "that the origin of the war is traceable to Germany, German statesmen, and German policies." [28]

Before the Reichstag in the same year Stresemann cited a speech of 1916 wherein President Wilson had declared that "no one could know how the war had begun and what had caused the conflict," and from denouncing the war guilt accusation as historically absurd, Stresemann went on to deny the moral basis of the entire Versailles Treaty.[29]

Declamatory speeches, however, do not measure the full extent of Stresemann's activities in "combating the war guilt lie." [30] He helped to create and represented his own political group in an inter-party organization established for this purpose, and correspondence between the Reichstag Deputy and the then Major Stülpnagel at the Bendlerstrasse reveals that Stresemann was instrumental in obtaining secret funds from the Foreign Office in 1921 to be used by the *Reichswehr* for propaganda in England and the United States against the war guilt clause and the treaty of which it was a part. He served as intermediary between the two agencies for the transfer of at least twenty-five thousand marks for the purpose described.[31]

What changed was not Stresemann's basic outlook but his position and responsibilities, and as Foreign Minister after 1923 he was not at all times able to express himself with the same freedom he had previously exercised. He might cautiously suggest, as he did shortly after accession to office, that other nations follow Germany's lead in opening their archives to permit a full investigation of the causes of the war.[32] In the heat of the Ruhr conflict he might dare to speak out to the people of Hagen in rejection of the "war guilt lie," calling upon the nations whose "consciences were clear" to be prepared as was Germany to submit the question to an impartial international tribunal.[33]

The precarious position of the German Foreign Minister, negotiating with the Entente Governments regarding the Dawes Plan, Locarno, and German entry into the League of Nations, while at the same time trying to placate the influential Nationalist forces within Germany, perhaps explains the frequently changing tone in the expression of Stresemann's war guilt views.[34]

It is clear, however, that Stresemann no more accepted Article 231 of the Versailles Treaty than did the German Nationalists. He differed from them in that he saw the denial of the charge not only as an emotional issue but also as a means of invalidating the entire peace treaty, and he worked consistently toward that goal. When, however, it appeared that concessions might be forthcoming from the Entente, he was willing to soft-pedal his views and demands insofar as pressures within Germany would permit him to do so.[35]

Despite the political sagacity which made him realize that German declarations would not make the Allies formally alter the peace treaty, he never put the war guilt question completely aside. In 1924 at the Dawes Plan meeting in London, in 1925 at the time of the Locarno meetings, in 1927 on the occasion of the dedication by Hindenburg of a monument at Tannenberg, Stresemann supported in varying degrees the repudiation of German war guilt.[36] In 1929 in one of his last parliamentary battles, which concerned the repara-

tions question, he reasserted his stand against the charge that
Germany alone was responsible for the war.[37]

3. English Economic Rivalry

Where, then, if not with Germany, did the responsibility
for the war lie? It is perhaps not unexpected that Stresemann,
a National Liberal, a member of the middle class, and associated with business interests, should point to England,
rather than to Russia against whom the Social Democrats
directed their antagonism at the outbreak of the war or even
France, Germany's traditional foe.[38] England was the *Haupt-
feind* and instigator of the war; economic rivalry and jealousy were the motives.[39] These were views which Stresemann
expressed from the beginning of the conflict.[40]

In his principal campaign speeches at Dresden and Aurich
in December, 1914, published in pamphlet form the same
month and widely circulated, Stresemann asserted that the
war was caused by the attempt to destroy the Reich by an
"England jealous of the growing strength of Germany" which
challenged her superiority, because England who "gloried in
the traditional invincibility of her fleet" was "envious of the
growing German colonies, fleet and commerce." [41] He refur-
bished the cliché wherein an Englishman had declared that
"the day the German fleet is destroyed, every Englishman
will be a pound-note richer," and remarked how apropos
had been the lines in parody of the German national anthem
which had once appeared in *Kladderadatsch:*

> Alles, alles ueber Deutschland
> An der Spitze Albion! [42]

Stresemann repeatedly stressed that the war was one of
"envy against German development—*propter invidiam!*" [43]
"[England] begrudged us the Reich and its economic development," he declared before the Reichstag:

They loved us and were friendly to us . . . as long as we were politically impotent, as long as we were a nation of poets and thinkers. When Michel the dreamer became Michel the seafarer, when the political unification and development of our economic strength came. . . . when we created the seaports for the German world trade that insured Germany's economic position in the world, then began the economic struggle even before the clash of arms came. England's whole history shows this struggle against us. . . .[44]

Stresemann frequently supported his strictures against England with references to a 1907 speech of Albert Ballin, the head of the Hamburg-America Lines, in which Ballin had referred to England's policies of ship subvention, patent laws, and discrimination against German-made goods.[45] These Stresemann cited as examples of "how, through England's envy and disfavor, the world war had been unfettered." [46]

As editor of *Saechsische Industrie* Stresemann also publicized his indictment of England in articles concerning the economic aspects and problems of the war.[47] A war aims petition of his Saxon industrial group to the State Ministry was justified on the grounds that the war involved not only political matters but economic questions as well, for it owed its origins "primarily to motives of economic envy of England toward Germany." [48] Similarly, his support, previously mentioned, of a like petition of the Six Economic Organizations rested on this same belief that "in this greatest of all economic wars" England led the battle directed toward Germany's destruction.[49] It is clear that Stresemann saw the war not as a clash of "national or cultural ideas" but as a "struggle of competitors" *(Konkurrenzkampf),* forced upon Germany by England, and one which would be "carried on in the economic field even after the cannons [were] silent." [50] Stresemann's private correspondence is in the same vein, and in addition he frequently called attention to the "encirclement policy" of Edward VII as an important contributory factor.[51]

Stresemann's extravagant charges against England terminated with Germany's defeat, which forced a more defensive stand against criminations of German war guilt. He was then more apt to ignore such long-range causes as the Anglo-German rivalry and to stress the proximate causes of the war and in so doing divide the blame among all the Powers. The heightened Franco-German tension during the Poincaré ministries at a time when England, whose intermediacy Stresemann sought, was assuming a more conciliatory attitude also silenced the war-time polemicist. It is difficult, however, to overestimate the importance of Stresemann's anti-English outlook during the war itself as a force in shaping his ideas on the conduct of the war.[52]

4. Historical Parallels

Stresemann was careful to point out that his strong reactions to England's efforts "to destroy German economic life" had nothing to do with "Pan-German shouting." [53] By this Stresemann meant that his statements were not mere emotional charges against an enemy but were based on facts supplied by a thorough knowledge of history as well as of economics.[54]

It was from this font that Stresemann frequently drew the comparison between the situation which Germany then faced and that which existed when Rome demanded ships, weapons, and means of defense from the Carthaginians, and then moved their cities from the sea "so they could never again carry on trade." [55] He added that the historical parallel was not an exact one, for Germany "with her idea of the state" resembled Rome more than Britain with its "mercenary armies"; and Germany, like Rome, would gain the ultimate victory in the war.[56]

It was in the Napoleonic wars of the early nineteenth century, however, that Stresemann found the parallel he sought.[57] Then, as now, the fight against England had been the fight for freedom of the seas, against her misuse of the blockade; then, as now, England's "hatred and tenacity to destroy" were directed at the nation which might challenge her world dominion. In both wars England controlled and misled public opinion, and instigated other nations to fight against her enemy. He noted as ironies of history that Germany, in fighting against England, was carrying out "the life work of the great man of another nation," while Napoleon's France was "giving its life blood for England." [58]

To the members of the Prussian Lower House, who had invited him to speak on this topic, in January, 1917, Stresemann noted that while the historians Treitschke and Sybel were justified "as Prussian patriots" in taking a narrow view of Bonaparte as a mere conqueror, the picture was different "in the frame of world history." He looked upon Prussia's battle against Napoleon and her defeat as part of a "painful history of diplomatic and military incapacity" on Prussia's part, pointing out that Napoleon had had no quarrel with Prussia and would have preferred an alliance with her to war; the Emperor's first action upon entering Berlin had been the proclamation of the Continental Blockade against England, and Tilsit, too, had been "only an episode in the Emperor's battle against Britain." Stresemann told the members of the Prussian Lower House that he would "stand with Ranke and Lenz" in the emphasis of the necessity of Napoleon's struggle against England, then as now "the disturber of the world's peace."

5. Russia, France, and Sarajevo

In placing the onus on Britain and stressing economic causes Stresemann glossed over French and Russian responsibility for the war. Concerning these two Entente Powers Stresemann wrote (for the press in September, 1914) that although the first war declarations had involved Russia and France "neither Petersburg nor Paris" was "the seat of the powers opposed to Germany." He labeled both as merely the "willing pupils" in a war conducted by England.[59]

Stresemann was able to view with a degree of equanimity the French and Russian roles in the war. The former (he asserted) fought "under the delusion that Alsace-Lorraine was French" and wished to return to France; also to erase the humiliation of Sedan and regain the prestige, the *gloire,* of the Napoleonic era. The Russian Tsar had indeed gone against all tradition in defending "the Belgrade assassins," but Stresemann expressed doubt that Russia, on its own, would have started a war with a stronger enemy so soon after its defeat by the Japanese.[60] "In spite of all the systematic attempts, through a distortion of history and incomplete dipplomatic documents to portray Russia as the incendiary of the war," he wrote, "although the external causes appear to lie in Petersburg, the real cause is England's determination to push Germany out of the world market." [61]

What he termed his "philosophic attitude" toward England's allies may well have been an expression of his confidence in a German victory over both of them.[62] Stresemann saw slight prospect by the end of 1914 of a French reversal of Sedan and believed that despite the preponderance of Russian manpower the Germans, with their courage and the generalship of Hindenburg, had little to fear from "the unspirited Russian mass-army." [63]

Stresemann tended to discount the events which followed the assassination at Sarajevo, declaring that "one should not portray as unqualified judges those who say that this world war was not decided upon in the last ten days of July [1914] . . . but that the basic causes lay in all the things which had gone before . . ." [64]

Yet, in Stresemann's comments on the events of the Serbian crisis a few deviations from the usual anti-English stereotypes are revealed. Early in the war he asserted that Germany "had held to her alliance with Austria in an hour of danger *in alter Nibelungentreue,*" [65] and in 1917, writing to General Ludendorff to urge that faltering Austrian morale be bolstered, he suggested that an appeal be made to "the natural instincts of the German in Austria" to reawaken the former love for Germany to the intensity shown "when Germany, through Austria, was drawn into the war." [66] Earlier, in answering Grey's charges concerning German mobilization, he had concurred with remarks of Bethmann-Hollweg, who had offered as evidence of Germany's desire for peace "the great efforts . . . to the last minute to persuade Austria-Hungary to be satisfied in the Serbian question with the occupation of Belgrade." [67] There is, finally, an interesting comment in a letter which Stresemann wrote on June 9, 1915, to Senator Biermann of Bremen:

The question who caused this war will always be answered with difficulty. The immediate reason, to be sure, lay in England's efforts to erect a strong power coalition against us in order to force us down. For we got a hint of that when, after the murder at Sarajevo, we left no doubt concerning our inclination to get started immediately. One cannot object to that if one keeps in mind that for us each year would have decreased the possibility of victory, and perhaps two years would have made it impossible.[68]

There is no reason to believe, however, that Stresemann was not truly convinced that England's role was exactly that which he so frequently voiced. Certainly his outlook was typical of the middle-class—merchants and professors alike— which found in Lissauer's *Hymn of Hate* the truest expression of its anti-English feelings.[69]

6. Some Broader and Narrower Views

Notwithstanding his occasional excursions into the realm of historical comparison, Stresemann prided himself on being one of the "circle of men of practical life," and his words were directed to business and industrial groups and to the general public.[70] Yet at times, in articles rather than in public addresses, he was able to look for a moment beyond the confines of a narrow nationalism to the larger implications of the war.

This war, which Germany did not want (he wrote) would be costly to all. Certainly England, which had made temporary economic gains by taking Germany's place in various countries, would not profit in the long run, for her temporary advantages would not compensate her for the loss of her normal trade with Germany. Regardless of the final outcome of the war, England would emerge from it "as the conquered one" in a certain sense, for while some countries "might be able to buy peace only through large concessions," England had already begun to make such concessions, as evidenced by her giving up control of her prized East Asiatic markets. "We need not rejoice over this," Stresemann soberly commented,

for connected with English defeat in East Asia is the defeat of the white race by the rising yellow race. White rule received its first setback when the Russian dreadnaughts were destroyed by the Japanese fleet in the sea battle of Tsushima; it ends now with . . . the self-confidence of that aspiring State of the East so strengthened that it has been able to treat China like a tributary nation and to extend its position as a world power in Hongkong, Nanking, and Peking. The great world commercial establishment of John Bull, London, has liquidated its East Asiatic branch, which belonged among the firmest pillars of its world businesses, and transferred it to Japan. Germany has lost in this war till now Kiaochow; England has lost her influence in all of East Asia, perhaps in part of India, and the collapse of a world prestige, till now strongly defended, is announced to the twentieth century.[71]

The military end of the war (Stresemann wrote) would not terminate its economic aspects. He predicted that England would turn to a protective tariff, and in place of the old England would arise "the imperialist Greater Britain of Joseph Chamberlain," closely bound to its colonies politically and economically through raised preferential tariffs. Whether or not this would allow London to maintain its position as a world shipping center Stresemann considered questionable, but conceded that in any event it would "increase Germany's difficulties in overseas markets," difficulties which would be real enough in the face of a "shattered world market" which hardly permitted hope of a lasting peace.[72]

In the rise of the United States in the face of this altered economic world the writer saw a new problem, not only for Germany but for all of Europe:

If one were to imagine Europe as a single great unit opposite the United States, how wretched then is the picture it offers! Our enemies estimate their war costs at more than a hundred billions; the sum that we and our allies spend will not be much less, and on these tremendous sums interest must be paid, which increases the state debt and makes new taxes and tariffs necessary. In contrast stands the mighty structure of the United States . . . which up to now has not only been spared the storms of this world war in a time of upheaval of all economic values in old Europe, but through a billion orders for war supplies has considerably increased its gold balance and strengthened its economic power. There can be no doubt that this will in future lead to a preponderance of American power or at least to increased difficulty for European trade in those areas in which European and American industry compete, just as in the East the strengthening of Japan's political influence will also create economic difficulties. . . .[73]

Stresemann did not confine himself to the economic field. He noted that after the war Europe would be "a convulsive and bleeding body." "We can indemnify and rebuild destroyed provinces in Europe," he wrote, "but the lost intelligence of hundreds of thousands who in the future would have been our collaborators in great new ideals, on great new works of culture, science, and technique, we cannot reclaim." [74]

In the intellectual field as well, he observed, the war had also "shipwrecked the union of nations"; it would not be easily recovered, and an understanding among the nations would be equally difficult to restore. "If a nation like Germany which has contributed so much to civilization is now to be branded Hun and barbarian," he wrote, "it will not be easy to build a bridge to those who use those names." While he would regret it if all these ties were cut, Stresemann averred, if any nation could stand "intellectual isolation" it would be Germany, which had "given the world much more" than the world had given back "in cultural things." [75] His speculation had led him back again to the narrow nationalism on which he based his concept of the "Greater Germany."

Chapter II

WAR AIMS: THE GREATER GERMANY

During the initial stages of the war little was said by the German Government regarding war aims: "Not lust of conquest" but defense of the Fatherland represented the official viewpoint.[1] The official censorship, which through supervision of press and meetings controlled to a great extent the expression of public opinion, actually enhanced the popular illusion of victory which came with the rapid unfolding of the Schlieffen plan in its initial stages; and even while the Chancellor, aware of the check to German arms, hoped to lighten the burden of war on two fronts by a conciliatory peace with one of Germany's adversaries, the German people began to think of war goals beyond the mere defense of German soil.[2]

The erroneous belief in an early triumph was not the only reason. Of major significance was the involvement of entire peoples in the war, for the passions and animosities, both instinctive and deliberately aroused in order to gain mass support, contributed to a situation which made it impossible to terminate the war in a compromise peace.[3] The insistence on tangible gains to compensate for the tremendous sacrifices, both human and material, made and to come; the desire to punish the enemy nations considered responsible for the carnage; and the appeal for security against the repetition of such a war—all these stimulated unofficial demands for an enlargement of German territories at the expense of her foes.[4]

With the rapidly mounting cost of the war a *status quo* peace came to be looked upon as one entailing losses which could not be borne, and there were few vocal Germans who were not inclined at one time or another toward an annexationist program, or at least to the belief that, where such a policy would not prolong the war, any territories taken in a defensive war should be retained when the peace was made.[5]

Economic demands, such as those for the acquisition of certain coal and iron regions of France and for the agricultural lands of the East, also played a strong role; while nationalism, with a strong suggestion of the racial motif of a later era, was a vital force behind the demand that the Baltic areas, peopled by Germans, should be made a part of the Fatherland. The requirements of military and naval strategy supported the call for annexation of fortified French territories, protective coastal areas, particularly in Belgium, and strategic bases for the fleet.

There was a further relationship between the demands for territorial aggrandizement and the problem of domestic reform. "Partisanship for large war aims and opposition against the so-called *Neuorientierung* usually went hand in hand," wrote Bethmann-Hollweg in 1921. "At least such a relationship developed during the course of the war." [6]

Due to the variety of interests indicated above, there was no single program among those classified positively as annexationists. Some advocated the gains in the West—annexation of Belgium and the French ore districts; some supported the acquisition of agricultural lands in the East; others spoke in terms of a new Central European bloc, a *Mitteleuropa*, under German leadership; [7] still others—with the Ottoman alliance —favored German penetration into the Middle East; and others yet emphasized an enlarged colonial empire in Africa or elsewhere. While some proponents of annexations held to one of these ideas, others were supporters of two, several, or all, and it was "the vicissitudes of the war . . . [which gave] . . . now to one, now to another, the chief prominence in public discussion and in the press." [8]

For the sake of domestic accord in the interests of the external struggle, Bethmann-Hollweg was compelled to make progressively stronger, if ambiguous, statements regarding Germany's war aims.[9] In the annexation question were soon disclosed the disparity of aims, the social antagonisms, and the internal disunity of the German Empire. It was the war aims controversy which destroyed the political truce of the parties and influenced the making of war policies, both military and diplomatic, which led to ultimate defeat.[10]

1. War Origins and War Aims

Stresemann's views on war aims for Germany can place him only in the category of "annexationist," and to broaden this description to "ardent annexationist" would perhaps bring it even closer to the mark.[11] Both his critics and supporters during the Weimar era have acknowledged (for their own purposes) this aspect of his wartime career.[12] Stresemann himself did not deny his previous stand on this issue, although he euphemistically referred to himself as a "wartime optimist." [13]

His affiliations and interests, both before and during the war, placed him in the camp of those who supported a positive war aims program and determined the scope and intensity of his annexationist views. Even his first brief political experience with the National Social Union of Friedrich Naumann had been for the young Stresemann primarily an expression of a strong national feeling, an exultation in the imperial idea,[14] rather than support of the social program of the liberal Naumann, from whom he soon separated.[15] He found what he sought in the National Liberal Party, which had prided itself on its "unswerving loyalty to Emperor and Empire" from the time of Bismarck and the *Reichsgründung*, a patriotic feeling which gradually found expression in a "forceful militant imperialism." [16]

The National Liberal Party was also the businessman's

party, and Stresemann was a businessman. Reference has already been made to his leadership of Saxon industry and high position in the League of German Industrialists, an organization of the finished goods industries. A war-time affiliation of the latter group with the Central Association of German Industrialists brought Stresemann into close contact with the leaders of heavy industry, the "chimney barons" who were predominant in the Rhineland-Westphalia circles of the National Liberal Party.[17] Stresemann's membership in the Hansa League reflected his interests in the promotion of foreign trade, the shipping and ship-building industries, and the navy.[18]

Stresemann became a member of the Pan-German League in 1907, when he first entered the Reichstag as a Deputy. It was in the National Liberal Party that the League, dedicated to the creation of a "greater Germany," found its greatest strength within the parliament.[19] During the war he was in close touch with such Pan-German leaders as Heinrich Class, Dietrich Schäfer, Baron von Vietinghoff-Scheel, and Freiherr von Gebsattel, as well as with Alfred Hugenberg, one of the League's most earnest supporters, and General Keim, the head of the Army League, one of the numerous off-shoots of the Pan-German organization. Stresemann had been a supporter of the Colonial Society and the Navy League, Pan-German affiliates, since the beginning of his active political career.

A National Liberal on close terms with Bassermann, the Party's staunchly imperialist leader; prominent, despite his youth—he was thirty-six at the time of the outbreak of the war—in German economic life; allied with men of a Pan-German point of view, Stresemann took a position on the war aims question which reflected these interests and associations.[20]

The conviction that Germany had been drawn into the conflict against her will, despite years of efforts to maintain the peace, drew from him the conclusion that Germany could place "no faith in agreements"; that only through her strength, and, more, through the assertion of that strength so as to obtain "real guaranties" as distinguished from "paper" ones, could she protect her interests and insure her future.[21]

Stresemann's conviction that England, in his opinion the instigator of the war and Germany's principal enemy, would wage war to the very limits of her capacity and never willingly "give up her control of the seas" or her efforts to dominate the world economy, led him to the conclusion that Germany must secure "real guaranties" rather than rely on treaties which would not be honored.[22]

He believed that Germany's future could not be assured by a *status quo* peace, since this would not provide the required assurances against England, nor compensate for the heavy expenses and sacrifices which thus far had been made in the war, and which "the German people were determined to make in order to triumph." [23]

If one could place no faith in treaties; if one could not trust one's enemies unless they were weakened until unable to make war; if one could not accept a *status quo* peace for the additional reason that it failed to compensate for the losses already suffered, the only remaining alternative was to carry on the war to the point where Germany could dictate the peace terms.[24] In short, there must be a German victory, one which would provide for the Empire's economic security through the opening of the world market to Germany, with freedom of the seas guaranteed by a strong German fleet. There must be a victory which would bring again into the Reich territories which "had once been German," a victory which would unite "Germans all over the world" in a "feeling of glory" for their Fatherland.[25] Stresemann envisioned a "Greater Germany" rising from the war, created by continental annexations to gain secured frontiers in the West and in the East as well as by such colonial extensions and increased seapower as might be demanded by German economic and military interests. With these would come a Central European tariff union on as large a scale as possible in order to counter the war-time loss of world markets and the boycott of German goods.[26]

2. The Western Expansion Program

While Stresemann did not deviate from this war aims program outlined above, except for what might be termed tactical reasons, his attention was directed at one time or another to different aspects of it, viz., in the spring of 1918, when Russia left the war, a "free Baltic" was for the moment of chief interest to him. From the beginning of the war, however, until the German collapse in the late summer of its fifth year Stresemann was primarily concerned with the western war aims, an attitude he shared with the leaders of heavy industry, the Pan-Germans, and much of the middle class from which these groups drew the preponderance of their membership.[27] The political, economic, and military aspirations of this vocal nationalistic segment of the German people were brought together in a comprehensive program of demands,[28] and to these, in numerous speeches, pamphlets, and letters, Stresemann gave expression.[29]

From France Germany must take a strip of coastal area from the Du Nord and Pas de Calais Departments. Boulogne, he hoped, would become German, and "the black-white-red flag must fly over the roofs of Calais," which would become a "German Gibraltar." [30] The Southern part of the Calais Department and that of Du Nord, together with the Longwy-Briey region, would provide the coal and iron ore which would insure German independence, at the same time weakening the French economy.[31] A part of Southern Belgium might be given to France in compensation in the hope of a later reconciliation, but in any case France must lose her border fortresses and any other areas, e.g., in the Vosges, which the military leaders might demand as necessary for German security.[32] In addition to this correction *(Berichtigung)* of continental frontiers, France must cede all rights which she had acquired in Morocco.[33]

Belgium must be attached *(angegliedert)* to Germany in some way, perhaps in a relationship similar to that between England and her colonies. At the least Belgium must be divided so that "Liege would be Prussian," Antwerp "a free Reich city," and Flanders and Hainaut German colonies "without representational rights in the Reichstag." [34] Stresemann later called for "absolute supremacy" *(Obergeltung)* over all Belgium with economic, military, and political domination *(Oberherrschaft)* by Germany.[35]

Stresemann prefaced his demands on Belgium with the explanation that until the nineteenth century its history had been a part of German history, culturally as well as politically. Its heroes, Egmont and Hoorn, had been Germans; the names of its cities had originally been German; and in 1815 Lüttich (Liege) had petitioned the Congress of Vienna to become German again. In its present form Belgium was not a real state at all in a national sense, only "an artificial buffer state, a forced, political creation." [36]

He supported his call for annexation of Belgium with a demand for the protection of the rights of the Flemish people; [37] and he also pointed out that a land "conquered with so much blood must not again be relinquished." [38] His basic argument, however, was that possession of Belgium was a guaranty of German seapower and of Germany's "military and economic future vis-à-vis England." This was interpreted by Stresemann and his colleagues not as a policy of conquest but rather as a means of guaranteeing "permanent peace," i.e., of preventing a renewal of the war by England.[39]

Annexationists differed on just how much of France should be placed under German control, and they did not concur as to the ultimate solution of the Belgian problem.[40] The Pan-Germans, including Stresemann, were in complete agreement, however, that Belgium had lost all right to independence, for a restored Belgium would be a "vassal state of England and France." [41] In the face of the German-English rivalry a neutral Belgium would be a fiction, a sham to be ended permanently—the Belgian coast must be a base either for Germany or her enemies.[42]

Stresemann deemed it of paramount importance that, together with the French coastal regions mentioned above, the Belgian coast be held so that German naval power might break out of the "wet triangle" and reach the open Atlantic.[43] Colonies and coaling stations for the fleet would follow, for by moving up to the "world ocean" Germany would be assured of her world position, not through dependence on treaties or on England's good will but through her own power.[44] With sea power all else would be added; without it Germany would be at England's mercy.[45] The Western annexation program would guarantee this sea power and with it peace. Belgium was the key, and "the man who would give up Belgium without having guaranteed Germany's economic freedom would deserve to be hanged from the gallows." [46]

3. The "Free Baltic"

In the East as in the West Stresemann's annexationist views were closely tied to those of the Pan-Germans, heavy industry, and to the proprietary agrarian interests allied with them.[47] The annexations made in the West were to be balanced economically in the East by "increased agricultural territory" and militarily by "better East Prussian borders." [48] Courland and Esthonia were to become colonies as part of an "absolute annexation of the Baltic sea provinces," which would include a strip of Polish land from Petrikau through

Grodno, and from Vilna as far as the Narew bay, "so that Petersburg would become a border city." [49] The Baltic lands would provide a settlement area for German war invalids as well as for Germans coming from the Russian provinces.[50]

In a nationalistic sense the German war aims for the Baltic represented to Stresemann the culmination of a seven centuries' struggle in defense of German culture,[51] for lands containing such old Hansa cities as Libau and Riga, for lands once conquered by "the blood and swords of the German knightly orders." [52] He considered the Baltic provinces as German, for the Baltic German racial stock although outnumbered there had "determined the character of the entire country through the imprint of its culture and intellect," had, indeed, influenced intellectual life in Germany as well through the professors trained at Dorpat, where "the second German fraternity had been founded," where "they feel and think German." As in the West where protection of the rights of the Flemish people provided a reason for German policy there, so in the East there was a like responsibility to safeguard those who under continued Tsarist oppression had "remained true to Germany." [53]

Once obtained a "free Baltic" should not, in Stresemann's view, be split up, nor should the states have complete independence, for politically the area was not ready as a whole for parliamentary institutions and economically would require someone to lean on.[54] He considered full autonomy for such small nations as utopian, for normal developments would drive them into union with a larger neighbor.[55] Stresemann's solution was a close relationship with Germany under her "military, political, and cultural protection." [56] Even if Lithuania were granted its own government eventually, it should still be tied to Germany by military convention, customs union, and a single system of money and communications.[57] This "close relationship" as spelled out by Stresemann was tantamount to the "union of the Baltic lands with Germany" for which he had "always hoped and wished." [58]

4. Mitteleuropa

Stresemann had supported the idea of a Central European customs union from the early days of the conflict.[59] In part he regarded it as a war measure to strengthen continental commerce against England's economic boycott.[60] It also held prospects for Germany's future economic development, for which he emphasized the need for a favorable position in the markets of Austria-Hungary, the Balkans, and Turkey.[61] He urged that Germany and Austria, fighting together on the battlefield, should not later fight each other economically, for a customs union would add to the economic strengthening of both, in that, as a combined population of 120 millions, they could ward off the economic attacks of their enemies better than if they opposed them singly.[62] He saw the threat of such attacks in an English preferential tariff system and the developing strength of the United States, a lasting French antagonism against Germany, and a Russian inclination toward economic and political absolutism.[63] While not unaware of the difficulties of maintaining an economic union, Stresemann believed the foundations were secure, resting on the generous peace offer made by Bismarck when the older German union with Austria in the Confederation had been dissolved.[64]

The appearance in the fall of 1915 of Friedrich Naumann's *Mitteleuropa* stimulated the discussion of a German eastward movement.[65] To the customs union was linked the idea of a new expansion to the Middle East with many divergent views both as to means and ends.[66] Stresemann, too, on occasion broadened his interpretation to include "the road to Asia Minor which the German spirit of enterprise already bestrides in the magnificently conceived Bagdad railroad project." [67] But neither as a customs union with Germany's

wartime allies nor as a means to eastern expansion did Stresemann regard the Central European proposal as a substitute
for the program of western annexation and expansion as did
many of its advocates.[68]

"I must make a decisive stand," he declared, "against those
extremists who believe that our economic development
should take only an Eastern direction. . . ." He continued:

> Our future does not lie in the East, and we will not give up the
> struggle for world markets; for if we give it up England's purpose
> has been achieved. With the first ship that leaves Cuxhaven and
> Bremerhaven this struggle for world markets begins anew. . . .
> The world was our field and will be so in the future. . . . For the
> present things are not such that a *Mitteleuropa* could and should
> be so conceived as if it were the fundamental trend of a future
> economic development. That it cannot and shall not be. . . .[69]

5. The Colonial Reich

If, in contrast to his repeated calls for increased sea power
and continental annexations, Stresemann less frequently
spoke out for colonial expansion, it was, nevertheless, from
beginning to end a basic part of his war aims program. Together with his like-minded associates in industry he demanded "security for Germany's colonial empire" and "a
colonial empire adequate for Germany's many-sided economic interests." Stresemann pointed out that England's trade
with her colonies represented her margin of superiority over
Germany in foreign trade and that therefore it was not
merely for the sake of prestige but necessary for the maintenance of Germany's economic life that Germany regain a
great colonial empire.[70]

He also emphasized the relationship between colonies and
fleet and pointed out the failure of pre-war Germany "to
pursue the colonial policy on a large scale and to provide the
necessary means for doing so." He warned that in the economic war which would continue after the termination of

hostilities Germany would need absolutely unhindered access to raw materials, "a large proportion of which" could be "imported from our colonial possessions if they are extended as they should be." Germany's export trade also had to be considered, and since England had already shown that there would be no "equality of opportunity for all nations in the colonies" it was clear to Stresemann that Germany could not "resign her position as a colonial power." [71]

Besides these economic arguments there were other more emotional and idealistic reasons to which he attributed "the demand regarding which the whole German nation" was in agreement—the restoration of her colonial possessions. "[The colonies] . . . were a home to thousands of us," he declared:

They have been drenched in German blood and were defended step by step till the flag had to be hauled down after an unequal struggle! Think of the work we have put into German East Africa; think what the Admiralty made of Kiaochow; think of the Germans who are yearning to get back to Samoa and our other territories! . . . The Empire has promised its protection to those who made their homes in the colonies under its flag and must extend this protection to them at the approaching conclusion of peace. We are not going to be cut off by England from a world policy any more than we are going to be starved out by her in the economic sphere. . . .[72]

To these ends Stresemann called for the return, enlargement, and economic development to the full of Germany's colonial empire "accompanied and supported by an energetic naval policy." [73]

6. Tactics and their Implications

In the preceding pages we have examined briefly the background and nature of Stresemann's annexationist ideas. If the war had come as a surprise, his response was immediate and clear not only regarding the war's causes and nature, but as to what was to come out of the conflict for Germany.

There was of course no uniformity of opinion in Germany concerning war aims. At one extreme were the positive annexationists; at the other were those "who never abandoned the idea of a purely defensive war"; between were groups whose opinions varied with the military situation.[74] Among the annexationists were many who advocated some single aspect of the war aims more than did Stresemann, and others who strove to a greater degree in some particular field of action; but it would probably be difficult to name many Germans during the first World War who actively supported a war aims program broader and more comprehensive than that of Gustav Stresemann.

With his first campaign speeches and war pamphlets Stresemann successfully attempted, despite the censorship, to force a discussion of the war aims question. He worked tirelessly to make his views dominant in the divided National Liberal Party; and, despite the *Burgfrieden,* he strove to gain among the middle-class parties an active parliamentary majority in favor of an annexationist program. Outside the Reichstag he worked with influential groups to create a new base for the conduct of the war, i.e., through defining the "Greater Germany" to move away from vague statements of defensive war by indicating what the fruits of the necessary and expected German victory should be. He sought to supply the Government with the backing of a united public opinion in support of annexations to serve as an instrument of pressure for the peace negotiations, and, perhaps most important, by all these means he sought to force a reluctant Government, personified by Bethmann-Hollweg, to accept unequivocally the annexationist program.

There were significant implications in Stresemann's war aims program. It demanded that the war be fought to a completely victorious end; that any and all means available be utilized for this purpose; and that any compromise peace be rejected. The acceptance of such a program rested on a complete faith in the capabilities of the German army and fleet and in the capacity of their leaders. His actions denoted a lack of faith and confidence in the civil Government's ability to carry the war to a victorious conclusion or to achieve the fruits of such a victory. To these matters we shall turn after first examining Stresemann's actions to effect his annexationist demands.

PART TWO:

THE STRUGGLE FOR THE GREATER GERMANY

Chapter III

THE FIRST ANNEXATIONIST CAMPAIGN
(1914-1915)

The struggle, with its illusory triumph, of the German annexationists to gain popular backing and, more important, force official acceptance of their positive war aims program was a continuing one throughout the greater part of the war.[1] It may be divided, like some cacophonous symphony, into distinct movements or phases, each marked by a change in tempo and a corresponding shift in the Government's position under pressure of the annexationist attack. Even in 1914, when public response was greatest to official declarations that Germany's was a defensive war, the annexationist music makers were already in the pit tuning up their varied instruments of discord. For more than two years the controversy mounted. It was marked by collapse of the political truce, heated parliamentary debates, petitions, and clandestine propaganda, culminating in the spring of 1917 in a major triumph for the annexationists. To these events and more specifically to Stresemann's role in them we now turn.

1. The Opening Assault

Stresemann's speeches in the summer and early autumn of 1914, when definite war aims demands were only beginning to crystallize, put him in the forefront of the annexationists.[2] In all thirty meetings held in his electoral district he declared "that Calais would become German." [3] In a brochure based upon his campaign speeches, particularly his outspoken remarks at Aurich and Dresden, he touched on almost all aspects of annexationist demands, emphasizing the "Greater Germany" to come as a result of victory.[4]

The pamphlet "had the effect of a bomb in certain circles"; the Government took immediate steps to persuade the Business Committee of the National Liberal Party to dissociate the official party position from that taken in Stresemann's pamphlet "because of its possible effects abroad," while the censor restricted distribution of the brochure.[5]

The newly elected Deputy protested to the Party Secretary against "the small group" in the Business Committee which presumed, without mandate, to speak for the Party electorate.[6] He called for an expression of the views of those of the Party who did not "spend every morning in the Government offices" and insisted that the Business Committee's action be reconsidered in the Berlin office of the Party as well as through an informal conference of the Party's parliamentary group.[7] His own views, he pointed out, had coincided with those expressed "to the cheers of the majority of the Reichstag *Fraktion*" by Bassermann prior to the latter's departure for military service, and in rejecting his pamphlet the Committee had encouraged the Government "in its weak attitude" by exposing "in an ostentatious manner a member of the Reichstag *Fraktion* who dares to support a Greater Germany before the honorable Government's highly esteemed diplomats have gotten around to it." [8]

Even while engaged, through public speeches and pamphlets, in spreading his ideas on war aims and while initiating action within his own Party toward a unified annexationist stand, Stresemann was participating in a third line of approach to the problem through meetings with industrial leaders.[9] On November 7, 1914, he took part in an interesting discussion as a member of a sub-committee of the War Committee of German industry at a meeting called to deal with war indemnity and trade policies, and to study from "an economic standpoint" the widening of German territory through annexations."[10]

There was unanimous agreement among those present that "on grounds of military defense it was necessary that Germany possess Antwerp, Calais, and Ostend, and that the French fortress area be annexed as well," but the question as to what to do with Belgium, from the beginning and throughout the war the principal subject of annexationist dispute, elicited conflicting opinions. Speaking for a minority, Siemens opposed annexation as bad economically, and politically as well, for "it would bring foreigners into the Reich." [11] Hugenberg, whose views represented those of the majority present, urged the annexation of Belgium as a sop to labor, whose growing power and demands in the post-war era could only be withstood without internal difficulties "by diverting attention" and "giving play to the imagination" through "the widening of German dominion" by territorial expansion.[12] Stresemann also spoke for German control of Belgium, but he remarked to Hugenberg that war annexations would have no bearing on the demands of labor for a share of the national wealth, for such demands were dependent on the country's economic situation, and even before the war the German workers had been on their way to achieving their aims. To Siemens he stated that there should be no worry about mixing Germans and Belgians since both were commercial peoples with common interests, and that industrial Belgium would be easier to acclimatize than agricultural Alsace-Lorraine. He noted that "annexation of Belgium as a province" was not the only possible solution of the question, for "Belgium could be treated as a German colony," with "many freedoms guaranteed" but with military and "certain other affairs" placed under the "supreme authority" of Germany. "If the necessity is stressed on all sides," concluded Stresemann, "that Antwerp, Calais, and Ostend be occupied by Germany, then we must also be concerned with the corresponding hinterland and take care that the area is not threatened in the rear by enemy powers."

The meeting of the War Committee led directly to a conference with the Chancellor early in December at which Stresemann and *Landrat* Roetger of the League of Industrialists presented the comprehensive war aims program which the industrialists had in the meantime prepared, a program which called for the annexation of Belgium and French coastal, mineral, and fortress areas in the West, while in the East the cession of Poland, Courland, and Esthonia was expected from Russia.[13] The Chancellor replied that it was difficult to take a position on these questions under the military circumstances then prevailing; that while he was soberly confident of victory and "under no circumstances would conclude an armistice-type peace," it was too early for the Government to commit itself to "something as programmatic" as the War Committee had presented.[14]

Stresemann interposed that the "Committee had considered it a duty" to present its unified program because there seemed to be completely lacking "the uniform demand in the masses" which had existed in 1870. Those occupying themselves with the question as to what would come after the victorious conclusion of the war were so far apart that at the peace conference the Government would be "unable to base itself on public opinion." He went on to say that the industrial group had acted in order "to put order and harmony into this chaos," to "influence" public opinion, and "to give the Chancellor the opportunity to base himself on industry, . . . united almost without exception in the War Committee."

Bethmann-Hollweg's assurance that his views and those of his callers were "not very far apart" was not borne out by the cautiously limited program, conciliatory to France, which he offered.[15] However, despite his reluctance to go along with the War Committee's sweeping program, the Chancellor had

already placed himself in a difficult position through publication of official Belgian documents showing the pre-war
military discussions of that country with England.[16] By thus
destroying the Belgian claim to neutrality, apparently to
justify the German invasion which he had previously termed
a "wrong" to be rectified as soon as possible, Bethmann
helped to strengthen the growing sentiment that the restoration of Belgium would be a threat to German security.[17]

As a result of pressures in which even some of those more
moderate than Stresemann and his associates joined, the Government made its first shift from the position it had taken
at the outbreak of the war. When early in December the
National Liberals united with the other middle-class parties
in the Reichstag to demand indemnities in compensation
for Germany's "enormous sacrifices," [18] the Chancellor accepted this viewpoint and himself declared "that Germany
must secure herself against future attacks by altering the
frontiers" so that "no one would again dare to disturb her
peace." [19] What these alterations would consist of, the Chancellor did not state.

The vague position taken by the Government merely
whetted the appetites of the annexationists without satisfy-
ing their demands. From this point the partisans, both for
and against annexations, began to speak out more sharply
in support of their views. That Stresemann had not moder-
ated his attitude at the end of 1914 is clearly illustrated by
his appeal to Bassermann, after he had recapitulated in a letter the opinions of the War Committee, the Chancellor's
slight concessions, and other points of view:

I urgently request you [he wrote] not to deviate one milli-
meter from the line which you have drawn in your speech at the
Fraktion dinner because of the *Berliner Tageblatt, Frankfurter
Zeitung* . . . and others. Now the great moment of world history
has come: we shall move up to the Atlantic *(Weltmeer);* we shall
be able to create in Calais a German Gibraltar. Let the Progres-

sives do as they please; for us the hour can command only one
thing, that is the support of these demands and their propagation
in public opinion.[20]

2. Correspondence and Pan-German Activities

In the spring of 1915 the threads of the parliamentary discussions of the December sessions were again picked up, and
in both plenary sittings and meetings of the important Finance Committee the debate was outspoken. The National
Liberal, Center, and Conservative Deputies maintained their
united stand, against the continued Social Democratic opposition, in support of a positive program of war gains, although, as in the case of Belgium, there was no uniformity
in the details of their schemes.[21] The efforts of the war aims
majority in the Reichstag—the so-called *Kriegszielmehrheit*—
were complemented by the work of the annexationists outside the parliament, and together they forced the Chancellor,
who had been steering an uneasy course between antipodean
views, to public statements which, although ambiguous,
moved the Government in the direction of annexationist
commitment.[22]

While Stresemann participated in the activities of the
Reichstag majority indicated above, his chief contributions
to the annexationist cause during this period were made
outside the parliament. His voluminous correspondence reflects the zealous support of the war aims and "their propagation in public opinion" which he had called for. He considered it to be his duty to speak out against anti-annexa-
tionists such as Gothein, who had written in the *Berliner
Tageblatt* that "Germany would not annex a single square
kilometer of French territory no matter how great the victory";[23] against anti-annexationist organizations such as that
formed in Berlin under "the beautiful name," *Neues Vaterland,* to unite those "opposed to annexation of Belgium and
the idea of a Greater Germany";[24] and against the gag-rule

(Mundtotmachung) of the Chancellor, who kept from the press those views which ran counter to his own desire "to propitiate England and France" through a renunciatory policy regarding Belgium and the coastal areas.[25] He wrote bitterly against "the old German stupidity" *(Michelei)* that permitted postcards "which insult the Tsar" while silencing those "who speak of the fact that Antwerp must be German." [26]

Complete confidence in a German victory which would realize the positive war aims program was exhibited in his bristling replies to the doubters.[27] To a cautious suggestion that one should wait for victory before talking about the annexation of Belgium, Stresemann brusquely rejoined that he had indeed been guided by the fact that "the military experts have repeatedly represented that the achievement of this prerequisite was certain." [28] He discounted pessimistic reports—even Bassermann made a doleful plaint [29]—with the assurance that the "unchanged military situation" was "a good one" if only the Government had the resoluteness to take for Germany "the Belgium which has been conquered with the sword." [30]

Stresemann also sought to find new support among the Progressives. He was convinced that the views of that Party were not represented by those who stressed the primacy of internal reforms, following the *Berliner Tageblatt,* or the ideas of Rohrbach and Jäckh, whom he unflatteringly labelled as the "Chancellor's vassals." [31] He appealed to known annexationists among the Progressives, such as Professor Max Apt, to prevent a breach "over world issues" such as that which had occurred in 1867 between the Progressive Party and the National Liberals.[32]

Whoever [wrote Stresemann] expects us to lower the flag and pettily give up the way to the Belgian coast, fought for with so much German blood, in order to carry on a so-called *Kultur-Politik* of conciliation in the sense of certain Progressive politicians stands further from us in world-political feeling than the greatest enemy of the Reich. World-political questions are in the order of business—first comes the fate of the German Reich, then come the internal conditions.[33]

In contrast to his voluminous correspondence, replete with annexationist enthusiasm, Stresemann's speeches at this time were devoted more to the economic problems of the war than to exhortations for the war aims program, for he had concluded that other types of action would yield better results.[34] "Everyone in Government circles and at the Headquarters knows that I stand for endurance till the final victory," he wrote to a Saxon constituent who had invited him to address a local gathering.[35] "I have been so active that if I spoke in Plauen now they would merely say, 'There goes Stresemann's artillery again!'" As a more fruitful alternative he suggested sending a resolution signed by prominent persons not active in political life to the Emperor, Chancellor, and leaders of the Saxon Government; and he counseled that the resolution should emphasize that "German national circles are no longer able to form a dam against revolutionary currents when they see themselves deserted by the Government . . . [regarding] . . . the development of the state." "The people at the top," he wrote, "have an absolutely childish fear of [revolution]. . . ."[36]

This temporary and self-imposed silence did not prevent Stresemann's working on behalf of the annexationist program through the leaders of the various Pan-German groups working zealously for the same cause, especially with Heinrich Class, director of the League itself and perhaps the key figure in the war aims movement outside the parliament.[37] In basic agreement with Class's views, he voiced objection in the Reichstag to the confiscation of a pamphlet of the Pan-German leader and tried to mitigate the Government's action.[38] Stresemann also took a leading part in the activities of the newly founded *Auskunftsstelle Vereinigter Verbände*, which "sailed completely in annexationist waters" as a "central clearing house" for the various Pan-German groups.[39] He was in close touch with the annexationist group which met in June, 1915, at the *Berliner Künstlerhaus* to approve the so-called "Petition of the Professors," which had been prepared with the guidance of Class and Reinhold Seeberg, a professor of theology.[40] When the petition, which boldly listed its demands under the heading *"Keine Kulturpolitik ohne Machtpolitik,"* was confiscated promptly by the Government, the directing group reconstituted itself as the Independent Committee for a German Peace.[41] This group became one of the most active annexationist organizations, and Stresemann played an increasingly important role in it.[42]

3. The Petition of the Economic Organizations

Stresemann was also occupied with the question of what effects the complete annexation of Belgium would have on German industry and commerce.[43] This activity required extensive correspondence with such prominent industrialists as Kirdorf, Duisberg, and Heineken, and called for personal conversations as well, since some found the problem "too complicated" to put into writing.[44] These talks and others with those who shared common views on war aims questions took place in 1915 at the meetings of the Wednesday Society, established by Bassermann but managed for the most part by Stresemann during the frequent absences of the former on military duty.[45]

In these leaders of industry Stresemann placed the greatest faith and hope in the struggle to put the Chancellor on the right path in the war aims question, and with them he continued to work, as during the previous winter, in furtherance of the annexationist views.[46] The result was a comprehensive statement of war aims, the product of the cooperative efforts of industrialists under the general leadership of Hugenberg, the Pan-German Heinrich Class, and Hirsch and Stresemann, who in addition to affiliation with the two groups mentioned, were also Reichstag Deputies of the National Liberal Party.[47] After several preliminary sessions a meeting was held during the first days in March in which four economic associations participated—Stresemann's League of Industrialists; the Central Union of German Industrialists, the voice of heavy industry of the Rhineland-Westphalia area; the Agrarian League, representing the large, proprietary interests in the land, and the League of Middle-Class Citizens in the German Empire. In spite of a hint from the semi-official *Norddeutsche Allgemeine Zeitung* that the economic associations refrain from making a declaration on war aims, the four groups outlined a general program of demands headed by "the unconditional refusal to give up Belgium." [48] The following week another meeting was held at which a fifth major economic group, the German Peasants' League, a small-farmers' association which Stresemann had long cultivated in the interest of his party, joined the other four in completing the petition.[49] It was presented to the Chancellor on March 10.[50] The five economic associations were joined by the Hansa League in a second petition directed to the Reichstag calling for a free discussion of the important questions concerning the peace.[51]

The petition which the economic associations presented to the Chancellor on March 10 was similar in content to the demands voiced by the industrialists of the War Committee to Bethmann in December, when Stresemann had been one of their spokesmen.[52] It called for an "honorable peace" which would "do justice to the sacrifices made," and because of enemy demands that the Fatherland be destroyed it declared that Germany must be protected not by treaties but by the "weakening of her enemies" economically and militarily. The petition called for the solution of the Belgian problem by a division of that country into Walloon and Flemish territories, both under complete German control. From

France cession was demanded of her coastal areas and the ore lands of Longwy and Briey. These gains in the West were to be balanced in the East by annexation of agricultural lands, at the same time providing a better East Prussian border. The colonial Reich was also to be restored. The petitioners explained that their demands did not represent a "policy of conquest" but merely what was needed "to guarantee a lasting peace" by removing the threats on Germany's borders, and that they were based on the military victory "which would guarantee these goals." [53]

The presentation of the petition of the economic associations concurrent with the pressures exerted in the Reichstag by the war aims majority there marked a crescendo in the annexationist outburst. An attempt was now made, in which Stresemann actively participated, to integrate the annexationist efforts of parliamentarians and industrialists.[54] The effort took the form of a joint meeting in Berlin on May 1 of the leaders of the economic associations, under the chairmanship of Hugenberg, and key members of the political parties supporting the positive war aims. The assembled annexationists listened to the Military Governor of Belgium, General von Bissing, emphasize the necessity of retaining Belgium, especially the coastal areas, and following the Bissing report it was decided to send two deputations to the Chancellor to point out to him that "behind this demand for the retention of Belgium there stood both the majority of the parties and the leading economic organizations." "Without talking against the Chancellor personally," reported Stresemann, "the idea was expressed that he was not sufficiently clear about the feeling of the German people in this question." [55]

Shortly thereafter both parliamentary and industrialist groups presented their views to the Chancellor, the former on May 13, at which time Bethmann reassured the Deputies, led by the Conservative Count Westarp, as to his stand on

Belgium, asserting that "Belgium must be rendered harmless" by becoming Germany's "vassal state." [56] The industrialists, including Hugenberg, von Wangenheim, Friedrichs, Hirsch, and Stresemann, the latter two linking industrial and parliamentary groups, were received by the Chancellor four days later. After pointing out to the Chancellor that Germany's need had brought together the usually hostile economic groups in a common program, they elaborated on the war aims which agriculture and industry had agreed would "strengthen and preserve these two basic elements of the German economy," which was the "starting point for the Germany to be striven for after the war." The delegation touched upon many aspects of the annexationist program in oral and written statements. They pointed out that they were willing to give up "any demands which could not be carried out militarily," but felt it important that "a goal be set up which would indicate to the statesmen what could be achieved" with victory.[57]

The Chancellor replied that he did not think a discussion of war aims opportune in view of the serious situation which Germany then faced. He admitted that the war was showing a development which eliminated the idea that it "could be closed with a reconciliation of the nations," and agreed that "a reconstruction of Belgium" was impossible, since a restored Belgium would only be "a French-English vassal state." He expressed doubts that the deputation's wishes for the East could be fulfilled as they conflicted with the needs of a separate peace with Russia which he hoped to achieve, but denied that he was "not in favor of complete exploitation of a German victory, and assured the delegation that he would request "the circles it represented to stand by his side" when the time came to participate in the discussion and solution of these questions.

On May 20, 1915, the petition of March 10, with only slight changes in content, and the addition of another signatory, the *Christliche Deutsche Bauernvereine,* was sent again to the Chancellor as well as to the Ministries of the federal states comprising the Empire.[58] Even though the contents of this so-called Petition of the Six Economic Organizations and of its forerunner of March 10 were restricted from circulation by the censorship, the very existence of the petitions stirred controversy. Whether through accident or design the petition found its way into the foreign press, and from this source the annexationist demands were divulged to the Germen people.[59] Thereupon the activities of the moderates increased, demanding in turn renewed efforts of the war aims proponents.[60]

Stresemann defended the petitions both inside the Finance Committee of the Reichstag and outside the parliament, prefacing his remarks with the warning that the petitions expressed the common aims of "the preponderant part of industry, agriculture and the middle-classes" and therefore could not be ignored.[61] He then stated the two "chief complaints" against the petitions, that they had been composed "without connection with the Government," and that they had been given to the public at a time when "the military situation was in contradiction to the war aims expressed." He pointed out that the economic leaders had talked at length with the Chancellor, who had not rejected their ideas, had said indeed that it was "deplorable that anyone would think him capable of not wanting to exploit the achieved victory completely for the future security of the Reich." "If the petition had been keyed to the military situation," noted Stresemann, "each change in that situation would require that one shape the petition anew." Instead the demands had been based on the "prerequisite of their military practicability"—"one should not reproach the Economic Organizations because their petition, written in a dark hour, had shown complete confidence in a German victory."

Although Stresemann disclaimed, for the Associations, any

responsibility for publication of the petitions, he declared that he saw no derogatory effect in announcing a "decisive will to victory" and the aim to exploit this victory; it was rather those who opposed the annexation policy who were guilty of extending the war "by awakening abroad the false impression that the German people [had] reached the limits of its capacity" and needed peace more than the enemy. "We do not want to see Germany again go through this battle for existence with these frightful sacrifices of blood and property," concluded Stresemann,

We see the guaranty of Germany's political and economic future only in a powerful policy which prevents our enemies from again daring to play the same game in order to undermine our existence. Our war aims demands arose from these motives; today there is no cause for us to change them; we shall support and defend them as soon as it is possible for us to do so with the removal of the unbearable censorship conditions.[62]

These pressures, according to Stresemann,[63] were responsible for the Chancellor's statement to the Reichstag on May 28:

The greater the danger in which we stand . . . the more we must persevere until we have created and won for ourselves all possible real guaranties and securities that none of our enemies . . . will again dare to engage us in armed conflict.[64]

Bethmann's statement led in turn to further declarations in the Reichstag by the party leaders and to strongly annexationist statements and resolutions by party committees and bodies outside the parliament.[65] None was more outspokenly annexationist than that issued in June by the National Liberal Party.[66] It was Stresemann who now imparted new vigor to the annexationist controversy.

Chapter IV

THE WAR AIMS CONTROVERSY CONTINUES
(1915-1916)

In May, timed to coincide with the visits of the leaders of the parties and industry to the Chancellor, the National Liberal Party Business Committee and the Chairmen of the Party's *Land* Organizations had issued a joint statement calling for a peace which would extend Germany's frontiers to provide security and to reward the sacrifices of the German people.[1] This was followed in June by another party proclamation which called in addition for "the development of Germany's overseas position," taking complete advantage of "the tremendous successes" of the "incomparable army and dauntless fleet." At the same time National Liberal leaders spoke out in the Reichstag, Prussian Diet, and in public meetings.[2] In these activities they were supported by the other middle-class parties and the growing number of Pan-German organizations, and opposed by the moderates, especially the Social Democrats. The war thus moved into its second year, the sound of the guns echoed on the home front by the shrills of the annexationists and their opponents.

1. The Cologne Incident

Stresemann, too, resumed his speaking on behalf of the positive war aims program. "All Germans," he declared in June in Frankfort to a joint meeting of an industrial group and the local organization of the Hansa League, "agree that all our acts of friendliness to other peoples could not protect us from world war, and that this war must now bring us a peace of security." As a step toward that goal he hailed the recent declaration of the King of Bavaria that "the new way to the sea, won by battle" should never be relinquished.[3]

As a result of Stresemann's speeches there occurred in July an episode which widened the gulf between party leaders and the Chancellor with significant effect in the war aims controversy. It began when Stresemann, along with Bassermann and other Party leaders, was invited to speak in Cologne at a joint meeting, attended by some eighty members, of the National Liberal directing committees of the Rhineland and Westphalia. Although Stresemann's topic for discussion ostensibly concerned Germany's economic tasks after the war, he had been secretly informed by the presiding officer, Professor Moldenhauer, that the "economic theme" had been chosen "with regard to the censorship," but that "above all" they wanted to hear a discussion of the National Liberal Party's war aims.[4] Stresemann complied, and in what an American newspaper described as a "violent speech" from the leader of the "Tirpitz Party," declared that Germany must be made so strong and her enemies "so ruthlessly weakened" by border changes in both East and West that none would dare to attack her again.[5] He added that the "Reich leadership" was often lacking in "sureness of aim," the Chancellor being "accessible to the most varied currents," so that strong pressure was necessary to prevent his falling into the hands of the "culture and conciliation" advocates (Kultur-und-Versöhnungs Politiker), thereby giving up "real guaranties." Following Stresemann's remarks Bassermann briefly warned that "they must keep their eyes open so as not to be cheated out of their rewards," while other speakers questioned the Chancellor's ability to get the kind of peace desired.[6]

Through what Stresemann noted as "apparently a misunderstanding," the sharp statements made at the supposedly confidential meeting were published in the *Westfälische Politische Nachrichten*. The result was a lively discussion in the

German press, the *Berliner Tageblatt,* among others, branding the talks as a "deliberate move against the Chancellor." [7]
In Berlin, where political circles were awaiting the publication of an Imperial Proclamation on Germany's war aims,
the rumor now spread that the Emperor's statement, against
annexations, would be a "stream of cold water" directed at
the National Liberal leaders for their remarks at Cologne.[8]
Erzberger, the influential Center Deputy, who claimed that
he had read a draft of the proclamation, informed Stresemann that it emphasized that Germany was "not waging a
war of conquest" and that it contained nothing about "guaranties for the future." In order to prevent such an "impossible declaration" Bassermann sent a telegram to *Reichsrat*
Buhl, a prominent Bavarian National Liberal, so that the
latter might use his influence with Count Hertling, Chairman of the Bundesrat's Committee on Foreign Affairs, but
the censor prevented Bassermann's message from getting
through.[9]

The Chancellor, upon receiving a report of the National
Liberal meeting at Cologne, had invited Bassermann, to-
gether with some of the more moderate National Liberal
Party members, to a conference, but as a result of Basser-
mann's attempt, by means of his telegram, "to play off the
King of Bavaria against the Emperor," the invitation to him
was withdrawn, and Bethmann spoke only with the others.
The Chancellor complained about the attacks against him,
which he regarded as a challenge he would have to answer.
Bethmann asked if any open distrust of him existed in the
Fraktion which would justify the action of the Party leader.
He added that he did not believe his war aims "differed
essentially" from Bassermann's.[10]

In consequence of the meeting with Bethmann-Hollweg
a crisis developed within the National Liberal Party over
the question of whether or not the Party should issue an
official statement to the effect that the Party did not mistrust

the Chancellor. Bassermann refused to issue such a statement, insisting on the concurrence of the entire Central Committee for such an action, and after some friction carried the majority in support of his policy. As a result no official statement disavowing mistrust of the Chancellor was issued.[11] Instead, there was an almost unanimous expression of confidence in Bassermann and approval of his war aims program—a new statement was issued on August 15 similar to that issued in May, which had called for the usual extension of boundaries in East, West, and overseas.[12] The Party leadership went further by rejecting the Chancellor's reproach to Bassermann for the telegram sent "in an overflow of patriotic worry," and expressed instead a criticism of Bethmann's "personal" use of the censorship. The Party members who had met with the Chancellor were criticized for having allowed themselves to be used as "batteringrams" *(Sturmbock)* against Bassermann.[13]

Four days later the Chancellor declared before the Reichstag that the war was destroying the old world and a new must be created; that Europe "could have peace only through the inviolable strength of Germany's position . . . Germany must build its position so strong and secure that the other Powers would never again dare to think of a policy of encirclement." [14] Meanwhile, the Emperor's Proclamation to the German People had already appeared—an appeal calling for perseverance until a peace was achieved which offered "the necessary military, political, and economic guaranties. . . ." [15] Bethmann, according to Stresemann, had claimed that Bassermann had been misinformed concerning the proclamation, for it had never been the Chancellor's intent to suggest to the Emperor a proclamation of a single sentence to the effect that Germany had no ideas of conquest—in addition it had been intended from the start to call for "military, political, and economic guaranties." [16]

As *rapporteur* for his Party, Stresemann with evident satisfaction pointed out that these events and their denouement had "clarified the position of the Party to those outside" concerning its position in "the important questions of Germany's future" and would help their ideas gain influence at the making of the peace. Indeed they had already had an effect, "for the Chancellor's last speech . . . was surely made under the impress of the National Liberal Party regarding the war aims question." [17]

2. Further Annexationist Petitions

The annexationists were not content, however, to rest on the basis of the statements issued by the Government in midsummer, and there was continued pressure from the parties making up the war-aims majority.[18] As Stresemann pointed out in evaluating the results of the Cologne incident, described above, "the more the Chancellor was influenced by the *Flaumacher*" and "so-called intellectual circles" for a conciliatory peace and the renunciation of Belgium, the more it was necessary to oppose such views decisively, "so that at least the Chancellor would be kept in a middle position." [19] This constant pressure was now considered even more necessary because of the conciliatory position taken by the Government on submarine warfare. Bethmann's success in maintaining predominance over Tirpitz in the *Lusitania* and *Arabic* crises was taken by the annexationists as a direct blow at their war aims program, for they saw in these events the augury of a weak peace through relinquishment of the Belgian coast and subsequent renunciation of the idea of control of the sea. The rumor was prevalent that the Government was preparing to come to an agreement with England on the basis of giving up Belgium in return for the restoration of the German colonies.[20]

To combat this supposed danger Stresemann utilized his position as syndic of the Union of Saxon Industry, representing five thousand factory owners, to appeal to Count

Vitzthum of the Saxon Ministry asking him to work through the Saxon Government and the Bundesrat to prevent any action which might entail giving up Belgium, which would indeed be the mark "of a lost war." The petition, which Stresemann personally presented on September 9, pointed out that the Belgians "in their hatred of Germany would join anew any hostile coalition"; and that England, controlling Belgium, would be in a position to start a second war. The appeal called for the rejection of any English peace offer and for continuation of the war until England was defeated.[21] On the same day the Hansa League, in which Stresemann had an influential voice, directed a petition to the Chancellor calling for the freedom of the seas, extension of the frontiers, restoration of colonies, and an indemnity.[22]

In November Stresemann and Freiherr von Wangenheim, as representatives of the economic organizations, were received by the Chancellor for a discussion of economic problems related to the war. Stresemann did not let pass the opportunity to interject some comments concerning industry's peace aims, among which he included a more favorable position in the markets of Austria-Hungary, the Balkans, and Turkey, as well as bases for the fleet so that trade could not be cut off in the future. The Chancellor utilized the meeting to advise Stresemann that all rumors regarding pending peace negotiations were incorrect, and he expressed the hope that no one would believe him capable of concluding "a rotten peace"—what he had said about the war aims in May was still valid.[23]

The annexationist controversy in 1915 had begun with discussions in the Reichstag, and the matter was aired officially in that body once again as the year drew to a close. The occasion was an interpellation by the Social Democrats, led by Scheidemann, who, on the ground that the Government had apparently moved from its declared position of August, 1914, on war aims, now raised the question, "On what conditions would the Chancellor be ready to enter into peace talks?" [24] As in previous debates the disposition of Belgium was the focal point of the controversy. In replying Bethmann stated that he could not discuss in detail what guaranties would be required regarding Belgium, but that Germany must insure herself militarily, politically, and economically, and that the longer the war continued the greater the pledges must be. "Neither in the East nor West," concluded the Chancellor, "will our enemy be permitted incursion gates from which tomorrow they can renew their threats more ominously than before." [25]

The Chancellor achieved a temporary internal harmony as a result of his declaration for both the Socialist and Pan-German press interpreted his "ambiguous wheelings" as favoring their own point of view.[26] Stresemann was depressed because of "the resigned tone" in the Chancellor's speech. "He merely spoke of guaranties," commented the National Liberal annexationist, "and used the expression 'pledges' *(Faustpfaender),* so that a Deputy . . . was able to say, not without injustice, 'One does not keep pledges, one gives them up.' Unfortunately the Chancellor did not contradict this interpretation, and the *Frankfurter Zeitung* has emphasized . . . that this omission means that the Chancellor agrees completely with [this] interpretation of his words. . . ." [27] This criticism formed the basis for attacks against the Chancellor's war aims stand when the conflict was renewed in 1916.

3. The Reichstag Debates of 1916 and After

Stresemann's major role in the annexationist movement in 1915 had been to voice outside the Reichstag the views of the annexationist majority of the National Liberal Party, to formulate and express the aims of the Economic Organizations, and to assist in concerting the efforts of industry and the majority parties in support of a common war aims program. Now, in addition, he began to share with Bassermann the role of spokesman for the National Liberal *Fraktion* within the Reichstag before the plenary sessions, and in 1916 he made eight speeches, two of them major addresses concerned in great part with the war aims question.[28]

The debate on the censorship in January gave Stresemann his first opportunity to express his annexationist views in parliament.[29] He had already spoken out strongly against the censorship in the discussions of the Finance Committee in defense of the right of the Economic Organizations to circulate their war aims ideas as confidential matter.[30] Now before the full Reichstag Stresemann emphasized that the *Burgfrieden* had never been meant to extinguish the differences between the parties or to limit free discussion of major questions, particularly concerning foreign policy and war aims.[31] Pointing out that these questions had been freely debated within the Finance Committee without worsening relations between the parliamentary groups, and "that everyone, inside and outside Germany, knew, despite the censorship, that these differences existed," he declared it was time "the whole German people" was given the opportunity "to debate the problems of the new Germany." "Let us now discuss the great issues," demanded Stresemann. Among these he included "the future relationship to the Baltic Germans and to the Flemish" and insisted that "the German people, as well as the diplomats, should have a say"—on this "both National Liberals and Social Democrats could agree" even though their war aims differed.[32] In explaining the motivation behind his annexationist activities the future Foreign Minister of the Weimar Republic displayed a remarkable näiveté as to the problems of the Government:

No leading statesman [he declared] need be angry with those who set up far-reaching goals which may go beyond what can be realized at the time. . . . It is the task of the military experts and statesmen to lead back to *Realpolitik* and consider what can be achieved militarily. It is desirable to strive for the impossible. If people make such demands, it might perhaps be easier for a Chancellor to push through a greater part of them than if a priori demands are renounced.[33]

In a short statement prepared as an unsigned editorial for the *Düsseldorfer Generalanzeiger* Stresemann continued his criticisms of the censorship, asking if a freer discussion of war aims would not "bring with it the possibility of an understanding." The editorial continued with the suggestion that such discussion would "mean the end of the confidential meetings" and, even more, "the death of all the anonymous pamphlets and protocols with which leading persons are daily flooded." [34] Despite this apparent disapproval of such techniques Stresemann seemed to find nothing distasteful in the brochures attacking the Chancellor which were circulating in 1916. He frequently exchanged views with Hans von Liebig, author of a rather harsh attack on Bethmann-Hollweg's pre-war policy.[35] He passed along copies of Wolfgang Kapp's attack—typewritten to avoid the censors—which expressed views on Bethmann's Belgian war aims similar to those made by Stresemann following the Chancellor's statement of December 9, as well as criticisms of the latter's domestic policies.[36] He also helped circulate copies of the pamphlet written under the pseudonym "Junius Alter," which attacked the Chancellor, particularly his pre-war diplomacy.[37]

In April, 1916, came what has been called "the high-watermark of annexationism in the German Reichstag during the first two years of war." [38] The debate was touched off by the demands of the Social Democrat, Hugo Haase, for the "political restoration of Belgium" as well as its "economic independence.[39] The Chancellor himself set the tone for the middle-class parties by his remarks on April 5, in which he declared that there would be "no *status quo ante* in Belgium." [40] Whether his view reflected an undue optimism regarding the anticipated results of the Verdun offensive or the inability to maintain a moderate stand when facing the leaders of the annexationist groups, his words had the effect of causing the majority party leaders to make new declarations based upon an interpretation of his remarks in a pro-annexationist sense.[41] Even the statement of the moderate Socialist Scheidemann, expressing regard for the Flemish people and the idea that "only a child in political things can persuade itself that when a whole continent stands in flames . . . not a single frontier stone shall be removed . . ." was construed as a call for favorable boundary changes, although he was quick to deny this with the declaration that Stresemann and Count Westarp, the Conservative leader, had both drawn false conclusions from his statement and from the Chancellor's as well.[42]

For his part Stresemann in a much discussed and frequently quoted speech reviewed the long history of Germany's peaceful pre-war policy, stressing the jealousy of England when "Michel the dreamer became Michel the seafarer," and developed all aspects of the annexationist program—the need of "safeguards in East and West," expansion through Central European economic ties, and an open road to world markets through seapower. "In complete agreement with the Chancellor, we too see in an unassailable Germany the best peace guaranty for Europe and the World," he declared, and added:

I know that there are other views based on the premise that peace is best secured by rejection of world-political expansion, by means of understanding and accommodation to other people. Such a view I should have regarded as debatable at one time but not after the experiences of this war.[43]

After the declarations of the preceding May, August, and December it might appear as almost impossible to inject anything new into these periodic annexationist pronounce-

ments. Yet on this occasion they went beyond earlier calls
for security of frontiers and spoke bluntly of territorial acquisitions and—in Stresemann's words—of "world-political
expansion." [44] There were other developments of significance
connected with the declarations: the Progressives as a party
joined in the expression of positive war aims; [45] the annexationist front appeared to be strengthened by a split of the
Social Democratic Party into two groups, although in fact
there was no change in the basic Socialist opposition to annexations; [46] and in addition the middle-class groups now
moved together in the question of unrestricted submarine
warfare. On the other hand, the issue of internal reforms, the
so-called *Neuorientierung*, began now to assume a greater
importance, and since the common outlook on war aims of
the middle-class groups did not extend to the area of class
privilege at home, the reform issue was to show its divisive
effects as the war moved into its third year.[47]

There was also manifested a growing antagonism toward
the Chancellor, for while the annexationists were ready
enough to seize upon his words as a proof of his support of
their views, he never went far enough to satisfy them, particularly in his statements regarding Belgium.[48] The belief
that the Chancellor would be willing to give up Belgium
for the return of the German colonies brought general criticism of Bethmann at a meeting held later in the month by
annexationist party leaders and prominent industrialists from
the Economic Organizations in Berlin.[49] All agreed with the
statement of Stinnes, the industrialist, that Germany must
retain its military hold on the Belgian coast and, if possible,
take Calais; [50] and all concurred with the assertion, probably
Hugenberg's, that Belgium, especially Antwerp, was vital
to heavy industry, which also required the French ore areas.
To give up Belgium, it was affirmed, would be a political
disaster, for German monarchial feeling would be so weakened that it would never recover, while the workers of Rhine-

land-Westphalia would revolt if their blood sacrifices had been made in vain. There were still darker tones added to this somber picture: "The people, deceived in its hopes would go over to the Social Democrats in the worst sort of opposition to the state," while "state-preserving circles" would lose their zeal and never support another war for a state which did not exploit its victories. In answer to all this "the newly created path to the sea would be a visible sign of the success of the war." [51]

From the beginning of the war Stresemann had adhered to the idea that Belgium must remain in German hands, but in 1914 when Hugenberg had made remarks similar to those just expressed, Stresemann had clearly differentiated between the demands of labor and the annexationist program. In 1915 he had pointed out to a constituent that the Government's "absolutely childish fear" of loss of support, even of revolution, was an excellent weapon for the annexationist propagandists. In 1916 he offered no dissent to these views now put forth as tenets by the annexationist directorate.

There was no petition, no delegation to the Chancellor as there had been following a similar meeting during the previous year. From the comments made at the gathering it is clear that Bethmann-Hollweg himself was regarded as the chief obstacle to acceptance of the annexationist program for a Greater Germany.[52]

Shortly after, on May 21, the Central Committee of the National Liberal Party repeated its declaration of the previous year, "confirmed by events since that time," that only an "extension of the land and sea borders of the Empire in the East, West, and overseas" could provide "real guaranties" for military, political, and economic security.[53]

After the National Liberal declaration of May 21 Stresemann's activities seemed to flag. He continued to defend the annexationist program in his correspondence: to the Saxon businessman who called for an early end to the war, he tartly replied that "Germany's entire future would be sacrificed" by such a policy.[54] While conceding to another critic that annexation of Belgium would "strengthen the Social Democrats" and "bring in Jesuits," he maintained his stand that domination by Germany was vital for economic, military, and political reasons.[55] To the Pan-Germans, however, he appeared to be withdrawing from the ranks of the leaders. True, he helped distribute the writings of Kapp and "Junius Alter," as previously noted, and granted permission to reproduce his own Reichstag speech against the censorship for a special edition of the *Alldeutsche Blätter,* the principal organ of the League.[56] However he forbade the Independent Committee for a German Peace the use of his signature on a proclamation they were readying for publication on the ground that Reichstag members could better support the annexationist program if they maintained a certain independence from the groups formed outside the parliament.[57] He ignored the protest that the absence of his name from the proclamation, which had been signed by other Reichstag members, would have a bad effect.[58] His letter to Dietrich Schäfer emphasized that the time was not right for such a proclamation. "All eyes are on Rumania and the fronts," he wrote, "and if the Chancellor would say, 'Conquer, then talk of the prizes of victory,' most would agree." To a National Liberal confidant he complained against the "hysterical scoldings of the Pan-Germans" which were not helping the annexationist cause.[59]

Stresemann's attitude did not betoken any despondency as to the ultimate outcome of the war. He no longer anticipated as he had in the spring that "if the harvest were good" the war would end "without another winter campaign." He was also aware that the Verdun offensive had not been the success which the Supreme Command had expected, and that there was a growing desire for peace in the country.[60] However, he still had faith in the ability of the

military leaders to bring the war to a successful conclusion.[61]
His despondency lay in Germany's internal situation, in the
failure of the Government to "keep up the spirits of the
people." "Patriots are praised everywhere," he wrote, "except in Germany where only *Flaumacher* who want peace and
understanding with England are allowed to speak out." [62]

From the beginning of the war to the summer of 1916
the waves of annexationist demands had washed against the
figure of the Chancellor; they had moved him slightly but
had not dislodged him from his basically moderate position
on war aims in which he had the full support of the Emperor.[63] There had been an equal lack of success, in the same
period, to get the Chancellor to approve the policy of unlimited submarine warfare, the means by which the Greater
Germany was to be achieved, and we must now review
Stresemann's ideas and efforts concerning the conduct of the
war during this period before taking up the renewed struggle
to achieve the acceptance of the annexationist program.

PART THREE:

THE CONDUCT OF THE WAR

CHAPTER V

THE UNRESTRICTED SUBMARINE WAR (1914-1916)

In the preceding pages we have followed the efforts of Stresemann and his fellow annexationists to gain official acceptance of their positive war aims program during the first two years of the war. If to win the war meant achievement of the war aims, conversely, to gain the Greater Germany it was necessary to win the war. The implications have already been noted—a compromise peace must be rejected and any and all weapons available must be utilized to attain the victory. To most annexationists, certainly to Gustav Stresemann, the submarine represented the ultimate weapon for this latter purpose.

Submarine warfare, which led to American entry into the war and eventual German defeat, first drew attention in the closing weeks of 1914 when Grand Admiral von Tirpitz, State Secretary for the Naval Office, declared to an American newspaper correspondent that through the use of the underseas weapon Germany, too, could play the English game of starving out her enemy; the creator of the German navy emphasized that Germany possessed enough submarines to carry out this mission.[1] Shortly thereafter, in early February, 1915, a policy of "enlarged submarine warfare" was announced through which the waters around the British Isles were declared to be a "war zone" in which enemy merchant vessels would be sunk, and neutrals were warned of the danger of accidental sinkings in this area.[2] It was declared that this new submarine policy, intended to counter the Allied blockade which prevented not only war materials but also food from reaching the Central Powers, would "bring

England around *(einlenken)* within six weeks." [3] Without achieving this objective it had the immediate effect of involving Germany in diplomatic controversy with neutral nations, particularly the United States: the sinking of the *Lusitania* on May 7, 1915, changed the hitherto correct relationship between the two countries to one of threatened war, and tension became more acute in August with the sinking of the *Arabic*. However, a détente was achieved in September through diplomatic assurances to America that the submarine warfare would be curtailed, a decision made by the Imperial Government against the opposition of Tirpitz, who, in addition to continuation of the unrestricted submarine warfare pressed for a strengthening of Germany's naval position through annexation of the Flanders Coast. [4]

While the Government's assurances eased the tension with the neutrals, within Germany the lines were being drawn for continuation of the struggle as to whose policy, the Naval Secretary's or the Chancellor's, would prevail. [5] The action of the Admiralty chief in offering the submarine as the key to a quick victory, coupled with his agitation for Belgian fleet bases, had the effect of widening the gap between moderates and annexationists which had already developed despite the *Burgfrieden* and the official limitation of discussion of such matters. [6]

1. The *Lusitania* Crisis

Stresemann, already in the forefront of the annexationists, lost no time in expressing his support of Tirpitz's submarine doctrine. "I am glad," he wrote to a National Liberal colleague in the first weeks of 1915, "that in Tirpitz we have a man who goes his way and does not let himself be distracted by weak characters." He went on to point out that the Chancellor's demand for consideration for the crews of enemy merchant ships as opposed to the Admiral's policy of torpedoing without such consideration "had dealt the U-boat

action a great blow." "I am on Tirpitz's side," he concluded.
"In certain places they apparently still have not grasped
the fact that we are fighting a battle for our existence. . . ." [7]

Espousal by Stresemann of the submarine program was
to be expected even apart from its role as a means to the
annexationist ends he sought, for his record of support of
the fleet program of Admiral von Tirpitz dates back to
Stresemann's first public speeches as a newly elected member
of the Reichstag.[8] Again, in his campaign for re-election in
1912 he emphasized his belief that the "fleet meant as much
to the workingmen" of his constituency as Germany's "power
position" meant to him.[9] "We [National Liberals] are all
united," he then declared, "in the belief in an imperialistic
policy. . . . Our economic interests are in danger without
strong weapons. There is no place in the National Liberal
Party for the pacifist movement." [10]

That Stresemann was ever aware of any contradiction between Tirpitz's pre-war "risk policy," which emphasized
the building of capital ships, and the Grand Admiral's ad-
vocacy in 1914 of the submarine as the weapon to "force
England to her knees" is nowhere evidenced.[11] Stresemann
considered England's antagonism to the growth of the German fleet as completely unjustified.[12] He was so convinced
of the primacy of the economic rivalry that, while he frequently inveighed against the "encirclement policy of Edward VII," [13] he could not grasp at all that England looked
upon the growing German navy as a deadly menace to her
very existence.

Neither did he seem to realize that the use of the submarine, involving as it did Germany's relations with the
neutral states, was primarily a diplomatic question, and that
the admirals—and later the generals—were "talking politics"
when they declared that the U-boats would bring the war
to a successful conclusion despite American intervention,[14]
while he, who took great pride in being an active member

of the "freely-elected Reichstag," was playing at soldier in concentrating almost exclusively on the military capabilities of the submarine. His enthusiastic regard for German sea-power, extending throughout his career as a National Liberal, made it easy for Stresemann to accept unquestioningly the program offered by the Naval Secretary which in addition promised to provide the means to make realizable the positive war aims program, the glittering promise of which seemed to blind Stresemann to the realities of the German situation.

In full support of the Admiralty Stresemann approved the sinking of the *Lusitania* and fulminated at the "clever British Foreign Office" which stressed the fact that the German submarine action had been directed against a passenger liner while concealing that the ship was carrying ammunition.[15] The later agreement by the German Government to submit American claims to an arbitration court filled Stresemann with dismay.[16]

Would it not then be opportune for the political parties to speak out concerning the submarine war in such a way that the Naval Secretary could utilize this support against the Chancellor? This question brought Stresemann to the Admiralty on June 19, 1915, for a long conversation with the Undersecretary, Eduard von Capelle. The latter advised Stresemann that the Grand Admiral had imposed "strictest reserve" on the Naval Office in matters touching on political relations with the United States. He explained that an action of parliamentary groups such as suggested by Stresemann would appear as having been planned by Tirpitz as an intrigue against the Chancellor, and with the admonition that the Grand Admiral "might be put into the embarrassing position" of having to repudiate it, Capelle requested the Deputy to refrain from any such action.[17]

Nevertheless, the Undersecretary fully shared Stresemann's views about the nature of the war. He did not hide his disapproval of the Government's policy, pointing out that the Foreign Office completely misunderstood the nature of submarine warfare, which, from a purely military side, could not be engaged in on a limited basis.[18] Although he discounted the recent warnings of the American Ambassador, Gerard, as to the effects of a break in relations—he doubted that it would change materially the situation concerning the American supply of ammunition or loans to the Entente—Capelle nevertheless recommended that if possible good relations with the United States should be maintained. To that end he recommended that Germany should settle the *Lusitania* claims, which he expected to be moderate. The Undersecretary concluded by stating that the Chancellor's office was the place for decisions in all these matters.[19]

The implication in Capelle's remarks that the political leaders should put their pressure directly upon the Chancellor was not lost on Stresemann. A few days later, on June 28, he participated in the presentation of a petition of the Economic Organizations, already active in the war aims question. The petition urged the Chancellor not to give up or even limit in any way the energetic prosecution of the submarine war, which was termed Germany's "most effective countermeasure" to England's economic warfare. The petitioners declared that Germany had no substitute for the submarine and that yielding to American demands "to stop and search merchant ships before torpedoing" them would end effective submarine warfare; that while they realized the importance of good relations with the United States, no restrictions to the use of the submarine should be considered until Germany had adequate guarantees that there would be no obstruction to the legal supply of foodstuffs and raw materials, and that Americans would not be passengers on merchant ships carrying ammunition to Germany's enemies.[20]

Stresemann's regret in the Government's failure to heed the petition and to strengthen its policy is reflected in both the tone and content of his correspondence: he had been informed by "reliable sources" (he wrote) that the submarine war was being further limited and Tirpitz's political activities closely restricted—he feared that the Grand Admiral would again submit his resignation and that it would be accepted. Changes had already been made in the Admiralty staff which would probably threaten the submarine program and the western war aims program as well.[21] That the Naval Office held high regard for Stresemann—certainly found his services on its behalf useful—is suggested by the invitation in July, 1915, from the commandant at Heligoland to address the officers at that naval base, and by the enthusiastic reception given to his discussion of the war, its causes, the importance of the German fleet and the submarines, and the Greater Germany to come with victory.[22]

Later in the month at Cologne, where the National Liberal leaders attacked the Chancellor's "weak" policy and spelled out their war aims program, they also made allusion to the submarine program: Bassermann criticized the censorship which allowed those in favor of "proposals for peace" to speak out while it suppressed the utterances of those "who demanded a policy of force devoid of any sentiment." Stresemann attacked Admiral Truppel for an article, supposedly written at the behest of the Chancellor, in which he had stressed the importance of maintaining good relations with the United States, even at the expense of the Tirpitz program.[23]

When, with the sinking of the *Arabic* in August and the attendant warnings from Count Bernstorff, the German Ambassador in Washington, it became clear to Stresemann that it was the intent of the German government to meet the demands of the United States, he was stirred to further action. It took the form of a petition from his Saxon industrial group to the government of that state. Pointing out that Saxon industry, despite the disastrous economic effects of the war and the dangers of enlarging the war, insisted that Germany carry on with "all military means" to the ultimate victory, he urged against any permanent slackening of the war effort against England through restriction of the submarine in an effort to maintain good relations with the United States.[24]

Stresemann was bitter over the way the *Arabic* incident was handled, both by Count Bernstorff in Washington and by the Foreign Office in Berlin and over the settlement reached—a pledge by the German Government that in the future no liners would be sunk without warning and that additional measures would be taken for the safety of noncombatants. "I hope," he wrote to Huldermann, associate of Ballin at the Hamburg-America Line, in reference to the *Arabic* matter, "that the time will come in this world war when we are free from worry over other places of battle and can take up the submarine war once again with full force. Then, however, we shall have to torpedo everything that is sent into the war zone!" [25]

2. The Tirpitz Crisis of 1916

The second controversy, or more precisely, the continuing battle between Tirpitz and Bethmann-Hollweg regarding the submarine warfare, reached its climax in March of 1916. It coincided with and was in part caused by an external crisis brought about by the extension of the submarine warfare to armed merchantmen at the end of February. This had resulted in the sinking of the *Sussex* on March 24, an event which had again tautened relations with the United States until the German Government, as in the previous year, yielded to an American ultimatum.

The internal dispute resulted in the resignation of Admiral von Tirpitz when the Emperor, at his headquarters in Charleville, upheld the Chancellor's policy, although the Admiral was now supported by both the Navy and the Supreme Com-

mand.[26] Expressing the views of the sea arm, Holtzendorff,
Chief of the Admiralty Staff, asserted that ruthless submarine warfare would force England to sue for peace within
five or six months. He declared that the submarine was the
"one surviving means of bringing the war to a successful issue
within a measurable time." The Supreme Command had earlier opposed unrestricted submarine warfare. Now General
Falkenhayn maintained that the military and political situation of Germany demanded that she no longer refrain from
using the only measure capable of saving the situation.[27]

The role of the submarine had become a topic of intense
interest and controversy among the German people, despite
the censorship restrictions, from the time of the Grand Admiral's sensational disclosure to the press in late 1914.[28] The
use of the U-boats against armed merchantmen in February,
1916, had been misunderstood by many to mean the waging
of completely unrestricted warfare, hence public discussion
was lively even before Tirpitz left his naval post on March 14,
an event which raised the clamor to an even higher pitch.[29]
Even the Chancellor acknowledged that at this time unlimited submarine warfare appeared to be the desire of the nation as a whole.[30]

Even after his resignation Tirpitz continued to press for
all-out submarine warfare, and under his influence the Admiralty office utilized contacts with the civilian advocates of
a "German peace," both inside and outside the Reichstag, on
behalf of unhampered use of the undersea craft as the means
to a quick, victorious peace.[31] In the dispute between the
military and civilian branches of the Government the Chancellor was able to maintain both his position and his political
control.[32] The Emperor, however temporizingly, had supported Bethmann, and Falkenhayn was not popular enough
to carry public opinion against the civil government even
before the failure of Verdun became apparent and shattered
all confidence in his military leadership.[33] Thus the summer

of 1916 found the submarine still restricted in accordance with the views of the Chancellor.

3. The Committee Hearings on the U-Boats

Stresemann once again emerged as a strong supporter of unlimited submarine warfare at the beginning of 1916. He was convinced that Germany's military and political situation would be the brightest since the beginning of the war if only Germany would make use of "the sharpest weapon" at her disposal, and as with the annexationist program he was active in the effort to clear the way for an open discussion of these problems.[34] When the *Baralong* affair was discussed in the Finance Committee in January, Stresemann called for action to prevent the recurrence of such a "disgraceful situation," implying that only ruthless submarine warfare would serve as a "basis of support against England."[35] He even took the matter, hitherto discussed only in the Committee, to the floor of the Reichstag and called for an end to censorship restrictions which prevented open discussion of "great questions" urgently requiring debate, among which he emphasized the submarine warfare and the manner in which the United States had repeatedly interfered in the German conduct of the war through its complaints. Stresemann asserted that the German people desired to give expression to the emotions which these issues aroused, and if that were allowed, Germany's diplomatic representations, offered in the name of the German people, would be greatly strengthened.[36] In a later address in the plenum he demanded that the Reichstag should not be eliminated in the discussion of such important questions.[37] Outside the parliament the Economic Organizations in January presented a second petition to the Government calling for energetic use of the undersea weapon.[38]

When public announcement was made of the resignation of Tirpitz, Stresemann, on behalf of the Union of Saxon Industry, sent a glowing telegram to the Admiral, praising him for his work in building up the fleet "with his eye on England"; [39] and in his first parliamentary speech thereafter he eulogized the Grand Admiral as the man who symbolized "the will of the German people to seapower in the face of the opposition of jealous peoples." [40] These actions also served to demonstrate openly his disapproval of the Government's submarine policy.

The resignation of Admiral von Tirpitz made it inevitable that the Government defend its submarine policy before the political party leaders. Involving as it did the discussion of numbers of submarines, their employment, and relations with neutrals, the debate at the end of March took place within the Finance Committee, which controlled the naval budget, rather than on the floor of the Reichstag.

Stresemann's position in the forefront of the proponents of full use of the submarine and his close connections with the Naval Office were well known to the Chancellor, who invited him to a private conference a week before the committee hearings. At this meeting Bethmann pointed out to Stresemann that the Navy surreptitiously released false figures to the public concerning the number of submarines available, figures which he could not correct because of security reasons. The Chancellor also discussed with his visitor the diplomatic complications tied to the unrestricted use of the submarine, but he did not succeed in changing Stresemann's viewpoint. The latter asserted that he knew exactly how many submarines there were, and insofar as the handling of Germany's diplomatic problems was concerned he stated bluntly that he would prefer to see Tirpitz in the Chancellor's chair. [41]

That Stresemann had an inordinate faith in the naval leader is manifest; in fact, he even belonged among those who, according to Erzberger, blindly trusted Tirpitz and followed him as the children followed the Pied Piper of Hamelin. [42] But that he was, with regard to the number of submarines, "taken in" by the naval leaders who "made good use of his gullibility," as has been asserted, is doubtful.[43] Although the number of available submarines was not the primary concern of the Committee, it was discussed; [44] and whatever figures the Admiralty may have surreptitiously circulated to the public, Stresemann heard in Committee the testimony of Admiral von Capelle, who had replaced Tirpitz as State Secretary, and Capelle's figures were not questioned by the Chancellor.[45] Even if it is impossible to reconcile the figures given by Capelle with those found in the memoirs of the Chancellor, Erzberger, and others, they are not greatly at variance, and in no case are they large.[46] Stresemann was also informed as to the number of undersea craft actually in operation against England at a given time, and his enthusiasm for the U-boat war was not effected by their paucity.[47] When the Admiralty in 1916 advised Stresemann that delivery of four submarines was being made each month, he wrote enthusiastically to a follower that the rate of increase ranged from thirteen to seventeen monthly.[48] At the beginning of 1917 he was giving figures on submarine production and performance far in excess of those given confidentially by the Admiralty in the Committee hearings.[49]

The Admiralty may well be blamed for failing to press to the utmost the building of submarines before it was too late.[50] Yet even in the depths of his despair in the collapse of 1918 Stresemann speaks only of failure and not of deception when bitterly castigating the naval leadership for the limited production of undersea craft despite the assurances of industry and the urgings of the party leaders.[51]

It would appear that it was in the evaluation of the capabilities of the submarine and more in the appraisal of the effects on the enemy of its use, even if its capabilities had been properly evaluated, that any duplicity lay. If there is some suggestion that the Admiralty used Stresemann to carry out its game, it is clear that both the military leadership, in the desperate hope of winning an otherwise lost war, and

those, including Stresemann, who shared a far-reaching positive war aims program, were suffering from a self-deception
which they could not afford to give up in their assessment of
the potentialities of the submarine employed without restrictions.

In the Committee hearings in March it was not the question of numbers but what the submarine could accomplish
if fully utilized which primarily engaged the disputants. It
was with the strong statement that "in the U-boat Germany
has the weapon to defeat England," Bassermann opened the
discussion.[52] He was followed by the Chancellor and then by
Admiral Capelle, who gave assurance that "the organization
and material for the beginning and carrying through of the
submarine war were available in sufficient measure," and
that six hundred thousand tons of shipping would be the
minimum destroyed monthly, as previously stated by the
Naval Office.[53] It was on the Admiral's testimony that Stresemann based his declaration that in six months English losses
would amount to approximately four million tons, a quarter
of her total tonnage. At this point Bethmann interposed that
"if and when he considered the submarine would bring closer
a victorious peace" he would be for it, but that it was clear
to him that the prospective English tonnage losses would not
"force England to her knees." [54]

Stresemann, supported by Capelle, rejected the Chancellor's phrase. "I do not know," he said, "how the Chancellor
arrived at this expression." [55] He maintained that he and his
friends had never claimed that the submarine would bring
England "to renounce sovereignty of the seas" and let Germany dictate the peace.[56] They were, however, of the "decided conviction" that through such destruction of English
tonnage as projected by the Admiralty for the next six months
Germany would "strike the English economy so decisively
that the inclination to make peace with Germany would
dominate in England." Stresemann developed his argument:

Unlike Germany (he explained) England depended upon her merchant fleet, and the Chancellor had erred in stating that England would have "world tonnage at her disposal," for even her allies could not give up all their ships to her. If England were to lose the predicted tonnage she would not only lose "world prestige" but would in fact collapse.[57] Stresemann pointed out that this was not offered as his own view alone, but as that of a board of "economic experts" consulted by the Admiralty, a board of "cool, calculating merchants"— no "Pan-German utopians without knowledge of the field" —which had agreed that such a destruction of tonnage would be catastrophic for England. Stresemann concluded that even if English power had not been broken in six months, Germany could continue the destruction of English tonnage and make the matter of imports a decisive one for England.[58]

The Chancellor cautioned that indignation against England was not a basis for foreign policy and widened the discussion by pointing out that the unrestricted submarine policy would endanger relations with the United States and other neutrals. Would the damage to England, which he did not believe would force her to make peace, outweigh the effects of war with America?[59] The party leaders were divided on this issue, but neither Bassermann nor Stresemann believed that the United States would go to war, and the latter cited aspects of American internal politics in support of his view.[60] Stresemann was of the opinion that there was more danger of collision with the neutrals with limited than with unrestricted submarine warfare and predicted that increased U-boat activity would cause the European neutrals to ship more goods to Germany. Stresemann admitted that an American war declaration could not be taken lightly—it would entail "loss of German investments" there and "difficulties in South America" as well, to say nothing of increased financial aid to England, but he averred that all these disadvantages would be more than balanced by the catastrophe which the submarine warfare would bring to England. He warned that there was no assurance that England would not tighten her blockade even if Germany did not extend the submarine war for the Allied Conference at Paris was even then planning economic actions against Germany, and finally that Germany's economic position was worsening from month to month.

The National Liberal spokesman summarized his views: In the limited submarine war he could see only "an occasional success and a certain risk." In the ruthless conduct he could see "a procedure promising success." It might—although he doubted it—lead to a war declaration by America, but on the other hand "it opened up certain prospects of economic victory over England," who, though not forced to her knees, would be forced to make peace.[61]

The Chancellor maintained his position that the unlimited use of the U-boat would not improve Germany's overall position but make it worse.[62] He was supported on economic grounds by State Secretary Helfferich, who suggested that perhaps after "a victory at Verdun," when Germany no longer needed "to fear the opinion of the neutrals," the situation might be different.[63]

The hearings came to a close when the National Liberals, with the backing of the Conservatives and some of the Center deputies, rejected Bethmann's explanation and refused a vote of confidence. Stresemann warned Helfferich that there was little time left, and the Government would bear the responsibility "if it waited too long." In departing, he directed two questions at the Chancellor: What sort of peace would Bethmann achieve if he renounced the submarine war? How did he propose to end the war if he did not "apply the means which Germany possessed for vanquishing her main enemy?" [64]

4. The Aftermath of the Second Crisis

The discussion of the unrestricted submarine warfare was interjected into the extensive debate over war aims which took place on the floor of the Reichstag in April and May. Stresemann vehemently attacked "American business circles" for exploiting a "one-sided conception of neutrality in a shameless manner." He supported the Conservatives' resolution for unrestricted warfare, warning that the effects of the Allied blockade compelled Germany to "strike England's economic life in its vital nerve." To the Social Democrats, who warned that the people wanted peace and that the extension of the use of the submarine would close every possibility of bringing the war to an end, Stresemann declared, with the support of his Party, that only through application of all means at her disposal could Germany shorten the war and bring it to a victorious end.[65]

The war aims proclamation which the National Liberal Party issued in Berlin on May 21 reflected these demands of the Party for full utilization of the submarine. Calling for the employment of increased power against England, the principal foe, the Committee declared it to be "the main task of German politics to assure the military leadership freedom in the use of all military means to guarantee a decisive victory." [66]

As with the annexationist program, however, the demands for unrestricted submarine warfare, despite pamphlets, petitions, and propaganda, had not succeeded in the first two years of the war in materially altering the government's policy. There were brief moments of hope, as when in early June the Reichstag was carried away with wild enthusiasm over the reports of the naval battle of Jutland, and the enthusiasts could envision a new predominance of the Naval Office in policy making; [67] or when, in July the successful transit to Baltimore of the cargo submarine *Deutschland* was hailed by Stresemann as the advent of a new economic weapon.[68] But these moments were few and of no import— the Chancellor had prevailed. Even Under State Secretary Zimmermann in the Foreign Office to whom Stresemann

looked as a guide toward a more aggressive policy informed
the Deputy that American entry into the war would be unde-
sirable; while Admiral von Capelle, although he did not
"overestimate" America and considered the maintenance of
the submarine war to be "a matter of prestige," told Stresemann that the U-boats alone could not bring England to her
knees even though the damage they could do would be
strongly felt.[69]

Stresemann, however, had not lost faith in the efficacy of
the unleashed submarine, and with the failure of the Verdun
offensive and the tightening of the Allied blockade, he was
more than ever convinced of the necessity of its use with renewed vigor as a means of settling England's fate.[70]

It is a question of our existence [he wrote] and the Government must be prodded again and again. . . . Every concession the
Chancellor has made concerning war aims and conduct of the war
has occurred only under our pressure, and it is all the more necessary to maintain this pressure.[71]

Chapter VI

THE VICTORY OF THE ANNEXATIONISTS
(1916-1917)

It was the change in the High Command in August, 1916, which enabled the protagonists of unrestricted submarine warfare and an unambiguously annexationist program to force through their demands.[1] Although Bethmann had thus far been able to resist the war aims majority within the Reichstag, which was now becoming a pro-submarine majority as well, to say nothing of industrialist and Pan-German pressures outside, he was not able to stand up against Hindenburg and Ludendorff, the heroes of Tannenberg, who, after the failure of Falkenhayn's Verdun offensive, not only took over the direction of Germany's military efforts but also began to encroach in areas normally under civil jurisdiction.[2]

The policy reversal did not, however, come about immediately. The precarious military situation which existed when the Chancellor and the new Supreme Command met at Pless in August enabled Bethmann to get the concurrence of the military leaders that "the time had not yet come for unrestricted submarine warfare," and even further, "that Germany had to do everything possible to gain peace," as well as to restore unity within the country.[3] As a result the Chancellor accepted the offer of President Wilson to "act in the interest of peace," and when various political considerations seemed to slow down Wilson's mediation efforts until after the November elections, the German Government initiated its own peace offer.[4] At home an effort was made to lessen tension by sanctioning officially the "objective discussion of war aims." [5]

In back of the acquiescence of the High Command lay the demand for unlimited submarine warfare in the event of the failure of peace negotiations.[6] Neither Hindenburg nor Ludendorff had hope of ending the war successfully in the sense that Germany would, "through military blows inflicted by the land forces," achieve the goals deemed desirable both by the High Command and the annexationists. They shared the view of the Admiralty that unrestricted submarine warfare offered the only means and a certain means of bringing peace through a military triumph, and even as they gave assent to the Chancellor's peace proposals the military leaders were furthering plans for the extension of the U-boat war. In December, even before the German peace offer had been officially rejected by the Allies and while the German Government was expressing its approval of Wilson's mediation proposals, Hindenburg had persuaded the vacillating Emperor of the necessity of unrestricted submarine warfare.[7] The new policy was unanimously agreed upon at a Crown Council at Pless on January 9, with February 1, 1917, set as the date for its implementation. The Chancellor offered no opposition.[8] The failure of his peace proposals, marked by the antagonistic attitude of the Allied powers, had a far-reaching effect in Germany. Not only did Bethmann suffer a great loss of prestige, but the Supreme Command rose to new heights of influence and power, backed by the demands of the annexationists for a victorious peace and the general determination of the people to see the war through to a finish.[9]

The triumph of the U-boat, the means to victory, was a triumph as well for the positive war aims program. By April the Emperor had moved away from the moderate position he had previously held, due in part to pressure exerted by the Supreme Command; and in May, despite his inner feelings, the Chancellor, to the cheers of the Reichstag, told that body he was "in full agreement" with the military leaders on the question of war aims.[10]

1. Stresemann and the Supreme Command

Stresemann quickly grasped the significance of the change in the High Command. In the summer of 1916 his attitude had been one of despair. "Our entire situation is slowly becoming such that one can hardly hold his head erect," he wrote to a National Liberal colleague. "One lets the best spirits of the people come to nothing, depresses them intentionally through the naive hope of the Chancellor that England will . . . come to agreement with us in the fall." [11]

To Stresemann the way to lift the spirits of the people was to stimulate them both through the pledge of the Greater Germany to come with victory and through the unrestricted use of the submarine. "In foreign policy," he wrote, "our position is geting worse and worse. I begin to doubt our victory, for if we do not conquer England now, the peace will be closed at our expense. . . ." [12] Yet withdrawal from the battle, as evidenced in his separation from the Pan-German activities of the summer, was not in keeping with the Deputy's character. His letter continued:

We must not let ourselves be eliminated any more in the Reichstag. When it is a question of our existence we cannot depend alone on the Emperor and his weak Chancellor. On the contrary, we must see to it that we steer toward victory or at least prevent approaching the abyss.[13]

Stresemann suggested discussion of these matters in a *Fraktion* meeting, but even before the Reichstag sessions Stresemann spoke out at a National Liberal gathering at Eisenach in September. With a sharpness born of despair he criticized the failures of German foreign policy, "wrong from its very foundations." Declaring that all annexationist hopes depended on defeating England through the use of the submarine, he charged that "not technical but political reasons" held up the unrestricted submarine warfare for which Germany could not wait. He demanded more influence for the Reichstag in the making of foreign policy decisions such as in the use of the submarine.

Stresemann's Eisenach speech was no call to revolution. In his criticism of the Foreign Office he went no further than he had gone in pre-war speeches calling for diplomatic appointments based on ability rather than birth. In asking for influence for the Reichstag he made it clear he was not calling for the parliamentary system, i. e., responsible government after the English pattern; in calling for reforms he sought no radical changes to be made during the war.[14] In 1906 at his first Party Day at Goslar the young Stresemann had accused the National Liberals of being "too governmental," "too doctrinaire," but during the *Daily Telegraph* Affair crisis which occurred shortly thereafter he had meekly followed Bassermann in the latter's policy of gentle criticism of the Emperor's "personal rule." [15] At Eisenach it was victory which Stresemann wanted rather than reform *per se,* and no more did he seek power for himself or the Reichstag despite his desire to shape the policies of the Government toward the achievement of the Greater Germany. It was this failure of Stresemann and his Reichstag colleagues to "put their weight into the balance" which accounts for the influence of the Supreme Command, under the "demigods," Hindenburg and Ludendorff.[16]

Although Stresemann later was known by the appellative "Ludendorff's young man," [17] he was not, at least before the war, a blind devotee of military leadership, a follower of any Captain from Koepenik. His reaction to the notorious Zabern affair of 1913—he denounced the military leaders in Alsace for their "arrogant breaking of the law," for their display "not only of ignorance but scorn [of the law] in the spirit of the military rabble of earlier centuries"—is clear proof of that, and on several occasions during the war he criticized military governors for excesses in their handling of civil lib-

erties under the war-time state of siege.[18] Early in the war
he had looked to Tirpitz as a successor to Bethmann, but the
issue was not one of military versus civilian authority, rather
one of "strong" leadership against "weak." [19] Now Stresemann turned to the new Army commanders. Adulation for
Hindenburg he did feel, along with the majority of the German people. It was not blind worship, however, which now
influenced him but the fact that in the Field Marshal and
his collaborator he saw a new power which could accomplish
what others had been unable to—force the Government to
the strong policy which would bring to fulfillment the annexationist dreams of a Greater Germany.[20]

Stresemann wrote carefully of these matters to a few of
his close constituents: Bassermann was in close touch with
the new military leaders and reported their strong influence
in matters pertaining to the political conduct of the war; he
would place confidence in them if their "leading position"
in political matters were guaranteed. Stresemann added that
he, too, would go along if it would bring results.[21] Shortly
thereafter he could advise that Bassermann had been assured
that the submarine question was being re-examined, and
that the Admiralty was preparing a new memorandum on
the subject. Stresemann added that the new military leaders
were "against a Chancellor change at this time" but supported
Bethmann only so long as the latter "supported a strong policy and a strong peace." [22] The Chancellor, Stresemann reported, had succeeded in getting rid of Falkenhayn only to
find himself in a more difficult position, for he had placed
himself "under the great shield of Hindenburg" in answering questions about the submarine with the phrase: "Hindenburg is examining the matter, and you can depend on his
judgment." [23]

It had been Stresemann's first reaction that there was the
danger that Hindenburg, "a military man and not a politician," might be "mis-used" in the submarine question by

telling him that it was primarily a political matter because
of the significance of American interference or an economic
matter "by smothering him in figures," and he took steps
through Bassermann to counter any such influences on the
Field Marshal.[24] By early autumn it was clear that this danger
was non-existent, and Stresemann, informed of the views of
the High Command ("Ludendorff," he wrote, "is far more
the politician" [25]) could say with confidence that the "question has now been moved entirely out of the realm of political discussion and is solely a military question" in which
"the Chancellor is no longer interfering." Stresemann's only
regret was that "with the passing of summer the best time
for the use of this sharp weapon [had] been uselessly wasted."
By the end of September he was even accused of looking at
things "in too rosy a manner." [26]

After Berthold Körting, one of the more phrenetic Pan-
Germans among the National Liberals, had unsuccessfully appealed to Bassermann to bring about the Chancellor's down-
fall,[27] he then urged Stresemann to take over the leadership
of the Party in the Reichstag to fight against the Chancellor
and for ruthless submarine warfare and the annexationist
program.[28] Stresemann replied that he had been requested by
Hindenburg, through intermediaries, to "hold back on the
domestic political battle," and for this and other reasons was
convinced that they should accede to the wish of the army
leaders." [29] He added that Ludendorff, in a similar manner,
had informed him of his position regarding the use of the
submarines; he assured Körting that "one could have confidence that Hindenburg and Ludendorff would solve the question in the proper manner." [30]

How one can achieve something [cautioned Stresemann] is a
matter of tactics, and a blind attitude against the Chancellor may
create just the opposite effect from that which we wish. . . . As for
the rest, I am not as pessimistic as you are regarding the war aims.
It may be that the Chancellor takes the stand which you men-

tioned, but it is just as true that Ludendorff does not share this viewpoint . . . and Ludendorff appears to me to be the far more powerful man, especially if we have a military success in Rumania.[31]

2. The Third Submarine Crisis

In this confident frame of mind Stresemann attended the Reichstag Committee discussions early in October, 1916, which Bassermann, as chairman of the Commission on Foreign Affairs, opened with a call for consideration of the "fundamental question" of submarine warfare.[32] During the deliberations which followed, both Bethmann and Helfferich defended the position taken by the Government in the spring, warning that Germany's position was becoming more difficult and that the submarine warfare would increase these difficulties by causing war with the United States without bringing Germany closer to a victorious peace. Stresemann reaffirmed his confidence in the U-boat as the means of forcing England to peace through the destruction of her vital merchant fleet and repeated his query of the previous sessions of the Committee, how, without this weapon, did the Government propose to bring the war to an end? [33]

Stresemann's prognostication as to the effects of the use of the unrestrained submarine on England was promptly challenged by the Center Deputy Erzberger.[34] He warned Stresemann that in his calculations he was forgetting the world tonnage at England's disposal and asked in turn how peace would be made with America once that nation was brought into the conflict through the unrestricted submarine war. This exchange hinted at the great debate which was to shake the Reichstag and the nation in the summer of 1917.[35] Now, however, it was overshadowed by the startling statements of another member of the divided Center Party, Gröber, who carried the Committee debates to a climax by proclaiming that the decision concerning the use of the submarine rested with

Hindenburg, for if he were for it neither the Chancellor nor the Reichstag would oppose his decision.[36] After this declaration, which exposed momentarily the true power of the Supreme Command, he offered a resolution, supported by the majority including the National Liberal representatives, calling for the prosecution of the unrestricted submarine warfare.[37]

In his first clash with Tirpitz in 1915 the Chancellor had had the support of the Reichstag except for the enthusiasts who had followed Bassermann and his lieutenant Stresemann; in the second crisis, in the spring of 1916, the middle-class parties had been divided in their attitude; now, the majority of the party leaders in the Committee had gone over to the side of the Supreme Command in support of full use of the undersea weapon. For the Chancellor there was but one card left to play, the Peace Note of December 12, which proved to be no trump, and even before the failure of the peace offer was known, the Emperor had proved too weak to stand up to his military commanders in their demand for unrestricted submarine warfare.[38]

Stresemann used the Committee hearings as a platform to support the recent activities of the Pan-German groups on behalf of the submarine and positive war aims programs.[39] He also became active once again outside the Reichstag in the annexationist campaign. On October 24, he delivered the main address at a meeting of the *Bund der Industriellen* in which he pointed to "the conquered areas in the West" as possible sources for the raw materials which Germany needed. The following day they joined with the *Zentralverband Deutscher Industrieller,* a cosignatory of the petitions of the Six Economic Organizations, to form a union of light and heavy industry; and the newly formed council immediately sent a message to the Emperor expressing the hope of industry that Germany would emerge from the war "strengthened, enlarged, and secured" in both East and West.[40] Stresemann hit hard at the idea of a "Scheidemann peace," one in which "each would bear his own burden." [41] "If a Scheidemann idea got abroad," he declared, "it would be be taken as a sign that Germany feels it cannot win." He warned that a peace which recognized "neither victor nor vanquished" would signify a war lost by Germany, for if the enemy did not pay the cost of the war through compensations, the German people would have to bear the cost through heavily increased taxes which would fall on all classes.[42] His reiterated warnings about increased tax burdens related to a peace without compensations led the way for the Pan-German campaign in 1917 in which they "raised the specter of financial ruin in order to convert people to their plans." [43]

The results of the Committee hearings, the announcements of military success in Rumania, and the reports of the marine specialists on increased effectiveness of the submarines all combined to strengthen Stresemann's optimism during the closing days of 1916. "If, as can be assumed practically with certainty, the Entente rejects our peace offer," he noted, "then the last doubts fall away with regard to our now using our sharpest weapon." [44] Stresemann had no doubts about the U-boat's bringing a favorable peace if used to the greatest extent.[45]

3. The Victory of the Annexationists

When the Entente did reject Bethmann's Peace Note in January, it was the signal for the opening of a new propaganda barrage in support of the unlimited submarine warfare, with Stresemann serving as one of the heavy gunners.[46] As his comparative silence on this issue, outside the Reichstag Committee, had been in accordance with the wishes of Hindenburg and Ludendorff, his sudden burst into print and speech seems also to have been at their behest; at least, he had been made aware, well in advance of the announcement to the Party leaders at the meeting of the Reichstag

Committee on January 31, that the unrestricted warfare would be resumed on February 1.[47] His writings seem geared to the nature of the coming event. In an article written for publication on January 10, the day after the Pless Conference, he presaged the yet secret decision of the Crown Council. He exulted in the rapidly mounting loss of Allied shipping due to German submarines, whose effectiveness had been increased through "stronger armament, extended radius of action, and greater numbers." He warned that England and France were attempting to stop the submarines by arming their merchant vessels and therefore demanded that the German submarines be freed from the restrictions which were limiting their effectiveness. Turning to the crisis in England caused by the lack of cargo space and the resulting food shortage, he predicted that through increased use of the submarine England would be "forced to the peace table despite all the loud words through which Lloyd George attempted to conceal his anxiety":

. . . Proud England, take heed! [he concluded.] The time will come when England will resemble a beleaguered fortress . . . and the economic life of the island will suffer such an annihilating blow that no state minister at the end of the war can deny to us what we must have for our German future! [48]

Throughout the month Stresemann provided a steady outpouring of written and spoken agitation for the resumption of the unrestricted U-boat war. He denounced the Entente for the attitude manifested in their reply to the German peace offer, and petitioned the Emperor on behalf of the Union of Saxon Industry "to use all means to the greatest extent" which would in the foreseeable future change both the military and economic situation of their enemies. "The German people," he asserted, are in favor of this policy." [49]

In a speech before the Prussian Diet Stresemann pointed out that Napoleon had gone down to defeat because his fleet

had not been equal to that of the British, but added that
where "Abukir" and "Trafalgar" had been the "fateful
words" which recalled that earlier drama, "Skagerrak" and
the "German U-boats" were the words which marked the
present struggle, and England must admit defeat in its attempt to prepare Germany for the fate which had befallen
Napoleon.[50]

The meeting of the Reichstag's Main Committee on the
last day of January proved an anti-climax. As in the preceding spring, when the Chancellor had rejected the demands
of the parliamentarians who had supported Admiral von Tirpitz, the policy decision had already been made at the Crown
Council at Pless. Now, however, the Chancellor "painfully
pleaded for policy he had passionately opposed" for so long,[51]
while State Secretary Helfferich demonstrated with figures
and diagrams the very opposite of what he had shown in his
reply to Stresemann in the fall.[52] Admiral von Capelle, speaking for the Navy, guaranteed that the submarines would sink
six hundred thousand tons a month and thus "soften England
within six months." [53] He gave the opinion that although
from a financial and economic point of view American entry
into the war would be important, she was already producing
as much ammunition as she was able and "from a military
point of view" her entrance would mean nothing. "Should
America finally raise and train an army," he concluded, "and
be able to provide transports for it, our submarines could not
wish for better hunting." [54] As in the October meetings the
Center Deputy Gröber led the parliamentarians in support
of the new policy, confident in the judgment of the Supreme
Command, and Stresemann followed Bassermann in calling
for the unrestricted submarine warfare "regardless of the
American attitude." [55]

Stresemann had already prepared a long article for the
press to greet the opening of the unlimited U-boat war on
the first day of February.[56] The new development (he wrote)

had come as a result of the "growing and complete agreement" among the people based upon "hatred of England" and the desire to bring about peace through her collapse. He indicated that Germany would be able "to stand the tests" which the new measures would bring with the European neutral, who would recognize the necessity caused by the Entente's rejection of the German peace offer and would also realize that "this new ruthlessness would shorten the war." Stresemann expressed the hope that the United States, too, would remain out of the war—he pointed to "the growing understanding of the German position" there, particularly in the Congress—but added that "should a small group of blinded war fanatics" not preserve the peace, no difficulties which might interfere with Germany's foreign trade would be of significance compared to the possibility of conquering England. The tide had now turned in favor of Germany and her allies, and the world war had achieved its high point. "In the spring," he predicted, "world historical decisions will be made on all fronts as the fleet steps to the side of the army to strike the enemy at its nerve center":

The Emperor's command for full battle for the U-boats has lifted a nightmare from the German people. . . . With beating hearts we await the decision. We believe that the peace which our enemies have insultingly rejected . . . will now be ours after we make the renewed attempt with all strength to force through the victory. We hope for an earlier peace and a stronger triumph.[57]

The American decision to break diplomatic relations with Germany with the warning "this means war," reached Berlin late on February 3, "when the National Liberal Party under Stresemann's leadership was approving the submarine policy and denouncing the *Flaumacher* who had warned against it." [58]

The annexationist program was not neglected by Stresemann, who had joined the Pan-Germans in their renewed campaign following the rejection of the German Peace Note.[59] With Schäfer, Traub, and Westarp he headed a great rally of the Independent Committee for a German Peace in Berlin; and his speech there neglected no aspect of the annexationist program.[60] Stresemann was warmly commended by the Military Governor in Belgium, General von Bissing, for his speech in Hanover, "A German Peace and the German Future," in which he emphasized the permanence of German interests in Belgium.[61] He also joined with the Six Economic Organizations in the reaffirmance of their adherence to their program of 1915.[62] To the National Liberal Deputies assembled in the lounge of the Reichstag on the fiftieth anniversary of the Party in February, Stresemann expressed adhesion to the Greater Germany to be achieved through the use of the nation's sharpest weapons.[63] The war aims, however, occupied but a fraction of his address for the annexationist program was now assured. When the Chancellor had yielded to the Supreme Command on the means of prosecuting the war it had become inevitable that he accept as well the detailed program of war aims which they laid down, with the Emperor's approval, at a series of conferences at the General Headquarters at Kreuznach.[64] In the spring the Government moved officially from the basis of "no war of conquest" of August, 1914, to a platform of positive war aims.[65] The torpedoes of the unrestricted U-boats were to bring the Greater Germany!

Chapter VII

AN ANNEXATIONIST'S DIPLOMACY (1914-1917)

As the unrestricted U-boat war followed logically from the annexationist war aims program, so did an unremitting and implacable opposition to the man who had stood in the way of both the desired ends and the means to their fulfillment, the Chancellor, Bethman-Hollweg. Stresemann's attitude toward the Chancellor, which has been brought out in the preceding pages in connection with both war aims and submarine questions, extended beyond these matters to encompass all aspects of the Chancellor's conduct of the war.

"This war was lost diplomatically for Germany before it began militarily," wrote Stresemann at the height of the controversy over the submarines.[1] The phrase indicates not only the deep-rooted opposition of Deputy to Chancellor extending back into the pre-war period but suggests also, at least in part, a reason—the phrase was not originally Stresemann's but Prince Bülow's.[2] It was in the triumph of the Bülow Bloc Program of 1907 that Stresemann had first won election to the Reichstag, and with Bassermann he had remained an ardent supporter of the Prince's imperial and domestic policies.[3] The attraction which the suave Prince had held in the first decade of the century for the educated son of the Berlin beer-dealer,[4] then the youngest Deputy in the Reichstag, endured throughout Stresemann's career: he supported Bülow's candidacy as Bethmann's successor during the crisis of July, 1917,[5] and as a replacement in the Chancellory both to Michaelis and Hertling in the months thereafter; [6] Bülow in his opinion would have been the best man to make peace at the end of the war,[7] and later the Prince was his first choice as candidate for the Presidency of the Weimar Republic.[8] The affinity on the part of Stresemann for the ideas of Bülow included the latter's strong distrust of and antagonism to Bethmann, the Prince's successor in the Chancellorship.[9] From their common appraisal, in which Bassermann joined, Bethmann emerged as timorous, weak, and irresolute. In addition they considered him to be both inept and inexperienced in foreign affairs.[10]

After Bülow's resignation following the *Daily Telegraph* Affair and throughout the pre-war period, including those years when Stresemann himself was out of office, the latter continued to follow Bassermann in opposition to Bethmann's policies.[11] He echoed Bassermann's remarks in 1913 that while "other nations get a piece of the world [Germany gets] only a new military bill" with the complaint against the pacifistic policy through which "all of Europe was convinced" that the powerful German army "would never start a fight, so that as a result the expenses remained without practical advantage." [12] In 1909, while yet a member of the Reichstag, he had called for a "more energetic policy" in Morocco, and he had branded the subsequent developments in that area as a "complete moral defeat" for Germany.[13]

With the coming of the war both the National Liberal leader and his lieutenant were more open in their expression of dismay at Bethmann's leadership. "The world is not to be conquered with Bethmann-Hollweg and his Under State Secretary Wahnschaffe!" wrote Bassermann from his military post in Belgium, "It is a pity for Germany that this weakling stays in office." [14] We have already seen Stresemann's caustic and contemptuous reaction in connection with the treatment of his first war-time brochure calling for a Greater Germany.[15] While Stresemann was not loath to offer Germany's pre-war policy as a proof on appropriate occasions of innocence of the charge of war guilt, in other contexts he termed it a "policy of concession" *(Nachgiebigkeit)* which had been costly to

Germany, and he criticized the Chancellor for "not having learned anything" from the experience of the past decades.[16]

The criticisms which the future Foreign Minister directed against the diplomacy of the Chancellor may be divided into three general categories, those related to the outset of the war, those concerning relations with Germany's allies, and those connected with Bethmann's peace policies, and they may conveniently be taken up in this order.

1. The Beginnings

Stresemann was highly critical of the Chancellor's war declaration against Russia, taking the position that since "Russia wanted war with Germany" and "a *de facto* state of war already existed," it was "unforgivable to burden [Germany] with the odium of the war declaration" with its effects on Germany's alliances. He rejected Bethmann's claim that the decision had been a military one in keeping with the requirements of the Schlieffen Plan, pointing out that the Chancellor had hoped to gain the support of the Social Democrats through his declaration against Tsarist Russia, despite the warnings of both Ballin and Admiral von Tirpitz.[17] These criticisms, however, did not come until late in the war and most specifically after the war was over. In 1914, as we have seen, Stresemann had upheld the correctness of the German action in answer to the Russian mobilization; he had said nothing at all with regard to the actual declaration, but clearly from the beginning had been an enthusiastic supporter of the war.[18]

Of greater concern to Stresemann, or at least commanding more attention, was the "unlucky beginning" on August 4, 1914, with Bethmann's reference in his official address to "the wrong to Belgium" which he promised to rectify.[19] "These unlucky words," declared Stresemann, "were not, as *Vorwärts* wrote, accompanied by a general applause but from the first were rejected as not binding by the German people." [20] He referred also to the Chancellor's conversation with the British Ambassador, Sir Edward Goshen, which Bethmann had later made "clumsy efforts" to disavow. "For hundreds of years," wrote Stresemann, "school children will learn that the German Chancellor portrayed the perjured neutrality of Belgium as a 'scrap of paper' but then, filled with remorse declared a few days later that Germany recognized its wrong and would make it right again." Germany had never recovered from the effects of these errors of the Chancellor, according to Stresemann, and to Bethmann's ineptitude of expression he tied the demands of the Entente that Belgium be restored and indemnified and their charges of German war guilt. [21]

The reaction abroad had also made more difficult the efforts of German propaganda in other countries. "Whoever has attempted to make propaganda for Germany in the United States or South America . . . could not get by this 'scrap of paper statement,'" exclaimed Stresemann. "Everywhere they point to this remark . . . which has done more damage than the enemy could ever have hoped to do!" [22] Not only had German diplomacy failed in the task of carrying German views abroad; the Chancellor had also deceived the people at home as to the true feelings of the outside world relative to the events of the war. [23] As Stresemann blamed the Chancellor for the failure to shape public opinion abroad, so too was Bethmann accountable for the censorship at home which, while allowing those who supported conciliation and understanding with England to speak out, "persecuted those who supported the Greater Germany." [24] In 1870 Bismarck ("who almost approached Bethmann in genius!") had utilized the pressure of German public opinion to support his diplomatic negotiations as well as to influence world opinion, but Bethmann's failure in this regard had had the effect of destroying the spirit which the German people had manifested at the beginning of the war. [25]

2. Relations with Rumania and Italy

Closely related in Stresemann's mind to these diplomatic blunders at the beginning of the war was the fact that Germany was fighting against enemies who had been "allies of the Reich since the *Bismarckzeit*." [26] Stresemann clearly imputed the loss of both Italy and Rumania to the blunders of the Chancellor and his Foreign Office. "If one were inclined to carry on such a war," wrote Stresemann in 1915, when, discussing the war's origins, he had admitted Germany's "inclination to get started immediately" after the Archduke's assassination at Sarajevo, "one had to be prepared with those securities on which Bismarck, in all his diplomatic actions, placed such great value, . . . one should have made sure that Italy and Rumania marched on [Germany's] side or at least remained neutral in a favorable sense." [27] Stresemann, of course, had known the solutions for these problems. The proper diplomacy, as he saw it, would have been to offer the Trentino to Italy, which would have been sufficient to have caused that state to put "several hundred thousand men on the French border" and thus "provide relief for Germany in the West"; and Rumania would have had no cause to change its alliance if, in view of the war, there had occurred a marked change in the treatment of the Rumanian minority in Hungary. [28]

In both cases, it will be noted, the remedial actions suggested by Stresemann lay with Austria-Hungary, whose immediate interests were at stake; the Foreign Minister-to-be fails to suggest the course to be followed to induce the ally for whom Germany had entered the war to make concessions as odious to the ruling classes in the Dual Monarchy as giving up the three-class suffrage or granting equal rights to the Polish minority had been and were to be to the members of the Prussian *Herrenhaus*. [29] The one valid question he might have raised concerning German diplomacy, why had Germany

allowed herself to get involved in a war allied to the desperate
and anachronistic Danubian State, which was now "such a
great problem for Germany," apparently did not occur to
him.[30] Although he was not completely cut off from minds
which dared to raise such queries, he was apparently too en-
grossed in English economic rivalry as the war's cause and
the Greater Germany which would result from it.[31]

Whatever the Chancellor's shortcomings as a diplomatist,
Stresemann, when he made his criticism, was aware through
Rumanian sources that the anti-German feeling in that country had been strong even in the time of the late King Carol,
and that at the outbreak of the war Rumanian neutrality had
been maintained only in the face of a strong current in the
people in opposition to the Central Powers and in favor of
the French, and he was also aware of the strong efforts of the
German Government to move Austria-Hungary to make the
concessions through which Rumania might be kept neutral.[32]
In the face of his criticisms of Bethmann's diplomacy and his
own ideal solution, he was in fact confident that an ultimatum to Rumania was the means to force her to maintain a
benevolent neutrality.[33]

The much-admired Bülow was involved in the attempt to
hold Italy within the Triple Alliance,[34] and Stresemann had
only praise for the Prince's activities in Rome in 1915, attributing to his skill the delay in the Italian war declaration
against Austria.[35] It was Stresemann's opinion that "Italy's
interference could have been prevented" if Berlin had given
Bülow better support, and that the Chancellor had prevented
a meeting between the Prince and the Emperor, following
the former's return from his unsuccessful mission in Rome,
out of fear that Bülow would state this unpleasant truth.[36]
In spite of Stresemann's awareness of the efforts of Bülow and
of last-minute attempts to persuade the Ballplatz to make concessions to Rome, he criticized the Chancellor for failing to
make public the possibility of a break with Italy until the last

week, although it "had known for a long time that the odds
for holding Italy were about one to ten." [37] Nevertheless,
Stresemann saw nothing in the Italian defection to change in
any way Germany's war aims. He even expressed the conviction that those in the Entente whose courage had been sus-
tained by the promise of Italian entry on their side would
quickly see that "military conditions would remain the same,"
and with this argument rendered useless a more favorable
situation would be brought about for Germany than would
have been the case without Italian entrance into the war.
Stresemann condemned the actions of both Italy and Rumania as "blackmail" and an "exploitation of distress" representing a "new moral low in the relationships between
states." [38] The contradictions in Stresemann's statements are
quickly apparent as is the conclusion that concerning dealings with both Italy and Rumania he was, out of enmity toward the Chancellor, more inclined toward captiousness than
candor.

3. Peace Efforts versus War Aims

More important than these criticisms of the diplomacy of
the first days of the war or the loss of old allies was the divergence in views of Chancellor and Deputy concerning the vital
matters of peace and peace negotiations, since these impinged
upon the annexationist program for a Greater Germany. The
Chancellor's tendency to equivocate, his tendency to tack between the demands of the annexationists and those calling for
a "peace of understanding" convinced Stresemann that the
peacemaking should not be left completely to the diplomats,
specifically not to Bethmann and Jagow, but that "practical
men" from industry and military circles should be called in.[39]
With Blücher he "prayed that the diplomats would not spoil
what the soldiers [had] won with the sword." [40]

Stresemann early viewed the war as falling into two stages;

the first, against a three-power coalition, would be terminated by a peace with France and Russia brought about through understanding or conquest by Germany; the second would find Germany concentrating her power against England.[41] Initially he had hoped to separate France from England as a result of the rapid advance of German troops. Although by 1915 he labelled as "utopian" the Chancellor's idea of a separate peace with France which would keep her from any future coalition against Germany, even bring about a real conciliation, he did not completely discount the idea of a settlement provided that the annexationists' basic western aims were met and that any compensation to France in Belgian lands would not make France larger than she was before the war.[42] Before Verdun he again spoke of settling with France by inflicting a military defeat, but after that campaign while he "dreamed sometimes of a march on Paris" he admitted he would be satisfied by the eventual collapse of France through loss of manpower.[43] With the accession of Hindenburg and Ludendorff to the Supreme Command Stresemann regained his optimism regarding a peace with France on the basis of the annexationist program.[44] After the first weeks of unrestricted submarine warfare he added to the report then circulating to the effect that "Briand would not last and would make way for Ribot," his own confident prediction that Ribot, in turn, "would make way for Caillaux and peace." He was convinced that peace with France, on Germany's terms, "lay on the street," and it was "only a question of picking it up" when desired.[45] Briand did make way for Ribot, but the latter was followed not by "Caillaux and peace" but by Painlevé and Clemenceau, whose policy was war to that "last quarter-hour" which would belong to France.[46] On these developments Stresemann is silent, and we find that as late as June, 1918, while Stresemann found comfort in Clemenceau's "subdued language" in the face of the German military advance to the West which would soon permit "the bombardment of Paris," he expressed hope rather than conviction that France would collapse.[47]

In keeping with his theory of a two-stage war, indicated above, Stresemann shared the view, widely held among the middle and upper classes, that a peace should be concluded with Russia as early as possible to allow for the major effort against England.[48] The Chancellor himself had expressed similar views on several occasions.[49] Nevertheless, in November, 1916, the Government had proclaimed the creation of the Kingdom of Poland, an action which few approved,[50] and one which many, including Stresemann, were convinced had destroyed any chance of a separate peace between Germany and the Tsarist Regime.[51] It was this Polish action which Stresemann singled out in his vehement attack on the Chancellor in July, 1917,[52] to exemplify Bethmann's failures in diplomacy, and he pointed to it again under less emotional circumstances in testifying before a Parliamentary Committee in 1927.[53]

The Stürmer Government in Russia, which seemed inclined toward peace, fell from power coincidentally with the German declaration on Poland. With the speculation whether or not this Government would and could have come to an agreement with Germany had the Proclamation not been made we cannot deal here.[54] Assuming the affirmative, however, there remain inconsistencies in Stresemann's views and actions regarding peace with Russia and in his criticisms of the Chancellor.

Stresemann ignored, for example, the fact that the interests of Germany's Austrian ally had to be met to some degree,[55] although he was present in 1915 at a meeting between Bassermann and Andrassy at which the Polish question was discussed from this viewpoint.[56] Of greater weight was the fact that the Chancellor's ultimate decision, whether or not it coincided with his own inclinations,[57] was based on the assertions of the High Command, through its representative, General von Beseler, the Governer General of Warsaw, that for imperative military reasons, i.e., the anticipated voluntary enlistment of four divisions of Polish troops to fight against Russia, the creation of the Polish State should be brought into being without delay.[58]

Although in his 1927 testimony he disclaimed such knowledge, Stresemann was also aware of the efforts of the Government to make peace with Russia through negotiations in Stockholm before the Polish Proclamation.[59] He had received unofficial reports that the German representative had not pressed the negotiations under the impression that if Russia would not then make peace on Germany's terms she would have to do so later.[60] He also knew that the industrialist Stinnes, with whose annexationist views he could agree, had met with Russian representatives in the Swedish capital, and at the time Stresemann had expressed confidence in the industrialist's ability to "handle the slimy money matters" which would be necessary in order to reach an agreement with Russia.[61]

If the inability to arrive at a peace with Russia was due to reluctance to make the requisite concessions, it must be pointed out that Stresemann had himself called for German control of Poland.[62] Both in 1914 and 1915 he had presented war aims programs to the Chancellor which included the annexation of Poland as well as the Baltic territories, and it had been Bethmann who had rejected these demands as incompatible with the idea of a separate peace, which he hoped for at that time.[63]

Despite his criticism of the Chancellor for the Polish Proclamation in 1916, we find that Stresemann in 1917 was fearful that the German Government would miss the opportunity afforded by the Russian Revolution to push through a favorable peace while Germany was at the height of its power.[64] Annexations were now no hindrance to a peace, as he pointed out clearly in a memorandum to Foreign Secretary von Kühlmann in November, 1917: "This is Germany's opportunity to gain a decisive influence in the Baltic," he wrote, "and we must not, for any momentary advantage give up these possibilities for Germany's future." [65] The fact that Germany had created an independent Poland was now used by Stresemann as an argument in support of his demands that Germany now take up the cause of the German Balts.[66] While it is true that Stresemann was willing at this time to talk of "border corrections" rather than "annexations," this signified only that the future Foreign Minister believed the treaty could be made more palatable to the Russians through euphemistic language and not any change in his war aims program.[67] In 1918, when the Brest-Litovsk negotiations were in progress, Stresemann supported that demanding treaty completely, asserting that the annexations called for would not prevent Germany from gaining Russian friendship.[68] Speaking in the Reichstag in June he indicated his willingness to annex Poland in support of any demands which the High Command might make "to improve the frontier by moving it further to the East in order to prevent future invasions." [69]

Although, theoretically, he favored a peace with France and Russia, in actuality Stresemann was opposed to any peace settlement which would not bring the annexations which went toward the making of the Greater Germany. It had not been German diplomacy, he had remarked in reference to newspaper praise of the Foreign Office, "but Hindenburg and the Army" which had brought Germany her successes.[70]

There is no question concerning Stresemann's belief that any negotiated peace with England, before that Power had been so weakened that she would be forced to yield dominion over the seas, would represent a defeat for the Greater Germany, and any peace without the prerequisite indicated would be only a temporary armistice following which a second "Punic War" would still have to be fought in order to settle the basic issues.[71] Although Stresemann did not follow the Pan-Germans to the extreme of denouncing the Chancel-

lor as an Anglophile who wanted a separate peace which
would both provide favorable terms and spare England the
effects of the submarine war,[72] he shared their fear that such
a peace might be made, if only through Bethmann's folly
rather than the sinister motives they implied.[73]

We have already seen how on numerous occasions during
the first two years of the war this prevailing fear of a negotiated peace with England had influenced Stresemann's actions. Although in the fall of 1915 the Chancellor had assured Stresemann "that neither officially, semi-officially, nor
indirectly" had he extended any kind of feelers in order to
indicate . . . readiness to conclude a weak peace," when the
two met privately during the submarine crisis in March, 1916,
Stresemann again spoke out strongly against the idea of a
separate peace with England.[74] In September, 1916, when
Stresemann sharply criticized the failures of German diplomacy at a National Liberal Party gathering at Eisenach—
a speech which drew considerable attention in Germany—his
basic fear was still that the Chancellor held to the fallacious
idea of a separate peace instead of forcing the issue through
the destruction of English shipping.[75]

For these reasons Stresemann opposed the Chancellor's
Peace Note of December 12, 1916—a negotiated peace could
not bring the fruits of the complete victory which he still
believed possible through "the invincibility of German
arms." [76] In public, pending the reply of the Entente, he
could only praise "the Emperor's noble striving toward the
peace for which all yearned." [77] In private, however, although
not as blunt as some of his Pan-German colleagues, he left no
doubt not only that he anticipated the rejection of the peace
offer but that in fact he desired it so that Germany might
utilize the submarine to settle the war according to annexationist desires.[78]

While the Peace Note required at least the courtesy of
waiting until its rejection by the Allied camp, such deference

was not accorded the effort of the American President, now
made public in Germany, to mediate between the warring
coalitions.[79] To Stresemann the failure of Bethmann's peace
move meant the removal of the final barrier to the unrestricted use of the submarine, and Wilson's efforts were to be
shoved brusquely aside. Stresemann's speeches and articles
in January, 1917, demanded the complete rejection of Wilson
as mediator.[80] He declared that "a Wilson peace conference
would be another Algeciras" with everything against Germany and her allies, and called for the weapons of war to
determine who would force the peace.[81] He was infuriated
by the report that Count Bernstorff, in Washington, had
promised post-war compensation for Belgium in a desperate
effort to attain peace through the intermediary of Wilson and
demanded that the Ambassador be recalled immediately if
the report were true.[82] In the Reichstag Committee meeting
of January 31, Stresemann and the National Liberals joined
the parties of the Right in disapproval of the Chancellor's
reply to the Wilson Note, outlining Germany's confidential
war aims.[83] They did so even though they knew that since
the decision to commence the unrestricted submarine warfare
had already been made (it was announced to the Committee
at the same sitting), the German reply, in general and not
immoderate terms, was merely an empty gesture marking the
end of the fruitless efforts to end the war through the offices
of a neutral America.[84]

Stresemann's rejection of Wilson's mediation efforts vividly
illustrates the change in his attitude toward the United States
since 1914. Then his predilection had been based on close
economic relationship and the conviction that America would
remain neutral, would, in fact, be inclined toward the Central Powers due to the support of German-American elements
in the United States.[85] Now, his attitude was one of bitterness
over a neutrality policy which he considered contrary to
international law.[86] Wilson himself served as the focal point

for Stresemann's criticisms of American neutrality policies.[87] In the future the annexationist leader was to inveigh against a "Wilson peace." [88] The permanence of his intense antipathy to Wilson is revealed by his action as Foreign Minister in 1924 notifying his Ambassador in Washington to refrain from lowering the German flag to half-mast upon the occasion of the former President's death, in spite of the adverse effect this might have upon current diplomatic negotiations.[89]

After the war Stresemann contended that he had not been aware of the negotiations between Wilson and the Chancellor going back to the summer of 1916, indicating that he might have placed a different interpretation on Wilson's efforts than he did when he became aware of them only a few days before the rejection of Germany's Peace Note by the Entente.[90] Erzberger also has criticized the failure to inform the Reichstag about previous American efforts to mediate, but where the Center Deputy was also critical of the tone of the Chancellor's Peace Note, the failure to prepare the diplomatic grounds for its delivery, and its interference with the efforts which Wilson had already started, as well as the inept public remarks of the Emperor prior to the receipt of the Entente's reply, Stresemann's silence on these points is revealing.[91] Members of the Supreme Command also claimed after the war that they had not been fully informed as to the nature of the peace prospects held out through Wilson's intermediary.[92] It is clear, however, that the High Command, aware of the precarious military situation, was determined to launch the torpedoes in an effort to redress the balance.[93] If Stresemann was uninformed as to the diplomatic possibilities, he was equally uninformed as to the true nature of the German military position, and, it may be doubted that any expectations of a successfully negotiated peace involving compromises would have altered his conviction that the war had to be fought out to a German peace to be gained through the use of the submarine. It is evident that at this state of

his career the later Foreign Minister of the Weimar Republic
had no diplomatic tools in stock other than the all-out use
of the submarine and an aroused public opinion to support
it. He did not, in fact, regard the use of the submarine as
a diplomatic matter at all but a military question and looked
to the military leaders for the answer.

4. Diplomacy and the U-Boats

Writing in February to Bassermann, who had withdrawn
from political activity because of ill health,[94] Stresemann
gave an optimistic report of the success of the unrestricted
submarine warfare, which during the first two weeks had
"surpassed all expectations": "It does not seem impossible
that we shall reach eight hundred thousand tons to one million tons. . . . The neutrals have almost completely stopped
their shipping. . . ." He added that there had been no difficulties except for the break with the United States, an action
which he interpreted as more of a difficulty for Wilson than
for Germany—he designated an offer of the Swiss Minister to
act as a middle-man to keep negotiations alive as one made
at the suggestion of the American President, embarrassed by
Germany's firm, energetic action.[95]

In the plenary sessions of the Reichstag, where the discussion of the submarine war was now open, Stresemann was
the leading spokesman for the new policy which, he asserted,
had permitted Germany to take the offensive in the economic
battle after two years of defensive war.[96] He pointed to England's increased difficulties, publicly admitted by Lloyd
George, as proof of this.[97] While he conceded that war with
the United States would increase Germany's difficulties and
hence would not be welcome, he maintained that it would
not really change the situation very much since the American conception of neutrality had worked in favor of Germany's enemies, and now America would also face unpleasant

consequences since she was dependent in many ways on the German market.[98]

He defended the unrestricted submarine warfare against the charge by the Social Democrats that it was a violation of international law, and pointed out that neutrals were free to avoid the danger if they chose to do so. That European neutrals had not been alienated Stresemann attributed to the diplomatic skill of the new Foreign Secretary, Zimmermann—it was thanks to him that Germany could carry on unrestricted submarine warfare without fearing the political results which so many pessimists had forecast. Stresemann was confident that based upon the successes of the submarine in February the Foreign Secretary's prediction of peace by early summer was fully justified.[99]

Stresemann had expressed his optimism as to American neutrality almost simultaneously with Wilson's announcement of the severance of relations. His praise for Zimmermann was expressed in the Reichstag just before the contents of the Foreign Secretary's telegram to the German chargé-d'affaires in Mexico were disclosed with disastrous effect for the German cause in America. In a letter to Ballin, who still sought to preserve American neutrality, Stresemann expressed the conviction that had it not been for her diplomats Germany "could probably have carried out the unlimited submarine war with all its gratifying results without breaking with the last remaining neutral power." [100] Although he now criticized the Foreign Secretary in the Reichstag Committee discussions,[101] he supported Zimmermann's action when writing to his National Liberal followers. He admitted that the "clumsy" diplomacy had provided Wilson with "a cheap triumph in the Congress," but there was another aspect to keep in mind:

. . . It must not be forgotten that the German offer to Mexico was preceded by an offer by Mr. Carranza to Germany of a U-boat

station. It does not seem impossible to me that in the case of conflict with the United States Mexico could offer a very desirable
base for possible U-boat action, and that for these reasons the
suggestion by Zimmermann in the final analysis will show itself
as in German interests.[102]

It was not until the end of March, when the submarine
warfare and its effects entered into the discussion of the new
budget that Stresemann, who had for so long pushed aside the
warnings that unlimited submarine warfare meant war with
the United States, acknowledged that increased estrangement
with the United States was likely.[103] This threat did not daunt
him, however; he believed that Germany was ready to bear
the military, political, and economic consequences, for he
was convinced that the war was entering a final stage with
the U-boat as the decisive weapon.[104] In the Reichstag he
commented enthusiastically on the report of Admiral von
Capelle on the first two months of the unlimited warfare
during the first half of which some eight hundred thousand
tons of shipping had been sunk.[105] In the Committee discussions he scoffed at Scheidemann's fear that America would
adopt universal military service, claiming that to do so the
United States would have to stop all exports of ammunition
and other matériel. Beyond that lay the task of training an
army and the insurmountable difficulty of transporting it
across the Atlantic.[106]

Throughout the spring of 1917 Stresemann continued to
provide an optimistic voice in support of the submarine program. He assured the readers of the *Leipziger Tageblatt* that
American pledges "to provide three million tons of merchant
shipping for England within eighteen months" would be of
no help for "after eighteen months of U-boat war England
[would] no longer possess a merchant marine." [107] The *Lokal
Anzeiger* of Essen records the enthusiastic reception to Stresemann's address in that city on April 12 in which he declared
that through the U-boat Germany had now "taken the offen-

sive in the economic battle also"; that Germany, which "had been the anvil, would now be the hammer," and the "methodical blows against England's economic nerve" would force her to the peace table "if only Germany would endure till then." [108]

PART FOUR:

THE COLLAPSE OF THE GREATER GERMANY

CHAPTER VIII

THE INTERNAL CHALLENGE

The declaration of unrestricted submarine warfare in February had at first met with the general approval of the German people, angered at the Entente's rejection of the Emperor's peace offer and anxious to bring the costly war to a quick and victorious end.[1] But the enthusiasm of February faded quickly before a growing unrest, attributable to war weariness and the food shortage resulting from the Allied blockade.[2]

The discontent found outlet in the demands for a "new direction in internal policies," the so-called *Neuorientierung,* which concerned primarily the call for a liberal change in the relationship of the parliament to the government and and for the democratization of the Prussian electoral system through elimination of the three-class suffrage. By means of the latter the Junkers since 1850 had controlled the State which in turn dominated the Empire created by Bismarck.[3] In addition to these basic issues there was a growing sentiment in favor of removal of restrictive security measures related to the State of Siege proclaimed at the beginning of the war; while there had been frequent debates concerning these war measures and the method of their enforcement by the military commanders, the laws had remained unchanged.[4] The fundamental questions concerning the Emperor's "personal rule" and the Prussian reform had been raised in the era of the *Daily Telegraph* Affair in 1908 at which time the Emperor had made promises which had subsequently remained unfulfilled.[5] It was not until the impact of the events of 1917 that the first step was taken toward redeeming these pledges through the Emperor's Easter Message.[6]

The debate over internal reforms merged with the crisis which developed in July, brought about by the growing realization that the submarine would not "force England to her knees." Where in the earlier crisis the annexationists' war aims program had appeared endangered by the threats of internal collapse and the demands for reform, in July there was the additional challenge in the Peace Resolution of the moderates which restated the German defensive stand of August 4, 1914, and called for a peace of understanding and conciliation.[7] The threat was averted, however, when the Chancellor's dismissal became the dominant issue of the debate. Stresemann played an important role in both of these crises.

1. The *Neuorientierung*

That the submarine would remove the last barrier to a German victory Stresemann firmly believed, but even while initial reports from the Admiralty served to buttress this conviction Stresemann had become fully aware before the end of March of the threat to the annexationist program in the developing internal unrest.[8]

"Conditions in the interior are at a breaking point," he wrote to Bassermann and warned that the decrease in the bread ration to be announced in April would most likely be met with work stoppages if not a general strike. Stresemann noted the formation of the Independent Social Democratic Party as a manifestation of the "radical current running through the people" and as evidence that the Russian revolution and propaganda against "the autocratic German Government" had not been without effect. "Even in intellectual circles criticism of the Emperor has been sharp, and I have heard a dozen times the evil words about a bomb on Charleville," he reported to the ailing National Liberal leader. "It is a question whether the U-boats will bring the decision more quickly than economic conditions in the interior drive toward catastrophic phenomena." [9] In his speeches Stresemann became the champion of "endurance" (*Durchhalten*), of "holding out behind the front" until the last hammer blow had been struck. At the same time he joined the debate over the *Neuorientierung* in an endeavor to strengthen that endurance until the final victory for which he so passionately called.[10]

The Chancellor had also reacted to the warnings by holding out the promise of reform, including changes in Prussia, to come after the war, and at the same time the Government moved quickly toward the modification or repeal of a number of the war-time controls concerning which it had previously taken an adamant stand.[11] Bethmann was no doubt quickened in his actions by Scheidemann's article in *Vorwärts* warning that in the matter of reform it was already "five minutes to twelve," [12] while at the other extreme the Conservatives in the Prussian House of Lords unloosed a violent attack against the Chancellor and denounced the Reichstag as well for daring, in discussing suffrage reform, to interfere in "an internal Prussian matter." [13]

"The Chancellor can no longer get rid of the spirits he has called upon," recorded Stresemann not without some evidence of satisfaction, and added that he too would enter the debate with a reply to Bethmann on March 29 similar to his Jubilee speech to the National Liberals in February.[14] On that occasion he had called for the support of the positive war aims of the Party in order to achieve "the greater, freer Germany of the future," and in so doing had talked in general terms of a "new relationship," which he did not clearly define, "between Crown, parliament, and people" to come after the war.[15]

On March 29 Stresemann went far beyond his general statements of the preceding month, and his speech, the "longest, most ardent plea in favor of immediate reform,"[16] put him in the center of the controversy which now engaged the attention of all Germany.[17] To the Prussian Conservatives who had called for "military absolutism" rather than more parliamentary power, he declared that while the German people "love their army and adore its victorious leaders" they did not want military absolutism and in calling for it the Prussians distorted history and the work of Scharnhorst, Gneisenau and vom Stein. While making it clear that "the parliamentary system was no demand of the National Liberal Party," he rejected the charges of incapability of parliamentary regimes by pointing to the success of "British and French amateurs against German professionals" in the field of diplomacy. He scored the German Government for failure to understand the mood of the people at home or abroad and for the lack of contact between the Chancellor and the party leaders. "There must be some mistake in a system if we suffer one diplomatic defeat after another and there is a growth of radicalism in spite of reforms," he asserted. "We should investigate to see if changes are necessary."[18]

Turning to the question of reform Stresemann announced that in view of the length of the war he now withdrew his earlier opinion that reforms should be deferred until the end of the war and called for "an immediate reorganization of affairs in Germany and in the *Bundesstaaten*." While willing to leave details concerning suffrage reform to the individual States, he maintained that the Prussian election rights issue was "a German question" which the Reichstag had every right to discuss.[19] On the grounds that the government had "not taken the initiative," he called for the creation of a Constitutional Committee to which the reform questions which had been brought up in the debate should be immediately referred.[20] The Committee was created, and in the wake of the parliamentary debate William II, as King of Prussia, hurriedly issued his Easter Message promising the post-war reform of the Prussian legislature and the end of the three-class voting system, a proclamation which served temporarily to mitigate the internal pressures.[21] To the congratulatory letter of a constituent Stresemann replied that he was "not entirely innocent of this Easter Message." [22]

2. Internal Reform and the War Aims

Some of Stresemann's biographers have painted him as a "champion of a far-reaching democratization," a portrayal based in great part on his stirring speech of March 29 which preceded the Easter Message.[23] Stresemann's correspondence, especially with Bassermann, revealing his motives, moods, and resourcefulness during the spring crisis, makes clear that endurance for the sake of the positive war aims program was the primary consideration behind his Reichstag speech and other activities at this time.[24] In making his parliamentary address Stresemann had gone far beyond the wishes of Basser-mann, who saw only "a victorious end of the war" as the "command of the hour." [25] Clinging to the conservative Westphalian industrialists in the party's right wing, Basser-mann wished to defer to the post-war period modest reforms which would not depart from the spirit and form of "Bis-marck's Reich." [26] But Stresemann, unlike Bassermann, was now able to comprehend the fact that external "fate of the Reich" could no longer be separated from "domestic questions." [27] He looked upon the Easter Message not only as "a political act which would take the people's minds off the food shortage and other hardships of the war," but one which would also strengthen the annexationist cause.[28] "The political feelings in South Germany against us were based only on the wrong presumption that our war aims policy had something to do with opposition against a liberal new orientation," wrote Stresemann. Such a view was no longer possible, and he could now probably "support the complete annexation of Belgium and Northern France" without it being related to a "reactionary policy." [29] It was his conviction that the actions taken within the country by the National Liberals "had done much in the fight against a humiliating peace." In July would come a clearer proof that for Stresemann war aims came first.[30]

3. The Annexationist as Liberal

There were other reasons, related indirectly to the annexationist cause, which had motivated Stresemann's actions. The "radical current" in the country had divided the National Liberal Party's Reichstag *Fraktion* as well, and in order to prevent the defection of the left wing to the Progressives he had been forced to take a stand in favor of reform.[31] "We must not forget," he wrote to Bassermann, "that in the party in the country at least ninety percent stand on a quite radical viewpoint as a result of the events of the war and that our future depends on holding these to the flag of the party, especially if the suffrage of the individual States becomes more democratized. . . ." [32] Stresemann saw that not only must the Party base itself upon the new conditions but must do so promptly. Since the Government itself had taken the first step by modifying some of the laws under the State of Siege, the National Liberals could no longer maintain their old position of waiting until the end of the war without the implication of being fundamentally opposed to reform.[33] Since a change of position was mandatory and the reform inevitable, why, maintained Stresemann, should not the National Liberals get the credit for the *Neuorientierung* in the Reichstag instead of the Social Democrats or Progressives? [34] To Bassermann he pointed out that the Easter Message had been a National Liberal triumph since the Emperor's declaration, following Stresemann's speech, had appeared to be based more on the National Liberal program than on the pledges which the Chancellor had made previously.[35]

After the war Stresemann declared that in March, 1917, he had fought for the equal voting right in Prussia; [36] yet his speech had not contained this demand, and he told Basser-mann that the call for reform had been made at the insist-ence of the *Fraktion*. In urging the creation of a Constitu-tional Committee to which all the reform proposals would be submitted without any prior voting action by the Reichs-tag he had skillfully prevented from coming to the floor a Progressive measure calling for the immediate establishment of the equal vote in all the States, a measure which the left wing of the National Liberal Party would have supported, "splitting the Party down the middle." [37]

Stresemann privately admitted that once the Party had gained the credit "it was another matter if the reform were immediately undertaken," and by May he declared to the press that since the Prussian Lower House was taking up the matter of suffrage reform the Constitutional Committee "did not need to occupy itself with this question." [38] He told inti-mates frankly that he preferred a plural voting system for Prussia, such as he had supported in Saxony before the war, to the equal suffrage.[39] As a result of his action he believed that the Government, if it would take steps promptly under the wartime conditions of the *Burgfrieden* might still "bring safely to harbor" a moderate plural suffrage bill, which would be impossible if it were to wait until after the war when "ten thousand wearers of the Iron Cross would demonstrate before the castle" demanding equal suffrage.[40] "I would have wished that the Emperor had immediately introduced the proposal of election reform himself," observed Stresemann after the Imperial Message, "for if one makes concessions . . . it is well to make them at once and not let oneself be urged to them." [41]

It was not until 1918, when Conservative intransigence in Prussia revived the issue, that Stresemann openly supported equal suffrage in order "to preserve and strengthen the mon-archy," although he still admitted privately that he preferred the plural vote.[42] "We are not in a position to deal with theories," he wrote, "since today equal suffrage is a political necessity for Prussia." [43] It is clear that in his activity for the *Neuorientierung,* whether to further the war aims or to benefit his party, an adroit political tactician had found his rightful medium.[44]

In the setting of the Weimar Republic Stresemann also asserted that he and the National Liberals had led the middle-class parties to the parliamentary system both before and during the war, especially in the events of 1917 described above.[45] Certainly no member of the bourgeois parties had talked more eloquently in general terms about strengthening the Reichstag, but it is difficult to find an instance where Stresemann's call for reform during the war was not related to the annexationist program.[46] It was primarily in criticism of the Government's diplomacy and conduct of the war or in demand of freedom to speak out in favor of the annexationist war aims and in foreign policy questions that Stresemann had espoused the cause of liberalism, and it was not the autocratic power of the Government which he protested but the inept use of that power. "If we now had a Bismarck we would have no cause to call for changes," he had declared in the Reichstag in 1916 and had promptly turned to the Supreme Command.[47]

In speaking of the strengthening of the Reichstag he made it clear that he did not advocate the parliamentary system for Germany through a "single legislative act" but rather on the basis of a slowly developed tradition.[48] "One ought not to expect that the Constitution of Germany can be changed like a garment overnight," he declared. Nor did he demand a full parliamentarization of the Government, declaring that "such a majority government in wartime" did not seem to him "to be practicable." [49] He was, to be sure, in favor of the use of members of the Reichstag in ministerial posts—he denied charges of personal ambition—asserting that Social Democrats would have to be called upon in order to negotiate with the new Russian Government.[50] In private he admitted to Basser-

mann that he preferred a parliamentary regime for despite
his loyalty to the Dynasty he could not give a "vote of confidence to William II to handle foreign and domestic policy"
after the war. "No one has so sharply criticized the personal
rule as you have repeatedly done during the war," he reminded Bassermann. "Are there no conclusions to be drawn
from this at all?" But at the same time Stresemann pointed
out that a parliamentary system did not "necessarily mean
full parliamentary rule"; he would consider it a parliamentary system if there were the power to discharge the Chancellor on a vote of no confidence, if it could "remove the man
who will not be able to bring a good peace to Germany." [51]
The path from Stresemann's call for the *Neuorientierung* in
March to the crisis of July is thus clearly illuminated.

4. The July Crisis

While the Easter Message only temporarily allayed the
discontent which had forced the unwilling Emperor to this
half-way measure, the continuing dispute over internal reform and the relationship of that issue to the war aims had
brought about a new alignment of the parties in the Reichstag. The National Liberals, on common ground with the
Center and Progressives in support of the reform program,
reached an accord on war aims through the annexationist
formula of the Centrist Spahn which indicated satisfaction
if the Government pursued "neither boundless plans of conquest" nor tied itself to "a peace without annexations or indemnities." [52] At one extreme were the Socialists, who demanded more reforms and whose published Manifesto called
for a renunciation of conquests; [53] at the other, the Conservatives, whose parliamentary interpellation on May 3 insisted
that the Government accept its broadly annexationist program.[54] As a result of the controversy over reform there were
rumors that the Conservatives were planning "strong action"
against the Chancellor.[55]

Stresemann reassured an alarmed constituent that he had relinquished none of his annexationist aims. "There is a difference between supporting the war aims and talking about them from the speaker's platform in the Reichstag," he wrote.[56] With the Austrian ally "preferring peace today rather than tomorrow" and the prospect of peace negotiations with Russia, he considered it advisable "to put the war aims in the background," especially since he had been assured by Zimmermann in April that "a peace of understanding" with Russia would include the German demand for Courland and Lithuania. It was for these reasons, and because it would also give Scheidemann an opportunity "to shout out his ideas of a peace of renunciation," and would strengthen the Chancellor's position as well, that he had not supported Count Westarp's interpellation.[57]

Stresemann's connection with the rumored action against Bethmann is a different story. One attempt had already been made in the so-called Adlon Conference in February, 1917, at the beginning of the discussions on the reform issue, to bring about the Chancellor's replacement by Hindenburg through a petition to the Emperor, but the conspirators, pro-annexationist and anti-reform extremists, had failed completely.[58] That Stresemann was aware of the attempt against the Chancellor and knew that a meeting which he himself was addressing at the same hour at the Adlon (on the state of Germany's chemical industry) was being used as a cloak for the conspiratorial session is beyond doubt, but his actual connection with the incident is less clearly determinable.[59] Whatever his connection with the Adlon affair Stresemann appears to have sensed its failure quickly and claims to have warned friends against participating.[60] Later in both the Party press and in the Reichstag he completely dissociated the National Liberal Party from the incident.[61] As with the Conservative interpellation on war aims, Stresemann's aloofness from the Adlon plotters had not been due to lack of sympathy with their objectives but to a correct appraisal of the results of their action.

If the Adlon conspirators were to be shunned, there were others who were more dependable. Early in June Stresemann was told by Zimmermann that the Army Headquarters was almost unanimously against Bethmann and that the only hindrance to action—finding a suitable successor—had been removed with agreement on Prince Bülow, who was also supported within the Foreign Office.[62] This information was confirmed when Stresemann himself visited the Headquarters the following week. "Ludendorff would like to see a Chancellor change," reported Stresemann to Bassermann, "but doesn't quite know the right means to bring it about. The thunderclouds are drawing together."[63]

In 1916 Stresemann had turned cautiously to the High Command in the submarine question; in 1917 he was completely "Ludendorff's young man."[64] It had been the Supreme Command, in the person of Colonel Bauer, who had counseled Stresemann in May that the Conservative interpellation was a "tactical error."[65] It was Bauer who arranged Stresemann's reception on his visit to the Great Headquarters in June and for the staff car at the young Deputy's disposal to drive him back through the Rhine Valley. Stresemann seems to have come away from the Headquarters as awed as though he had talked with the gods in Valhalla. "I need not tell you how deep were the impressions I received in the conversations with Hindenburg and Ludendorff," he wrote to Bauer along with profuse thanks, "and how very much I continue to hope that in the important question of the Chancellor they will supply the initiative of the Great Headquarters and contribute to the solution of this really burning question."[66]

In July the storm broke. By the summer of 1917 it had become clear to a growing number that the submarine would not bring the triumph which the Supreme Command and the annexationists expected of it.[67] Stresemann was not unaware of these doubts, for Ballin after a visit to the Supreme Head-quarters in May had written that he "would wish Ludendorff judged the U-boat war somewhat less optimistically," and by June the shipping magnate had written bluntly that "the U-boat war [had] unfortunately not accomplished what the Admiralty Staff had promised against England," regardless of what other successes it may have achieved.[68]

The Center Deputy Erzberger voiced these doubts in the Reichstag's Main Committee when its sessions opened the first week in July.[69] On Friday, July 6, he followed with a second speech in which he cited statistics on the submarine campaign and world tonnage to prove that the undersea war-fare could never force England out of the war. From this Erzberger drew the conclusion that Germany could not get a better peace a year later than she could at that moment and therefore called for a renunciation of the positive war aims stand and a return to the German defensive position of Au-gust 4, 1914, as the basis for peace negotiations.[70]

Out of the uproar which Erzberger's speech created in the Committee Room came the growing demands for a resolution embodying the kind of peace suggested by the Center Deputy. Along with this came the demands for prompt action in car-rying out the Prussian election reform, and for a greater role for the Parliament in the decisions of the Government. On the same evening the Progressive Payer initiated action to create an inter-party committee to work with the Government and by July 10, as its chairman, he had carried the first de-mands to the Chancellor.[71] On July 19 the Reichstag ap-proved a Peace Resolution which called for a "peace of under-standing and the permanent reconciliation of peoples" and declared that "forced territorial acquisitions . . . [were] irrec-oncilable with such a peace." [72] Earlier, on July 11, the Em-peror had promised that the next elections in Prussia would be held on the basis of the equal voting right. There was a

growing optimism that "a new chapter had begun in the relations between the Government and the Reichstag." [73]

It was now, in days which contained "the most violent excitement" in his political life, that Stresemann played what
was perhaps his most important role in the Great War by
creating at this juncture a Chancellor crisis which resulted
on July 13 in the dismissal of Bethmann-Hollweg, an event
which proved of deepest significance.[74]

5. The Fall of Bethmann-Hollweg

On Saturday morning, July 7, Stresemann was summoned
to the Army Headquarters in Berlin to meet Hindenburg
and Ludendorff, who had hurried there immediately upon
receiving word of Erzberger's speech.[75] Stresemann records
that he briefed the Commanders on the political situation,
urging the prompt removal of the Chancellor for "the sake
of internal peace" and quick action by the Government on
the Prussian suffrage bill and other reforms to prevent being
forced to these concessions. He also recommended parliamentary representatives as ministers "as discussed at the
Headquarters" in June.[76] He was informed that the Quarter-
master General would take these matters up with the Emperor that same day.[77]

On that same morning in the presence of Colonel Bauer,
and twice thereafter during the week-end together with
Lieutenant Schlubach, also of the General Staff, Stresemann
held conversations with Erzberger in order to persuade the
Center Deputy to assist in getting rid of Bethmann, who
would be replaced by Prince Bülow toward whom Erzberger
was favorably inclined.[78]

Stresemann made his first overt move on Monday, July 9,
when the Committee sessions were resumed, in a speech before that body. He declared that he did not share Erzberger's
pessimism about the submarine warfare for the time would
come "when England could no longer function" if Germany

would only keep on.[79] At the same time he did not reject a peace on a *status quo ante* basis, "if that were all that Germany could get." [80] Equivocal on this point, he left no doubt as to his meaning when he began to talk about the status of the Reichstag. The Peace Resolution, he pointed out, would have no value so long as the world considered that the Reichstag had no real power. "If the relationship between the Reichstag and the Government is amended regarding parliamentary rights," he declared, "we face a different problem." Calling for co-responsibility of the Reichstag, he demanded the dismissal of the Chancellor as the first step on to this path.[81] Stresemann's speech now became a tirade against Bethmann both for his failure to keep up domestic morale through proper handling of the reform issue and for a complete bankruptcy in foreign policy. Charging that Bethmann's Polish policy had prevented an earlier peace with Russia, he declared that no one was "more poorly equipped to conduct peace negotiations" with either Russia or America. Branding the Chancellor unfit for his post, he demanded that Bethmann "draw the consequences and get out." [82]

Although Stresemann's speech created great excitement the reaction to it was a mixed one, for with the exception of the Conservatives the parties, including Stresemann's own, were divided in their opinion concerning the Chancellor.[83] The latter, visibly shaken, indicated his willingness "to withdraw for the sake of the Fatherland" but defended his policies in a long reply to Stresemann in which he attempted to separate the Deputy from the other members of the National Liberal *Fraktion*.[84]

On the following day Stresemann resumed his attack and succeeded in arousing rancor against the Chancellor by charging that Bethmann had refused to convey to the Army leaders a request which Erzberger had made at the beginning of the Committee sessions that Hindenburg and Ludendorff, known to be in Berlin, personally explain the military situation to

the members of the Committee.[85] Stresemann also carried the
issue to the meeting of the inter-party committee created by
Payer at the beginning of the crisis, which had already
achieved some success in the Prussian election reform issue,
and which was now drafting a peace resolution and working
on matters of parliamentary privileges.[86] Stresemann, on behalf of the National Liberals, demanded "first and foremost
a Chancellor change," promising that his Party would then
be willing to cooperate by participating in a Government
pledged to the program discussed in the group and willing to
make peace on the basis of no annexations or reparations.[87]

The climax came on July 12 through help from another
quarter. The Crown Prince, who had been summoned to
Berlin by his father in order to become acquainted with the
Prussian election reform, was given permission by the Emperor to determine the views of important persons concerning Bethmann's remaining in office.[88] In a meeting that morning arranged by his Adjutant, Freiherr von Maltzahn, and
that ubiquitous conspirator, Colonel Bauer,[89] the Crown
Prince interviewed six party leaders, carefully selected "to
serve the common wish" and keep "the easily influenced
Prince on the leash." [90] The interviews, including the
strongly-worded statement of Stresemann, who represented
the National Liberal Party, were carefully recorded by military aides so that the Prince could present to his father the
documentary evidence of the opposition to the Chancellor.[91]

On the same day Stresemann, having won over the dissi-
dent members of the National Liberal Party, presented a resolution to Valentini, Chief of the Emperor's Civil Cabinet,
calling upon the Emperor to dismiss the Chancellor. A copy
of the resolution was given to the press with great effect; the
previously divided Center Party passed a similar resolution
the same evening, and the Conservatives also voted against
Bethmann's remaining. At the request of the Crown Prince
copies of the three resolutions were given to him so that he

might give them to the Emperor along with the reports of his interviews.[92]

Stresemann himself delivered a copy of the National Liberal resolution to Helfferich at the Chancellory so that he could inform Bethmann of the National Liberal action. The Minister attempted to persuade Stresemann to refrain from further attacks against the Chancellor in the plenary sessions soon to open, claiming that the majority in the other parties were willing that Bethmann remain in office. Stresemann refused to accede to this request and added that if Bethmann did not resign it would be necessary to inform his party that Ludendorff had stated: "If this Chancellor stays we lose the war even if we kill ourselves winning (*totsiegen*)." [93]

From the Chancellory Stresemann hastened to the Army Headquarters where he reported the events which had just transpired, and a telephone call was immediately put through to Kreuznach.[94] The requests of the Army leaders to be permitted to resign, because they had no confidence in the Chancellor, were submitted to the Emperor that evening. Summoned to Berlin they were advised on the morning of July 13 that Bethmann's request to resign had already been accepted.[95]

Stresemann wrote triumphantly to Bassermann to inform him of Bethmann's fall:

. . . I hope to have given you joy with this, for in the course of this war you have repeatedly stated to me how much Germany has suffered under this man. For that reason I feel that I have done what you would have wanted in playing an active role in his overthrow.[96]

Chapter IX

TRIUMPH AND DISASTER

The fall of Bethman-Hollweg, the gradual nullification of the Peace Resolution, and the events which followed revealed the power in the hands of the Supreme Command and cleared the way for the full exploitation of the annexationist program through military victory. The treaties of Brest-Litovsk and Bucharest disclosed how completely that program would be adhered to.[1] In the spring of 1918 the military power was turned to the West for the final blows by which the Greater Germany would be realized.

The annexationist triumph was almost complete, but in contrast to the long struggle toward its achievement which we have followed in these pages, it was short-lived. In midsummer the German offensive on the Western Front was halted and then thrown back. Events moved rapidly. By November with the fall of the Empire and the Armistice which followed, the harsh terms of which presaged the nature of the peace yet to come, the hegemonic dreams of the German annexationists were destroyed.

1. The Nullification of the Peace Resolution

The elimination of Bethmann-Hollweg was both a personal triumph for Stresemann and a triumph for the annexationist cause. Whether or not, as Conrad Haussman wrote in 1920, Stresemann had been "more acted upon" than the initiator of the events of July, 1917, and the instigator had in truth been General Ludendorff,[2] it is certain that Stresemann never regretted Bethmann's fall and both desired and claimed credit for its accomplishment.[3]

Would Bethmann have fallen without Stresemann's attack in the Main Committee? The Emperor, although resentful over the concession to which he had been forced concerning Prussia, had still supported his Chancellor against the first demands of the military leaders.[4] The action of the Crown Prince in interviewing party leaders would hardly have been taken without the prior expression of opposition to the Chancellor which Stresemann had provided; there is reason to believe that the reports themselves would not have succeeded in influencing the Emperor without the accompanying party resolutions which were to a great extent the result of Stresemann's efforts.[5] Without the cover of parliamentary opposition the Supreme Command could not have pressed its ultimatum and yet maintained its pretence of not interfering with political affairs.[6]

Among the parties, only the Conservatives were united against Bethmann, but with their record on both internal reform and annexations they could not successfully have led a parliamentary action against him, and as much as they hated the Chancellor they did not desire his fall to be brought about as an action of the Reichstag.[7] Erzberger's motivations merit additional study, but it is questionable whether he raised doubts on the submarines and opposed the annexationist stand for the purpose of bringing down the Chancellor, even though he later was identified with that cause.[8] While few of the party leaders were completely satisfied with Bethmann, and while almost all—the Progressives and Social Democrats to a lesser extent—momentarily welcomed his departure,[9] without Stresemann's direct attack it is doubtful that any demand would have arisen among the Deputies for the Chancellor's dismissal.

Appearing as it did to have been the result solely of parliamentary demand, the fall of Bethmann-Hollweg suggested that the Reichstag had achieved a new level of power, as Stresemann had intimated in his speech against the Chancellor. In fact it resulted in the negation of the gains which had appeared so close to realization in the work of the inter-party committee in the days following Erzberger's speech. Had he remained as Chancellor, Bethmann could with little difficulty have moved on to the new ground in conjunction with the leaders of a co-responsible Reichstag and would have been able to work with the liberal majority in carrying out its aims, including those to be expressed in the Peace Resolution.[10] At the least Bethmann had held off the complete domination by the Supreme Command, now without significant opposition, and he had restrained the annexationists, with whose war aims the military leaders were to show themselves in full accord. While the expediential appointment of Michaelis as Bethmann's successor well served the purposes of the Supreme Command, it proved deadly for the aspirations of the Reichstag majority.[11]

The tactical mastery which Stresemann had displayed earlier in the spring concerning the *Neuorientierung* he again demonstrated in the July crisis and the events which followed. In calling for Bethmann's dismissal Stresemann had stressed its relationship with peace and parliamentary power. His words in the Main Committee had seemed to support the Peace Resolution, and he had clearly promised such support in the inter-party committee if action were first taken against the Chancellor. Once he had accomplished his purpose he refused to cooperate further with the inter-party group and insisted that the National Liberal Party would neither agree to the Peace Resolution nor participate in the government if such agreement were a prerequisite.[12]

In keeping the National Liberal *Fraktion* together behind him in the resolution against Bethmann and in rejecting the Peace Resolution when even the Supreme Command and the new Chancellor had nominally accepted it,[13] Stresemann achieved a major political victory. In order to hold the Party's left wing to these objectives he was forced to accede to a separate resolution "which tended toward a peace of understanding" but which called for other means to achieve that peace than an untimely public announcement.[14] Although he personally disliked this resolution he recognized that it would be impossible to attempt to stand along with the Conservatives in complete opposition to the parliamentary majority.[15]

It has been suggested that Stresemann in July had indicated that he was "willing to end the war short of a German victory," but even the compromise resolution of the Party did not renounce territorial gains if the peace permitted them.[16] The Party was still working for a peace in accord with German power.[17] Stresemann defined the National Liberal position in an article in *Deutsche Stimmen* in July: In the Party they were neither basically annexationist nor anti-annexationist; they did not demand that Germans "bleed till they have conquered Boulogne or Lake Peipus"; they were willing to negotiate on the basis of pledges held. But he added the following statement: "If our flag should be waving over Calais and if we should thus establish a German Gibraltar on the Atlantic, who could make us relinquish it, if we were able to maintain ourselves militarily?" [18] In private he was even more explicit in stating that he had given up none of his annexationist aims: they must carry out a firm policy in Belgium if they were to succeed in expanding to the West, and no security could be better than holding the Flanders coast. He expressed the hope that "military deeds" would soon permit putting an end to the Peace Resolution, which he termed "the folly *(Unfug)* of the Reichstag." [19]

Stresemann quickly returned to the meetings of the inter-party committee for he realized that his absence had deprived him of influence on the decisions made there. He reassured a critic that the National Liberal Party had not thus become a part of the Reichstag majority, for in returning to the discussions Stresemann had "reserved the right of independent decisions, especially in foreign policy." He added that this was "no idle phrase" and made his purposes clear: while keeping contact with the Conservatives to prevent their isolation, he was working cautiously with members of the Progressive and Center Parties, particularly those who had opposed the Peace Resolution, in order to prevent the two parties from joining solidly with the Social Democrats into a solid bloc under the "radical leadership of Scheidemann, Haussmann, Gothein, and Erzberger," which would "exploit its power ruthlessly." By not breaking this connection he hoped to achieve "that this majority would soon fall apart" and then many of its nominal adherents would "free themselves of the renunciation formula." [20]

Stresemann demonstrated his independence in foreign policy as a member of the Committee of Seven, created in late August to discuss with Michaelis and Kühlmann, the new Foreign Secretary, a reply to the Peace Note of Pope Benedict, which had suggested mutual renunciation by Germany and the Entente of indemnities and territories as a basis for negotiations.[21] When the majority wished to make a clear statement of Germany's position on Belgium in order to meet the conditions of the Papal Note, Stresemann sided with Westarp in rejection of this policy—if Belgium were mentioned he would insist on raising anew "the Flemish question." [22] At the second meeting of the Committee of Seven early in September he opposed even Kühlmann's compromise proposal, to which the majority agreed, through which a vague reference to the Peace Resolution of July 19 took the place of a specific statement on Belgium.[23]

Stresemann's post-war testimony suggests that had he been fully informed as to the significance of the Vatican's mediation offer his attitude might have been different; yet both his public and private comments at that time make it clear that he was completely aware of the importance of this avenue to peace through renunciation but was not prepared to travel it.[24] "I am very close to the Supreme Command," he wrote on August 17, "and do nothing in the field of foreign policy which it does not approve." The Supreme Command would conduct the peace negotiations and with regard to Belgium "it was not prepared for renunciation." [25]

Domestic matters demanded the same tactical considerations as foreign policy. The National Liberals had no further reform demands for themselves—"they had gained more in the last months than the left wing would have dreamed of years ago." But the Social Democrats must be induced to vote for the war credits, they must be prevented from either calling or condoning strikes which would interfere with military operations. It was "not pleasurable" but it was necessary "to gnash one's teeth together and sit with Scheidemann at the same table," and to make the necessary concessions. Here, too, Stresemann acted at the direct request of Hindenburg and Ludendorff who placed "unlimited confidence" in him.[26]

By the end of September it had become clear that the Social Democrats and their moderate allies in the Reichstag would no longer tolerate Michaelis.[27] Stresemann moved quickly to join in the demand for the ouster of the Chancellor so that the necessary change could be effected without an internal crisis. He worked secretly through the Duke of Schleswig-Holstein to insure that the Emperor's Chancellor-designate would accept the program of the Reichstag.[28] Stresemann again had wanted Bülow, but the appointment of Hertling in October on the basis of the Reichstag committee program which Stresemann had helped to shape meant success for the annexationist cause.[29] A new *Burgfrieden* was achieved in domestic affairs on the basis of a broad social program offered by the Social Democrats, one which Stresemann described as "bearable to the National Liberals." [30] In return it was agreed that in matters of foreign policy the new Chancellor's hands would not be tied. Theoretically, the German program was to be based on the answer given on September 19 to the Papal Peace Note, which had contained a vague reference to the Peace Resolution. But as Stresemann pointed out then and frequently thereafter, with the agreement of many who had originally supported it, the Peace Resolution of July 19 was now outdated, for it had been superceded by events.[31]

Stresemann had not been wrong when he had stated in the Main Committee in July that the Peace Resolution would have importance only if the position of the Reichstag were also amended, and it had been he at this crucial moment who had helped deflect the party leaders from the path which might have led to power.[32] His tactics had assisted Michaelis, between July and November, in diluting further the significance of the Resolution. The utter collapse of the Russian armies and the negotiations which began in November and culminated in the Treaty of Brest-Litovsk in March completed the route of the annexationist opposition.[33]

2. The Triumph of the Annexationists

Once again Stresemann could speak out for the Greater Germany.[34] "The God who gave us Hindenburg did not mean that Germany end this war other than victoriously," he declared at Cologne, and for the party press he wrote that Germany could not accept a peace without extension of territories and financial compensations; Germany's future depended upon her power, and the military situation was such as to guarantee the attainment of her objectives.[35]

"I hardly dare express all the hopes which fill me," he wrote to a constituent in December, 1917. With Russia "mortally wounded" Rumania, too, would soon be forced to make peace, and the Baltic states would move to close union with Germany. Now the German armies would be free for the battle in the West. "It is my firm conviction," he predicted, "that this will mean revolution in Italy." Then would come the collapse of France, and, "if proper policy" were adopted, England's position "would be at stake." [36]

In the spring he developed to the full his program for "a

free Baltic." He welcomed the first treaty, that with the Ukraine in February, as the initial step.[37] When the Russian treaty followed in March he joyously supported its extreme provisions—peace was not to be had by resigning the rights of expansion. It was no longer necessary to consider leaving Russian territories intact—"the old unified Russia" was gone —and for Germany's security needs, which demanded first consideration, they must depend on their own security measures, not on Wilson's League of Nations, which would "burst like a soap-bubble." [38]

"Germany's position was never more favorable," Stresemann told his Party's Central Committee on March 11 in Berlin. "We are now preparing to strike the last great blow, and when we remember the calmness and certainty with which our High Command has always made its preparations and how they have never miscarried, we now can face the coming fighting with the greatest of confidence." [39] The enemies who had rejected the German Peace Note of December, 1916, bore the responsibility for the blow which would now fall upon them and for any change in Germany's policy "as to territorial questions and indemnities. . . ." [40]

When the Chancellor in an address to the Reichstag on February 25 suggested, with a reference to the Papal Note of August 1, that Germany might be receptive to proposals for negotiations from the Belgian Government in exile at LeHavre,[41] Stresemann in his reply two days later noted that he had heard "with misgivings" the Chancellor's suggestions and that "in view of the whole situation" he would regard a fresh peace offer as a mistake. Belgium, if restored at all, was not to revert to her pre-war status; nor could Germany forget the "solemn pledges" made to the Flemish people. In any event, he concluded, the disposition of Belgium must be reserved to the final peace, where any German renunciation must "be sought by great concessions," i.e., the territories occupied by Britain and control of the seas.[42] A premature renunciation would represent "the height of political naïveté," he had written to Ballin, for then, at the peace conference only the demands of the enemy would be discussed; on Germany's, "the debate would be closed." [43] Implicit here was the admission that England could not be defeated and that Germany would not dictate the peace. The logical inference should have been to strive for negotiations while Germany, with the triumphs in the East behind her, had powerful armies poised to strike in the West. Stresemann could not have been unaware of the importance of a clear statement on Belgium as a necessary first step toward any possible negotiated peace, if such were desired, but the future Foreign Minister saw no need for diplomacy now— military power alone would resolve the issue. On March 21 the German artillery began a heavy bombardment which heralded the new offensive in the West.

3. The Collapse of the Greater Germany

The story of the failure of the great German offensive of 1918 is too well known to require retelling here. There remains to be related only the account of Stresemann's forced retreat from one self-deception to another until backed against the reality of utter defeat.

There was one last display of intransigent annexationism. On June 2, Foreign Secretary von Kühlmann, in an impromptu speech before the Reichstag, suggested that "military decisions alone, without recourse to diplomatic negotiations," could hardly bring an end to the war. [44] Stresemann joined at once with Count Westarp in the demand for the Foreign Secretary's resignation. [45] Yet even before this incident the National Liberal leader had been cautioned by Colonel Bauer not to overvalue the results of the Western offensive, and from Maltzahn, the Crown Prince's adjutant, he had received reports of the growing difficulties being encountered at the front. [46]

Despite these warnings Stresemann, when the Reichstag was adjourned on July 13, still had the general impression of successes in the West "which would lead to great decisions." [47] However, at the end of the month in a letter to Frau Bassermann he had to acknowledge that the offensive had been temporarily halted and that he was not too certain that its renewal would bring the completely favorable outcome previously anticipated; yet he assured his reader that there was "no real danger" to Germany for even American troops could not make up for the fact that with Russia's defeat "the nightmare in the East" had been removed. [48]

Despite a professed optimism the tone of his correspondence in August suggests a growing concern. On August 8, the day British tanks spearheaded an Allied advance in the Amiens sector, breaking the German lines and marking the end of the German offensive, he wrote to Colonel Bauer that while he was "confident of a good end to the war" he could no longer maintain this feeling in his party, and he pleaded that Ludendorff "force the political leaders to speak out against enemy propaganda" in order to keep the people "out of the morass of psychological collapse." He urged that some consideration be given to Russian demands in the East so that an economic agreement might be reached. He noted that in Southern Russia Germany had "already gone beyond the lines drawn at Brest-Litovsk" and suggested that the manpower tied up there might be used on the Western Front unless plans of which he as a layman was unaware "such as a move toward India" necessitated their remaining. [49]

To the National Liberal Party Secretary, who asked how to answer those who questioned the outcome of the military engagement at the Marne, he replied that there was "no reason to let heads hang as if [they] had lost a battle of Leipzig." He expressed full confidence in Hindenburg and gave assurance that his own "total view" of the war's outcome had not changed. [50]

By September he admitted privately that the Western offensive had been "a chain of failures" after Rheims and that there was no hope of ending the war through military victories that winter, and he acknowledged that Germany would have to bury her earlier aspirations in the West. "Perhaps in the future the entire face of Germany will turn somewhat more to the East," he wrote, "and we shall find there some substitute for that which for the time being cannot [elsewhere] be achieved." [51]

The party leaders had been told in late August by State Secretary von Hintze, Kühlmann's successor, that both Bulgaria and Austria-Hungary were war-weary and wanted to end the fighting, and that it would therefore be necessary to work promptly through diplomatic channels toward peace.[52] However, even the misgivings aroused here did not prepare for the blows which rained down at the end of September.[53] First came the sudden announcement of the resignation of Hertling and his replacement by Max von Baden, authorized by the Emperor to form a cabinet on a parliamentary basis. On October 1 the party leaders were first informed that Ludendorff had insisted that Germany make peace at once on the basis of the conditions laid down by Wilson in his Fourteen Points; a representative of the High Command present at the meeting added that "a delay of even a few hours might be fatal for Germany." [54] Stresemann emerged from this meeting "visibly shaken." He returned to his office in the Reichstag and after long reflection wrote a note to Hintze expressing opposition to the unconditional acceptance of a peace on the basis of Wilson's terms. However, by this time he had been able to put through a telephone call to the Supreme Headquarters and learned, with great agitation, that Germany "stood in hopeless battle" and required an immediate armistice.[55]

The news of these events could not long be withheld from the country and in answer to the accusing letters of surprised party members Stresemann now had to explain that it had been the Army which had demanded the step toward peace to which the National Liberals along with the other parties had felt obliged to accede. It was now necessary, he wrote, to abandon a war aims program no longer achievable and to support the new government in a unified front in its efforts to obtain peace.[56]

In blackest despair Stresemann summoned the provincial leaders of the National Liberal Party to Berlin for a confidential meeting to explain these events which lay behind the sudden fall from the heights of the long-held war aims. In a highly emotional and disjointed speech he bitterly condemned the military leaders for underestimating the enemy and for failure to achieve the technical production, both of tanks and airplanes, which industry could have provided.[57] He singled out the Admiralty for the failure to build enough submarines and for having completely discounted the influence of the American entry into the war. He now blamed Bethmann and Helfferich for having told the Reichstag in 1917 that the time had arrived for the unrestricted submarine war which would force England to make peace. He condemned the "zigzag course" in foreign policy and lack of leadership on the part of the civil government which, he asserted, could have had peace with England in the fall of 1917. The system which had led them to this situation, he concluded, "had forfeited its right to continuation of its existence."[58] Instead of the hoped for Greater Germany they must now use their last resources to insure the survival of the Reich and its people.[59]

From this despair there was a brief revival during the second week in October to be found in the knowledge that the military leaders "had now recovered their nerve," and he therefore had great expectations that if "they could endure six weeks longer the enemy would get over its feelings of victory and be willing to conclude a decent peace." He was convinced that Germany's territorial integrity would not be in doubt—Wilson's Fourteen Points were merely a basis for negotiations, not an accepted fact. It had been *Realpolitik* to make Wilson's position their own, he wrote later, for they had merely to prove the German character of the *Ostmark,* for example, to insure its retention. The fact that German troops were still in Belgium and France made it possible to demand a clear statement of the enemy's peace aims without allowing Germany to be exposed like "material to a tailor's scissors." [60]

By the end of October the newly roused hopes had also faded. That German troops still held enemy territory was of no help. Peace was needed at once, and it had therefore been correct to place persons "known abroad as democrats and pacifists" at the head of the new Government. But in the same paragraph he protested that it was "nonsense for the press to speak about a lost war," even though it could "no longer be won." [61]

When Ludendorff's dismissal was announced in the Reichstag and the Center Deputy Herold urged a popular levy for the national defense, Stresemann confessed that "it was all over." [62] There was "no further use in fighting"; the only hope was for a Talleyrand capable of saving Germany at the peace conference.[63] To a constituent who still called for "deeds" he replied that a demonstration in Berlin to urge carrying on the war would result in counter-demonstrations leading to a general strike and revolution, which must be avoided at all cost. It was vital to keep the Social Democrats in the Government to avoid "a duplication of Russian conditions." The main concern now was to save the monarchy which was the sole guaranty of the unity of the Reich.[64]

By the beginning of November there was a growing demand even within the National Liberal Party for the abdication of the Emperor and Crown Prince in order to clear the way for peace.[65] Stresemann, however, urged the *Fraktion*

to stand behind the Hohenzollerns, for he saw in the Monarchy on its new constitutional base no threat to successful
peace negotiations.[66] If the Emperor could no longer be
maintained, at least the dynasty must be saved, he wrote, for
they "must not break with that tradition which looked from
the old Germany over into the new." [67] On November 9
he was still urging that even if abdication should prove necessary the Social Democrats should at least guarantee the
monarchial principle, but even as he wrote the Emperor was
in flight and in the heart of Berlin the Republic was being
proclaimed.[68] Through four long years of war Stresemann
had fought for the Greater Germany. Now this dream had
vanished and the old Germany itself lay in ruins. The years
of rebuilding were ahead.

CONCLUSION

It has been the purpose of this study to provide an integrated account of Gustav Stresemann's ideas and activities as an annexationist during the Great War. The very fact that Stresemann's annexationism has been taken for granted (he himself never denied that he was one of those who during the war had "hoped for victory," and his definition of that term was tantamount to German hegemony in Europe), together with the overriding importance of his later career, tended to obscure the significance of his wartime activities, the full story of which has heretofore not been told. That Stresemann later became Foreign Minister makes them even more significant, and if once we grant the importance of the war years in shaping the period which was to follow, the brief stopover on the road to Locarno which his biographers have provided can hardly be considered adequate. The emphasis in the present account has been placed on Stresemann himself rather than on the annexationist movement as such, the story of which has been told elsewhere, and in illuminating the war aims proponent of the period of the Great War it has been the intent as well to throw light on the man who, in the period of reconstruction which followed, rose to new heights as a diplomat and political leader.

Stresemann's outlook on the German "world policy" of the pre-war era and on the causes of the war and the related war guilt issue was typical of the *Bürgertum* of which he was a part, and despite his conviction that a doctoral degree evincing study of economics and history lent some particular quality to his views which was lacking in those of his Pan-German associates, there is in fact little to distinguish be-

161

tween them. His hatred of England proved stronger than his knowledge of either history or economics and distorted his judgment both in the formulation of war aims and in supporting the means to achieve them.

Although Stresemann's war aims encompassed all aspects of the annexationist program, he placed emphasis on western expansion, for he saw in the control of Belgium the key to access to if not control of the sea, and he was convinced that the restoration and enlargement of the colonial Reich would follow once the western objectives were obtained. Looking to the East, he called for a "free Baltic," by which he meant the union of that area with Germany in the interests of the latter and the German Baltic minority. In addition to this expanded political power one of Germany's economic arms was to be outstretched across Central Europe to the Middle East while the other reached across the Atlantic "world-ocean." The Greater Germany which Stresemann supported not only signified political and economic hegemony backed by military power but represented a nationalistic idea as well, one which would serve as a beacon to Germans outside the Reich, drawing them together through a common feeling of glory for their Fatherland.

As Reichstag Deputy, party leader, and particularly as one in the inner councils of the Great Economic Organizations, Stresemann played an important part both in formulating and voicing the war aims program as well as in the attempt to unify the annexationist movement as a pressure group. His purpose avowedly was to provide a united public opinion upon whose force the Government might draw at the peace negotiations. Since, in fact, his war aims could be realized only through a victory associated with a dictated peace, a more fundamental and important purpose of his annexationist activity was to move the Government itself from its defensive stand of August 4, 1914, to a positive commitment to the Greater Germany.

These aims determined as well his espousal of the unrestricted submarine warfare, through which the annexationist program was to be achieved, and he was one of the leaders of what Ballin termed "the noisy minority" whose vociferous efforts cleared the path on which the Government later traveled to war with the United States.[1]

While one can thus state that Stresemann played a vital role in the German annexationist movement, it is difficult to evaluate the importance of the movement itself within the framework of history. It must be pointed out that the Pan-Germans had no world monopoly on chauvinism or far-reaching war aims, but if it is agreed that the activities of the German annexationists lengthened the war by making it practically impossible to negotiate reasonably and thus to end the conflict short of a complete victory, then indirectly it was responsible for internal disunity, the stimulation of the demands for internal reform, and the exposure of the weakness of ruler and regime, thus paving the way first for military dictatorship and later for revolution. Its demand for unrestricted submarine warfare in order to gain its war aims was an important determinant of Germany's somber destiny.

In both the fight for the war aims and for unrestricted submarine warfare Stresemann found his chief opposition in the Chancellor, Bethmann-Hollweg. The latter was the object of an intense antagonism, dating back to the pre-war era, which reflected the strong influence on Stresemann of both his party associate Bassermann and Prince Bülow. The climax of the struggle between Deputy and Chancellor came in July, 1917, when Stresemann succeeded in bringing down his antagonist and in so doing deflected the bid of the Reichstag for power into the barren wasteland of a Chancellor crisis. There is, of course, much room to speculate as to what might have happened had not Bethmann been forced out at this critical juncture. The view herein expressed was that Bethmann, in spite of, or perhaps even because of his weaknesses might have moved without great difficulty on to the new ground of the Peace Resolution with the support of a parliamentary majority. The Papal Peace Note, too, would have received treatment other than that which it found in the hands of Bethmann's successor. We have seen what did in fact occur— the avenue to peace through the Vatican was deliberately blocked, and the Government deluded the parliamentary majority by hypocritically professing adherence to the Peace Resolution until the events on the Eastern Front allowed the dropping of the mask. The July Crisis represented a turning point in German history, and Stresemann's mark is upon these events.

It is evident that Stresemann's thoughts were turned toward foreign affairs from the beginning of his political career as a National Liberal in 1906. His early call, "Freie Bahn dem Tüchtigen," the demand that Foreign Office positions be filled on the basis of ability regardless of social position, was frequently repeated and was the theme of his Eisenach address of 1916 when he also called for more power for the Reichstag in foreign affairs. Foreign policy aims also governed his actions against the official censorship and on behalf of internal reforms.

To suggest, however, that a future Foreign Minister was pointed ineluctably toward his destiny would be to ignore the plain truth that both before and during the war Stresemann showed little understanding of either the nature or the problems of diplomacy. In criticizing Germany's pre-war policies as weak he remained blind to the fears they aroused in the Powers which were to make up the Entente. He would not have been averse to a greater readiness to use the threat of German military might in support of diplomatic policies. There is no suggestion that Stresemann desired war, but when it came he was convinced of the complete righteousness of Germany's cause, and the very policies which he had branded as "weak" in the pre-war era were now adduced as evidence of Germany's earlier submissiveness and complete freedom from any taint of war guilt. Once the war began the prospects which it held out for the Greater Germany far outweighed any negative considerations, even in those rare moments of insight when he recognized the costliness of the world struggle. Here, again, he was typical of the society of which he was a part.

Stresemann frequently declared that "the war was lost diplomatically for Germany before it began militarily," but while his criticisms of Bethmann's policies were not necessarily invalid, the grounds for his criticisms were often partisan, and they were frequently made with the benefit of hindsight. He showed little realization of the difficulties of maintaining the alliance between Germany and Austria and as little appreciation of its necessity for carrying on the war. He saw the Foreign Office chiefly as an agency with the task of countering the effects of enemy propaganda at home and abroad and of presenting to the enemy at the end of the war the peace terms detailed by the annexationists, particularly the Great Economic Organizations, on the basis of the victory to be provided by the Supreme Command.

Stresemann's fanatic support of the submarine program again illustrates his complete lack of understanding of the nature of diplomacy. He never saw any contradiction between the submarine policy of Tirpitz and the "great fleet" policy of the pre-war period, any more than he had seen in the latter a source of friction between Germany and England. An early supporter of the U-boats, he heralded the unrestricted submarine warfare in the early months of 1917, defended it against Erzberger's attack in July, and never in the period which followed did he lose faith in this means to victory. Even in the post-war period he still maintained that he would have used the submarine from the first day of the war, and he remained convinced that utilized earlier it would have accomplished the task of forcing England to make peace.[2]

In his infatuation with the idea of bringing England to her knees he was convinced that the submarine war could be carried out without a diplomatic break with the United States, and completely misjudged the significance of hostilities with America despite his travel there, economic ties, and his own words concerning the looming importance of America through her economic might.

It was only in the shadow of defeat that one can find, in his changed ideas toward Russia, some hint of an understanding of the nature of foreign relations. Here we find suggestions which were to materialize only later at Rapallo and to be carried still further in his own skillful Treaty of Berlin. The Stresemann who cried for joy over the dictated Treaty of Brest-Litovsk became aware of the art and nature of diplomacy only when Germany was bereft of power. One can only speculate as to what his policy might have been had Germany completely regained her freedom from the restrictions of the Treaty of Versailles, the end toward which he devoted his years as Foreign Minister.

It is the theme of one major study of the Weimar era that Stresemann, despite foreign policy successes, in 1927 failed with disastrous results to grasp until too late the significance of domestic issues in relation to his tasks as Foreign Minister.[3] Whatever the validity of this thesis for the Weimar period, it is certainly true that in the first years of the Great War Stresemann did not appear to recognize this vital connection. Once aware, however, he demonstrated, as shown in the spring of 1917, far more flexibility and comprehension in meeting the necessities of domestic politics, which were after all closer to his own experience, than he displayed with his rigid annexationism in the field of foreign affairs. During his entire career as a National Liberal, Stresemann had been the follower of Bassermann, who could imbue his lieutenant with the imperial vision but who in political leadership could offer only weakness and indecision. In taking command of the National Liberal Party during the crisis over internal reforms Stresemann had his first opportunity to exercise party leadership. Out of this experience emerged the skillful politician, able to estimate a situation and to act quickly when an opportunity presented itself in order to obtain his objective, able to read the political barometer and to make even the storm work to his advantage.

It is hardly necessary to postulate a metamorphosis to account for Stresemann's successful transfer on to Republican grounds. For the Conservatives a victorious war was the surety for the maintenance of the status quo. Those who called for democratization generally supported the idea of a non-annexationist peace. Stresemann had not been bound by either formula. The *Neuorientierung* had been to him secondary to victory with its annexationist reward, but if it was secondary it at least had a place in his thinking, and he was willing to adjust his position when internal dissension over the Prussian electoral reform issue threatened to jeopardize the unity requisite to maintain the war effort. If the democrat portrayed by some of Stresemann's biographers has disappeared before the evidence provided by his own documentation, nevertheless he showed a political realism beyond the comprehension of most of those with whom he shared the vision of a Greater Germany. Although, in calling for a "greater, freer Germany," "greater" came first, it does not follow that he did not sincerely want a more liberal state as well. The relative position of these demands had perhaps been settled long before the war when he first chose to become a member of the National Liberal Party.

Despite the National Liberal credo of "unswerving loyalty to Emperor and Empire," Stresemann was far more critical of the German ruler and his "personal rule" as well as of the general spirit which had pervaded the Empire, than his later sentimental attachment to the memory of the monarchial idea during the early Weimar period would suggest. While he both regretted and condemned the Revolution of 1918, the Republic which it brought into being eventually provided far greater opportunity for him to achieve a position of responsible leadership than he could ever have hoped to achieve in the monarchy as it was constituted before October, 1918. Stresemann may have lacked the will to power, as manifested in 1916 when he turned to the Supreme Command,[4] but he was not wanting in ambition. The political leader created in 1917 was already engaged, as the curtain fell on the last scene of the Imperial drama, in finding a political role for himself in the new activity about to begin.

Here we find a lingering significance of his war-time annexationist stand. It was the reaction to this record and to his support of the submarine warfare which temporarily shunted him aside in the period following the Armistice, rather than any unwillingness on his part to assume office. Not only did his previous annexationism keep him out of power for three years, forcing him into narrow opposition, but it was also responsible in part for his exclusion from the newly created Democratic Party, which might have flourished under his leadership. This led to the formation of his own People's Party from elements only slightly less dedicated to the past than were the extremists of the German Nationalist Party. It is conceivable that the political history of the Weimar Republic might have been different had a united bloc of middle-class parties been created at its beginning. It is certainly true that Stresemann outgrew his own party in the years to follow.

Stresemann himself was no less a nationalist in the Weimar period than he had been during the Wilhelmine epoch. The fantasy which has made him a European first and a German second is something which only the era which produced the Kellogg Pact could create. True, one can ask if he was any more a nationalist, any less a European, than the statesmen with whom he dealt—in fact point out that Europe has moved most closely toward unity in the field of economic cooperation which he stressed. The valid contrast, however, is between the nationalist who was able to make the transition to the Republic and to work for it both out of love for country and from personal ambition, and those who made up the German Nationalist Party—those whose intransigence had been in part responsible for the collapse of the Monarchy and who now "subordinated national interests" to the venting of their hatred for the Republic.[5] Stresemann had run with and even led the nationalist pack in the clamor for the war aims and for unrestricted submarine warfare and in bringing the Chancellor to bay; in the Weimar period he himself became the victim of the pack.

Ambition, flexibility, and a practical political sense were traits which Stresemann had clearly displayed. Beyond these was a German patriotism which transcended the form of the state. The man who had once looked to a Greater Germany to come as a result of conquest under the leadership of others was able, because of these qualities, to undertake courageously the task of rebuilding through his own efforts without military power. The talent demonstrated in 1917 in domestic politics proved eminently adaptable to the field of diplomacy. In that area he proved able to work realistically and effectively within the limits set by defeat, even if to remove those limitations. What his ultimate goals were has not yet been disclosed.[6] Necessity may have tempered them, but it is doubtful if Gustav Stresemann ever lost the vision of the Greater Germany.

NOTES

Introduction

1. "Adenauer und Stresemann," *Das Ganze Deutschland, Wochenzeitung fuer Politik, Kultur, Wirtschaft,* Jg. 1, Nr. 10 (1949), 1; *Economist* (London), XVII (1949), 1113; Gordon A. Craig, *From Bismarck to Adenauer: Aspects of German Statecraft* (Baltimore, 1948), pp. 125, 136 ff.; Fritz Stern, "Adenauer and a Crisis in Weimar Democracy," *Political Science Quarterly,* LXXIII (March, 1958), 1-27.
2. For example, see T. H. Tetens, *Germany Plots with the Kremlin* (New York, 1953), pp. viii; 144-148; 273 f.
3. These include Rochus Freiherr v. Rheinbaben, *Stresemann: Der Mensch und der Staatsmann* (Dresden, 1928); Rudolf Olden, *Stresemann* (Berlin, 1929); Heinrich Bauer, *Stresemann, ein deutscher Staatsmann* (Berlin, 1930); Antonina Vallentin, *Stresemann; Werden einer Staatsidee* (Leipzig, 1930); Friedrich Hirth, *Stresemann* (Paris, 1930); Walter Görlitz, *Gustav Stresemann* (Heidelberg, 1947); Hubertus Prinz zu Löwenstein, *Stresemann, das deutsche Schicksal im Spiegel seines Lebens* (Frankfurt a. M., 1952) and Annelise Thimme, *Gustav Stresemann; eine politische Biographic zur Geschichte der Weimarer Republic* (Hanover, 1957).
4. Gerhard Zwoch, *Gustav-Stresemann-Bibliographie* (Düsseldorf, 1953).
5. A. J. P. Taylor, *The Course of German History* (New York, 1946), pp. 197-202; 208, offers a typical British wartime view; see George Boas, "Stresemann-Object Lesson in Post-War Leadership," *Public Opinion Quarterly,* VIII (Summer, 1944), 232-243, for an American counterpart.
6. Hans W. Gatzke, "The Stresemann Papers," *Journal of Modern History,* XXVI (March, 1954), 49-59.
7. Important among champions of Stresemann's European outlook are Felix Hirsch, "The Portent of Stresemann," *Commonweal,* XXXI (Summer, 1945), 486-489; Edgar Stern-Ru-

barth, *Three Men Tried . . . Austen Chamberlain, Stresemann, Briand* (London, 1939). All the biographies cited
above (n. 3) are sympathetic toward their subject and
his policies. Important critics include Robert, Lord Vansittart, *Lessons of my Life* (New York, 1943), pp. 68 f., and
F. J. C. Hearnshaw, *National Review* (London), CV (November, 1935), 678 ff.; *ibid.*, CX (February, 1938), 254-266; *ibid.*,
CXIV (June, 1940), 755 f.

8. Marvin L. Edwards, *Gustav Stresemann, A Study in Appraisal, 1923-1948,* unpublished Master's Essay, 1951, Columbia University Libraries, New York, *passim.*

9   Gustav Stresemann, *Vermaechtnis: Der Nachlass in drei Baenden,* ed. Henry Bernhard (Berlin, 1932-3); see also English
edition, Gustav Stresemann, *Diaries, Letters, and Papers,* ed.
and trans. Eric Sutton (3 vols., London, 1935-7).

10. Stresemann's letter of September 7, 1925, to the former Crown
Prince, first published in these volumes (*Vermaechtnis*, II,
553 ff., Sutton, II, 503 ff.) has served as a source of many of
the charges of insincerity and as a proof of Stresemann's
ulterior motives and duplicity in his dealings with Briand
and Austen Chamberlain. See Edwards, *op. cit.*, pp. 14 ff.,
35, 37 f., 84 ff.; also H. Wickham Steed in the introduction
to Hubertus zu Löwenstein, *Tragedy of a Nation* (London,
1934), p. 2, for a typical English reaction. For the French
response see Raymond Poincaré, *L'Illustration*, No. 4655
(May 21, 1932), p. 90, and Pierre Bernus, *Journal des Debats*,
XXXIX, Pt. 1 (May 6, 1932), 694 ff.; (May 13, 1932), 751;
(May 20, 1932), 781; (May 27, 1932), 817. See Gatzke, *op. cit.*,
esp. p. 55, regarding Bernhard and his editorship of the *Vermaechtnis.*

11. Edwards, *op. cit., passim,* esp. pp. 79 ff .

12. Erich Brandenburg, *Von Bismarck zum Weltkriege* (Berlin,
1924), pp. 300 ff. For interesting, brief comments on Bülow
see Norman Rich and M. H. Fisher, eds., *The Holstein Papers* (Cambridge, 1955), I, 156, 159 ff., 172; Hans Peter
Hanssen, *Diary of a Dying Empire* (Bloomington, 1955), pp.
253 f.; Joachim v. Kürenberg, *The Kaiser, a Life of Wilhelm*

II, Last Emperor of Germany (New York, 1955), pp. 160-163; Craig, *op. cit.*, pp. 30, 32, 45-53. On Bethmann-Hollweg see Brandenburg, *op. cit.*, pp. 301 ff.; Otfried Nippold, *The Awakening of the German People* (New York, 1918), pp. 23-27.

13. Olden, *op. cit.*, pp. 20-23. Stresemann attended the universities at Berlin and Leipzig. His thesis concerned the development of the bottled beer trade in Berlin: Gustav Stresemann, *Die Entwicklung des Berliner Flaschenbiergeschaefts* (Berlin, 1900). During the Weimar period he was derisively called the *Flaschenbierdoktor* by his adversaries.

14. Hajo Holborn, *The Political Collapse of Europe* (New York, 1951), pp. 80 ff.

15. Germany, Auswärtiges Amt, Politisches Archiv, "Nachlass des Reichsministers, Dr. Gustav Stresemann," microfilm, National Archives, Washington, D. C. (henceforth cited as Stresemann, "Nachlass").

16. Hans W. Gatzke, *Stresemann and the Rearmament of Germany* (Baltimore, 1954), makes extensive use of the "Nachlass" for the period of the Twenties; Henry L. Bretton, *Stresemann and the Revision of Versailles* (Stanford, 1953), uses it slightly for the same period.

17. Annelise Thimme, "Gustav Stresemann, Legende und Wirklichkeit," *Historische Zeitschrift*, Heft 181/2 (April, 1956), 287-338, uses the "Nachlass" for the war period, but her article emphasizes the post-war era. This applies also to her biography of Stresemann cited above (n. 3).

18. Germany, Nationalversammlung, *Das Werk des Untersuchungsausschusses*, 4. Reihe, "Die Ursachen des Deutschen Zusammenbruchs im Jahre 1918" (12 vols., Berlin, 1925-29), VII (Pt. 2), 300 (henceforth cited as *U.A.*, 4. Reihe).

Chapter I

1. Theodor Wolff, *Vollendete Tatsachen* (Berlin, 1918), pp. 9 ff.
2. Germany, *Reichstag, Verhandlungen des Reichstages, XIII. Legislaturperiode, II. Sitzung, Stenographischer Bericht*

(henceforth cited as *Reichstag*), vol. 306, pp. 1-3. The "enthusiasm and exultation" noted by Koppel S. Pinson, *Modern Germany, Its History and Civilization* (New York, 1954), p. 313, perhaps reflects the controlled press as much as popular feeling. See Ebba Dahlin, *French and German Public Opinion on Declared War Aims, 1914-1918* (Stanford, 1933), p. 15, on the German press, and Hanssen, *op. cit.*, pp. 13 ff., for an eye-witness account of gloomy reactions in Berlin.

3. R. H. Lutz, ed. *Fall of the German Empire* (2 vols., Stanford, 1932), I, 9. The Emperor's declaration was made to assure the favorable war credits vote of the Social Democrats to whom he had once referred as "fellows without a Fatherland," and "a gang unworthy to be called Germans." See Kürenberg, *op. cit.*, pp. 308 f.; Hanssen, *op. cit.*, p. 15.

4. A. Rosenberg, *The Birth of the German Republic, 1871-1918* (New York, 1931), pp. 74 f.

5. For the military events of 1914 see C. R. M. Cruttwell, *History of the Great War, 1914-1918* (New York, 1934); B. H. Liddell Hart, *A History of the World War, 1914-1918* (Boston, 1934); E. O. Volkmann, *Der grosse Krieg 1914-1918* (Berlin, 1934).

6. R .H. Lutz, ed., *Causes of the German Collapse in 1918* (Stanford, 1934), p. 257; Hanssen, *op. cit.*, p. 183.

7. Stresemann, "Nachlass," container 3054, serial 6838, frame 126799 (cited hereafter as 3054/6838/126799).

8. *Ibid.*, 3053/6824/124185 ff.; 124217-8; 124233; 124273. From the university Stresemann had moved into the field of industrial organization in Saxony. After a brief affiliation with Friedrich Naumann's National Social Union he moved to the National Liberal Party, whose imperial stand he favored although he criticized its conservative "governmental" stand on domestic issues. Elected to the Reichstag in 1906 as its youngest member at 29, he was close to Bassermann, the Party leader, and became a member of the Party's Central Committee despite opposition of leaders of the conservative right-wing. Stresemann ran unsuccessfully for re-election in 1912 on a platform combining a liberal domestic program

with an imperialistic foreign policy. His defeat, the result of strongly concerted Conservative efforts in his electoral district, was not regretted by conservatively inclined National Liberal leaders who ousted him from the Party's Central Committee. For an account of Stresemann's early Reichstag career, 1907-1912, see Olden, *op. cit.*, pp. 39 ff.; Rheinbaben, *op. cit.*, pp. 62-86. For a general account of the political developments in Germany during this period see Th. Eschenburg, *Das Kaiserreich am Scheideweg* (Berlin, 1929), *passim*, and Ludwig Bergsträsser, *Geschichte der politischen Parteien in Deutschland* (7th ed., Munich, 1952), pp. 165-173.

9. Stresemann, "Nachlass," 3054/6835/126108 ff.
10. *Ibid.*, 3053/6824/124233; 124273 ff.; *ibid.*, 3054/6838/126734; 126746; 126751; 126759 ff. In spite of this desire Stresemann had declined to be a candidate in opposition to his earliest political leader, Friedrich Naumann, and saw to it that the Nat. Lib. Party did not oppose Naumann's re-election. See Theodor Heuss, *Friedrich Naumann, der Mann, das Werk, die Zeit* (Stuttgart, 1949, 2nd ed.) pp. 295 ff.
11. Stresemann entered business in Saxony in 1900 and had been instrumental in organizing the Association of Saxon Industrialists: see Olden, *op. cit.*, pp. 26-38. Eight volumes of the "Nachlass," contained in reels 3051, 3052, and 3053, are devoted to his business activities; see Marvin L. Edwards, *Index to Stresemann Microfilm Collection*, unpublished, Columbia University Libraries; a recent dissertation is based on this material: Donald Warren, Jr., *Gustav Stresemann as Organizer of German Business Interests, 1901-1914*, unpublished, Columbia University Libraries, (New York, 1959).
12. Olden, *op. cit.*, p. 39. Stresemann was on the directing boards of the League of Industrialists and the Hansa League and active in other business associations.
13. Stresemann, "Nachlass," 3055/6840/127093 f.
14. *Ibid.*, 3054/6835/126223; *ibid.*, 6838/126829. He had previously visited the United States and Canada in 1912 on business: Rheinbaden, *op. cit.*, pp. 87-90.
15. *Ibid.*, 3055/6839/126871; 126993 ff. Due to the *Burgfrieden*

opposition candidates were not put up in the predominantly National Liberal district from which Stresemann ran as a candidate.

16. Stresemann, "Nachlass," 3055/6840/1271477 ff.; see also Gustav Stresemann, *Deutsches Ringen und Deutsches Hoffen* (Berlin, 1914), pp. 2, 10.

17. Gustav Stresemann, *Das Deutsche Wirtschaftsleben im Kriege* (Leipzig, 1915), p. 12. Later in a Reichstag speech Stresemann again used this argument to disprove the charge "that Germany had carefully prepared for a war of world conquest." In this instance he was asking for the reorganization of the Ministry of the Interior because of the fact that the economic mobilization in 1914 had not measured up to that of the military. The emphasis now seems to have been placed on the word "carefully" rather than on "prepared": *Reichstag,* 307 (May 19, 1916), 1141 f.

18. Stresemann, "Nachlass," 3104/7178/153425 ff. Stresemann blamed the error on "journalistic overzealousness."

19. Stresemann, "Nachlass," 3104/7158/153425.

20. *Reichstag,* Vol. 307 (April 6, 1916), pp. 866 ff.

21. Dahlin, *op. cit.,* p. 16.

22. Stresemann, "Nachlass," 3056/6843/127565 ff.

23. *Ibid.,* 3076/6900/135193 ff.

24. Gustav Stresemann, "Eine Atempause im Weltkriege," *Deutsche Stimmen,* Jan. 10, 1917.

25. Stresemann, "Nachlass," 3078/6916/136839.

26. Hajo Holborn, "Diplomats and Diplomacy in the Early Weimar Republic," *The Diplomats, 1919-1939,* ed. Gordon A. Craig and Felix Gilbert (Princeton, 1953), p. 138.

27. Gustav Stresemann, "Kaiserreich, Revolution, Wiederaufbau," *Reden und Schriften* (2 vols., Dresden, 1926) I, 286 f.

28. Stresemann, "Nachlass," 3095/7004/142747 ff.

29. *Reichstag,* Vol. 348 (March 5, 1921), pp. 2672 f.

30. Stresemann, "Nachlass," 3095/7004/142694.

31. *Ibid.,* 142665; 142690; 142697; *ibid.,* 3094/7002/142396; *ibid.,* 7003/142505. Hugo Stinnes was involved in this matter as was Dr. Simons of the Foreign Office, and the funds came to

Stresemann from Director Heilbronner of the Foreign Office Press Department. It would appear that Ebert was also aware of this affair.

32. *Frankfurter Zeitung*, 25 August 1923, No. 626.

33. Stresemann's address at Hagen, 2 October 1923, "Aufgabe des Passiven Widerstandes im Ruhrgebeit," *Reden und Schriften*, II, 109.

34. Bretton, *op. cit.*, chap. V, "The War Guilt Question," pp. 46-53, analyzes Stresemann's position during the Weimar period.

35. *Ibid.*

36. Stresemann, *Vermaechtnis*, I, 432; II, 185, 214; III, 198.

37. *Reichstag*, Vol. 425 (24 June 1929), pp. 2814 f.

38. Rosenberg, *op. cit.*, p. 99; Hans W. Gatzke, *Germany's Drive to the West* (Baltimore, 1950), p. 5; Stresemann, "Nachlass," 3055/6839/126993 ff.

39. Gustav Stresemann, *Englands Wirtschaftskrieg gegen Deutschland* (Stuttgart, 1915), *passim*.

40. Stresemann, "Nachlass," 3055/6840/127100 ff., speech, Chemnitz, 28 Aug. 1914, "Erster Monat eines Weltkrieges"; *ibid.*, 127105 ff., article, *Hannoverscher Kurier*, 28 Sept. 1914, "Krieg und Wirtschaftsleben,"; *ibid.*, 127111 ff., speech, Aurich, 4 Oct. 1914, "Die Weltlage und die Aufgaben von Volk und Vaterland"; *ibid.*, 127129 ff., speech Wilhelmshafen, 12 Nov. 1914, "Krieg und Wirtschaftsleben."

41. Stresemann, *Deutsches Ringen und Deutsches Hoffen*, p. 6.

42. *Ibid.*, p. 8.

43. *Reichstag*, Vol. 307 (April 6, 1916), pp. 866 ff. See also speech at Dresden, 28 Oct. 1917, reprinted in Gustav Stresemann, *Macht und Freiheit* (Halle, 1918), p. 120.

44. *Reichstag*, Vol. 307 (April 6, 1916), pp. 866 ff.

45. Stresemann, "Nachlass," 3055/6842/127311 f.

46. *Ibid.*, 3057/6847/128453 f.; also Reichstag speech cited in n. 44., above; *ibid.*, Vol. 310 (Oct. 10, 1917), p. 3133. That Ballin, despite these quotable phrases of 1917, took a different view, is evidenced by his correspondence with Stresemann. In a letter of March 23, 1915 ("Nachlass," 3056/6843/

127601), acknowledging receipt of a copy of Stresemann's *Englands Wirtschaftskrieg gegen Deutschland,* he states that he cannot agree on all points, especially the statement that "England planned the war and put it into motion," for he knew "partly from his own outlook, partly from unquestionable sources" that Grey had "tried honestly to the last moment to avoid the war," and the "greatest reproach" against him was that of vacillation, in failing to make a clear declaration of the war danger on the first day. Ballin indicated a desire to talk to Stresemann about the war, which he termed a "terrible crime" *(Verbrechen);* Stresemann apparently did not reply. For other comments of Ballin on the war's origins, see *ibid.,* 3065/6872/130738-44.

47. E.g., Stresemann, *Das Deutsche Wirtschaftsleben im Kriege,* p. 3.
48. Stresemann, "Nachlass," 3057/6849/128786 ff.
49. Stresemann, "Nachlass," 3056/6843/127579 ff.; *ibid.,* 127595 ff.
50. *Ibid.,* 3055/6842/127326 ff.; see also Stresemann, *Das Deutsche Wirtschaftsleben im Kriege,* p. 3.
51. Stresemann, "Nachlass," 3055/6840/127105 ff.; *ibid.,* 3057/6847/128453. Typical is an exchange of letters in December, 1914 between Stresemann and Eduard von Capelle, who in 1916 succeeded Admiral von Tirpitz as State Secretary for the Naval Office. They agreed completely that England was the instigator of the war and that economic rivalry and Edward VII's *Einkreisungspolitik* were the causes. Stresemann urged Capelle, through his contacts at the Naval Office, to see that these opinions were emphasized more by semi-official sources than was then being done: *ibid.,* 3055/6839/127026 f.; 126993 ff.
52. Viscount Edgar D'Abernon, *Lord D'Abernon's Diary* (3 vols., London, 1929-30), I, 209 f., II, 231.
53. Stresemann, "Nachlass," 3055/6842/123326. Despite his tendency toward nice distinctions between himself and the Pan-Germans, Stresemann was a member of the Pan-German League and shared its outlook; see below, pp. 38, 58.

54. *Ibid.*, 3060/6828/124928 ff.; Olden, *op. cit.*, p. 3. Although he took his doctorate in political economy, Stresemann's university program emphasized the study of history and literature, and he once considered an academic career: *Vermaechtnis*, I, 1. One of his close associates in the Pan-German movement, Dietrich Schäfer, was a prominent historian.

55. Stresemann, "Nachlass," 3055/6842/123326.

56. *Ibid.*, 3056/6843/127595. In 1919 Stresemann noted ruefully: "The comparison Rome-Carthage occurred to many of us during the war, only we thought that we were the Romans": Stresemann, "Wilsons Frieden," *Von der Revolution bis zum Frieden von Versailles* (Berlin, 1919), p. 166.

57. Stresemann prided himself on being a student of Napoleon: *Vermaechtnis*, I, 2; and his National Liberal associate, Ernst Bassermann, also an admirer of Napoleon, owned a large collection of Napoleon pictures, coins, and busts: Eschenburg, *op. cit.*, p. 18, n. For Stresemann on Napoleon see "Goethe und Napoleon," *Reden und Schriften,* pp. 350-367. For French comments on Stresemann and Napoleon see Maurice Muret, "M. Stresemann, Homme des Lettres," *Journal des Debats,* 34 pt. 2 (Oct. 14, 1927), p. 646; Millian Schömann, Les Jugements de Stresemann sur Napoléon," *Revue d'Allemagne,* VI (June 15, 1932), pp. 493-502.

58. For this and the following, Stresemann, "Napoleon und wir," *Reden und Schriften,* II, 329-350, *passim.*

59. Stresemann, "Nachlass," 3055/6840/127105 ff., for *Hannoverscher Kurier,* 28 Sept. 1914; *ibid.,* 3057/6847/128460.

60. Stresemann, *Deutsches Ringen und Deutsches Hoffen,* pp. 3 ff; Stresemann, "Nachlass," 3055/6839/ 126993 ff.; 127026 f.

61. Stresemann, *Das Deutsche Wirtschaftsleben im Kriege,* p. 40.

62. Stresemann, "Nachlass," 3055/6839/126969 ff. His sharp attitude toward England perhaps stemmed in part from the realization that she could not be so easily defeated and if not "completely conquered" would after a while "rekindle the war"; *ibid.,* 6892/127326 ff.

63. *Ibid.* Whether Stresemann ever fully recognized the truth about the Marne is difficult to say; e.g., early in 1915 he

hailed it as "the first great victory in the West" (*Ibid.*, 3057/6847/128451); but he was definitely aware of its limitations by the time of the Verdun offensive in 1916; *ibid.*, 3062/6851/129082 ff.; *ibid.*, 3055/6242/127318 ff.

64. *Reichstag*, Vol. 310 (Oct. 10, 1917), p. 3833.

65. Stresemann, *Deutsches Ringen und Deutsches Hoffen*, p. 12.

66. Stresemann, "Nachlass," 3075/6881/132049 ff.; see below, ch. viii, n. 66. Although, after the war he tended to stress the clumsy diplomacy of all the powers Stresemann did "acknowledge a certain responsibility on the part of Count Berchtold, the Austrian Foreign Minister": see Bretton, *op. cit.*, p. 47.

67. *Ibid.*, 3104/7158/153425. While undated, these remarks were probably a comment on the Chancellor's Reichstag speech of Aug. 19, 1915: F. Thimme, ed., *Bethmann-Hollwegs Kriegsreden* (Stuttgart, 1919), pp. 37 ff.

68. *Ibid.*, 3056/6843/127707 ff.

69. Stresemann, *Deutsches Ringen und Deutsches Hoffen*, p. 16. See also, Gatzke, *Germany's Drive*, p. 5; Kürenberg, *op. cit.*, p. 307; Pinson, *op. cit.*, p. 315.

70. Stresemann, "Nachlass," 3055/6839/127016 f.; *ibid.*, 6842/127324.

71. Stresemann, *Deutsches Wirtschaftsleben im Kriege*, pp. 46 ff.

72. *Ibid.*, pp. 55 f.

73. *Ibid.*, pp. 57 f.

74. *Reichstag*, Vol. 307 (April 6, 1916), p. 866.

75. Lutz, *Fall*, I, 338 f.

Chapter II

1. *Reichstag*, Vol. 306 (Aug. 4, 1914), pp. 1-3.

2. Gatzke, *Germany's Drive*, pp. 8 f.; *U.A.*, 4. Reihe, VII, (1), 133 f.

3. E.g., by the so-called "rainbow books," the official collections of documents relating to the crisis, none of which was entirely accurate or complete. Stresemann in 1915 criticized the German White Book, charging that in the desire to provide

quick information for the Reichstag it had not been produced with the proper care and consideration of the fact that it would become a "world historical document": "Nachlass," 3104/7158/153425.

4. Dahlin, *op. cit.*, p. 13.
5. Even among the Social Democrats, despite the official stand of the party, annexationist demands were not absent: e.g., while opposed to Western annexations they were not unwilling to liberate Baltic Germans in the process of ending Tsarist rule: see Rosenberg, *op. cit.*, pp. 105 ff.; Gatzke, *Germany's Drive*, pp. 19, 110 f.; and Holborn, "Diplomats and Diplomacy in the Early Weimar Republic," *op. cit.*, pp. 138 f. For representative positions of various political parties on the war aims question see S. Grumbach, *Das Annexionistische Deutschland* (Lausanne, 1917), pp. 114 ff.
6. Th. von Bethmann-Hollweg, *Betrachtungen zum Weltkriege* (2 vols., Berlin, 1921), II, 31; Conrad Haussmann, *Schlaglichter* (Frankfort a. M., 1924), p. 14.
7. See Henry Cord Meyer, *Mitteleuropa in German Thought and Action 1815-1945* (The Hague, 1955), for a clear analysis of a frequently misinterpreted subject.
8. Edwyn Bevan, *German War Aims* (New York, 1918), p. 5.
9. Gatzke, *Germany's Drive*, pp. 16 f.; F. Thimme, *Bethmann-Hollwegs Kriegesreden*, pp. 14, 23; K. Westarp, *Konservative Politik im letzten Jahrzehnt des Kaiserreiches* (2 vols., Berlin, 1935), II, 46-50.
10. Rosenberg, *op. cit.*, p. 96.
11. Philipp Scheidemann, *Memoiren eines Sozialdemokraten* (2 vols., Dresden, 1929), I, 280, 297 f. "Arch apostle of the policy of annexation" is the term used by J. H. Wheeler-Bennett: *The Nemesis of Power, The German Army in Politics, 1918-1945* (New York, 1954), p. 38.
12. The anti-Stresemann group, e.g., A. Gauvain, "De Stresemann à Bülow," *Journal des Debats*, 35:1 (May 18, 1928), pp. 807 f., and Jacques Bainville, *L'Allemagne* (Paris, 1939), II, 147 f., have cited Stresemann's World War annexationist views in order to make suspect his Weimar policies. Strese-

mann supporters such as Ernst Jackh, *The New Germany* (London, 1927), p. 50, stress the contrast between the wartime National Liberal leader and the Weimar Foreign Minister who initiated the Locarno Pact. Rheinbaben in his biography of Stresemann goes so far as to say that the latter, during the war "opposed emphatically the annexationists." (Rheinbaben, *op. cit.*, p. 107). Scheidemann's sharp criticism of what he termed Rheinbaben's "nonsense" (Scheidemann, *op. cit.*, pp. 297) would indicate that Rheinbaben's assertion met prompt rejection.

13. Stresemann, *Vermaechtnis*, I, 12, autobiographical sketch. See also, *U.A.*, 4. Reihe, VII, pt. 2, 309.

14. Gustav Stresemann, "Zum Tode Friedrich Naumanns," in *Von der Revolution bis zum Frieden von Versailles*, pp. 212-218; See also Olden, *op. cit.*, pp. 19 f.; Rochus v. Rheinbaben, biographical sketch in Stresemann, *Reden und Schriften*, p. 22.

15. Personal communication from Theodor Heuss dated 27 October, 1953.

16. Walter H. Kaufmann, *Monarchism in the Weimar Republic* New York, 1953), pp. 21 ff.; George N. Shuster and Arnold Bergstraesser, *Germany, A Short History* (New York, 1944), pp. 94 ff.; Ludwig Bergsträsser, *op. cit.*, pp. 88-98.

17. Gatzke, *Germany's Drive*, p. 5.

18. Rheinbaben, *op. cit.*, pp. 62 ff.; Olden, *op. cit.*, pp. 34 f.

19. Mildred Wertheimer, *The Pan-German League 1890-1914*, (New York, 1924), pp. 134 ff.; 204; Gatzke, *Germany's Drive*, pp. 4, 24-29.

20. Stresemann, "Nachlass," reels 3054 and 3061, contains the correspondence between Stresemann and Bassermann from 1907 to 1917; for Stresemann on Bassermann see his essay in *Reden und Schriften*, pp. 140-163, and his critical introduction to Eschenburg, *op. cit.*, pp. vii-xii. See also Eschenburg's study, based on the unpublished Bassermann papers which have since been destroyed, *passim*, esp. pp. 283 ff.

21. Stresemann, *Macht und Freiheit*, pp. 28 f.; see also his speech

to the Hansa League at Frankfurt, June 8, 1915, quoted in Grumbach, *op. cit.*, p. 73.

22. Stresemann, *Macht und Freiheit*, p. 37; Stresemann, "Nachlass," 3057/6849/128786 ff.

23. Grumbach, *op. cit.*, p. 36: report of National Liberal Party resolution in whose making Stresemann participated.

24. *Ibid.*, p. 74, Stresemann's speech to the National Liberal Party of Rheinland-Westphalia, July 25, 1915.

25. Stresemann, *Deutsches Ringen und Deutsches Hoffen*, p. 11.

26. Stresemann, "Nachlass," 3054/6835/126264 f.; 3055/6839/ 126925; 3056/6843/127565-72; Stresemann, *Macht und Freiheit*, p. 37; Stresemann, *Deutsches Ringen und Deutsches Hoffen*, pp. 12-15.

27. Gatzke, *Germany's Drive*, pp. 4 f.; Wertheimer, *op. cit.*, pp. 49 ff.

28. There was of course no single, exactly defined program to which all who shared certain general aims could agree. The *Drang nach Westen* was dominated by the view that England was the chief foe; against her Germany must gain control of the seas and to that end annex the European land areas which would make that possible; Gatzke, *Germany's Drive*, pp. 3 f.; 12 ff.

29. Stresemann was but one voice, albeit a stentorian one, in a group which produced a tremendous "literature" of pamphlets, petitions, articles, and speeches: Grumbach, *op. cit., passim;* Lutz, *Fall*, pp. 74 ff.

30. Stresemann, "Nachlass," 3054/6835/126264; *ibid.*, 3055/ 6839/126925-7; 127002 f.; *ibid.*, 3056/6843/127565-72; *ibid.*, 3065/6873/130912; Stresemann, *Deutsches Ringen und Deutsches Hoffen,* p. 15; Stresemann, "Gedanken zur Krisis," *Deutsche Stimmen,* XXIV (1917), pp. 417-432.

31. Stresemann, "Nachlass," 3055/6839/126969 f.; *ibid.*, 3056/ 6843/127670-4.

32. *Ibid.*, 3055/6839/126925-7; 126969 f.; *ibid.*, 6842/127345-54; *ibid.*, 3056/6843/127565 ff.

33. *Ibid.*, 3055/6839/126969 f.

34. *Ibid.,* 126970; 126993; *ibid., 6842/127331;* 127491; *ibid.,* 3054/6835/126264 f.; *ibid.,* 3064/6869/130189 ff.

35. *Ibid.,* 3055/6839/127016 f.; *ibid.,* 6842/127345 ff.; *ibid.,* 3061/6833/125812 ff.; *ibid.,* 3062/6850/126964 ff.

36. Stresemann, *Deutsches Ringen und Deutsches Hoffen,* pp. 12 f.; "Nachlass," 3055/6839/126925 ff.; *ibid.,* 6842/127331 f.; 127345-54; *ibid.,* 3064/6869/130189 ff.

37. Stresemann, "Nachlass," 3075/6882/132315 f.; *Reichstag,* vol. 307 (April 6, 1916), pp. 886 ff. On the Flemish question see S. B. Clough, *A History of the Flemish Movement in Belgium* (New York, 1930). According to Scheidemann (*op. cit.* I, 419) the Flemish question was "constantly mooted, especially by Stresemann," with the thought that Belgium would thus be divided and "by this means prepared for incorporation." See below, pp. 60, 151.

38. *Ibid.,* 3054/6835/126264; 3056/6843/127660 f.

39. Stresemann, *Deutsches Ringen und Deutsches Hoffen,* p. 15.

40. Grumbach, *op. cit.,* p. 357; Gatzke, *Germany's Drive,* pp. 119, 242.

41. Stresemann, "Nachlass," 3056/6846/128279 ff.; *ibid.,* 3057/6849/128786.

42. *Ibid.,* 3055/6842/127494 ff.; *ibid.,* 6892/127313 f.; *ibid.,* 3056/6843/127565 ff.

43. *Ibid.,* 3055/6842/127331; 3056/6843/127662; *ibid.,* 3062/6850/128899. The "wet triangle" was a phrase of Albert Ballin's by which the *Hapag* director referred to the area of the North Sea "between Heligoland and the river estuaries"; it was considered vital that Bruges, Ostend, and Zeebrugge be in German hands to assure passage from the "wet triangle" to the open sea: *ibid.,* 3077/6909/135519; Grumbach, *o.p cit.,* pp. 17, 97.

44. Stresemann, *Deutsches Ringen und Deutsches Hoffen,* p. 14; Stresemann, "Nachlass," 3057/6849/128765; 128786; *ibid.,* 3075/6882/132246 ff.; *ibid.,* 6884/132578 f.

45. Lutz, *Fall,* I, 341.

46. Stresemann, "Unsere Lage," in *Macht und Freiheit,* p. 126; Stresemann, "Nachlass," 3055/6842/127318 ff.; *ibid.,* 3057/6849/128786 f.

47. Gatzke, *Germany's Drive,* p. 5 and f.n.
48. Stresemann, "Nachlass," 3056/6843/127565 f.; 127670 f.; Bevan, *op. cit.,* pp. 3, 25, 47.
49. *Ibid.,* 3055/6839/126969; 127016 f.; *ibid.,* 3054/6835/126266; Grumbach, *op. cit.,* p. 367; Bevan, *op. cit.,* p. 26.
50. *Ibid.,* 3055/6839/126969 f.; *ibid.,* 6834/127670 f.
51. *Ibid.,* 3078/6915/136752 f.; *Reichstag,* vol. 311 (Feb. 20, 1918), pp. 4018 f.; Lutz, *Fall,* I, 810.
52. Stresemann, *Deutsches Ringen und Deutsches Hoffen,* p. 12.
53. *Reichstag,* vol. 307 (April 6, 1916), pp. 866 f.; see also Stresemann, "Nachlass," 3067/6887/133159 f.; Grumbach, *op. cit.,* p. 69. Stresemann in his "great joy" contributed a thousand marks to Dresden's relief fund when, at the peace settlement with Russia in 1918, the "old university of Dorpat and the internally so wonderfully German Reval" were "again under the protection of the German Reich": "Nachlass," 3078/6914/136438.
54. In the Reichstag when Scheidemann and Fischbeck demanded that the peace treaty with Russia provide for "self-determination of the border provinces," Stresemann was noncommittal: *Reichstag,* vol. 310 (Nov. 29, 1917), pp. 3948 ff.; see also Dahlin, *op. cit.,* p. 135.
55. *Reichstag,* vol. 311 (Mar. 19, 1918), pp. 4453 f. There were other dangers about which he wrote warningly to State Secretary von Kühlmann: the creation of a Northern Balkans; the destruction of German influence through the spread of socialism in independent small states; and British penetration of the Baltic: Stresemann, "Nachlass," 3067/6887/133159 f.
56. *Reichstag,* vol. 311 (Feb. 20, 1918), pp. 4018 f.; Lutz, *Fall,* I, 783 f.
57. *Ibid.,* (March 19, 1918), pp. 4453 f.; Lutz, *Fall,* I, 783 f.
58. Stresemann, "Nachlass," 3068/6890/133721 f.
59. *Ibid.,* 3055/6839/126969 f. In December, 1914, when Stresemann represented the War Committee of German Industry at a discussion with the Chancellor and State Secretary Clemens von Delbrück on war aims (see below, pp. 54 f.) he strongly supported the idea of such a customs union. He

would also have included the Scandinavian countries and hoped that even France and Russia would join, after their defeat, making a continental bloc against England.

60. *Ibid.*, 6842/127326 f. It was the impact of the Entente's blockade which stimulated the *Mitteleuropa* enthusiasm in Germany. It had been outside the mainstream of German political and economic history from 1871 to 1914: Meyer, *op. cit.*, pp. 29, 116-136.

61. *Ibid.*, 3056/6846/128279 f.; Stresemann traveled to Bulgaria in 1916 to promote economic intercourse: *ibid.*, 3063/6867/129885-129956; Stresemann, *Reden und Schriften*, I, 122-119. He also made several trips to Vienna and Budapest to develop trade associations and spoke at numerous meetings on their behalf; see also Meyer, *op. cit.*, pp. 154, 160.

62. *Reichstag*, vol. 307 (April 6, 1916), pp. 866 f.; Meyer, *op. cit.*, p. 171. Despite his public emphasis on German-Austrian partnership, Stresemann, in a personal letter to Bassermann (Dec. 30, 1914) emphasized that *de facto* control of the customs union must be in German hands: "Nachlass," 3054/6835/126264 f.

63. Stresemann, "Nachlass," 3066/6879/131767 ff.; Lutz, *Fall*, I, 787 f.

64. Lutz, *Fall, I,* 218 f., 345. The war briefly stimulated a new "Faith of the Nibelungs" and reinvigorated the *grossdeutsch* ideas of the early nineteenth century, Bismarck was frequently hailed as a father of *Mitteleuropa* despite the fact that the unification of Germany had come about through his exclusion of Austria: Meyer, *op. cit.*, pp. 23-29; 137 f.; 248.

65. Meyer, *op. cit.*, pp. 206 ff.; 218.

66. While Naumann's book was not intended as war aims propaganda it was often taken in that sense: *ibid.*, pp. 136; 194-205; 264; see also Gatzke, *Germany's Drive*, pp. 105 f.; Bevan, *op. cit.*, pp. 14 ff.; Dahlin, *op. cit.*, p. 74; Rosenberg, *op. cit.*, pp. 106, 313. Ballin's comments are of some interest: ". . . Naumann . . . has already broken many window panes for which the working classes will have to pay after the war. If we had such an idea . . . we could have done much better

with it before the war than now or after the war. The idea
... has come at a most unfortunate time and with a propaganda which will call forth counter-measures by our enemies at Paris. ...": Stresemann, "Nachlass," 3075/6884/132559; see also Meyer, *op. cit.*, p. 211.

67. Stresemann, *Deutsches Wirtschaftsleben im Kriege,* pp. 58 f.
68. Stresemann, "Nachlass," 3064/6870/130470; see also, Dahlin, *op. cit.,* p. 67.
69. *Reichstag,* vol. 307 (April 6, 1916), pp. 866 ff.; Meyer, *op. cit.,* pp. 236 ff. But see below, p. 157.
70. *Reichstag,* vol. 307 (April 6, 1916), pp. 866 ff.; Lutz, *Fall,* I, 343.
71. Stresemann, "Brauchen wir Kolonien?", *Reden und Schriften,* I, 108 ff.
72. *Ibid.,* p. 110. Despite Stresemann's emotional plea regarding the desire of German colonists to return to Samoa and the other colonies, official German statistics reveal that among 34,000 Samoans recorded by the 1914 census there were only 329 Germans; out of 12,230,000 inhabitants in all of Germany's overseas possessions, only 24,152 were Germans: *Statistisches Jahrbuch fuer das Deutsches Reich* (Berlin, 1914), p. 464. The number of Germans in all the colonies was less than the number of Pan-Germans, with their Colonial League affiliates, in Germany: Wertheimer, *op. cit.,* pp. 49 f.
73. *Ibid.,* p. 111.
74. Lutz, *Causes,* p. 4; *U.A.,* 4. Reihe, I, 20-25. To these middle groups E. Müller-Meiningen gave the name "tree-frog *(Laubfrosch)* annexationists": Scheidemann, *op. cit.,* I, 162.

Chapter III

1. For full treatment of German war aims see *U.A.,* 4. Reihe, vol. XII (1), Volkmann, "Die Annexionsfragen des Weltkrieges" (Berlin, 1929); see also, Gatzke, *Germany's Drive,* and Dahlin, *op. cit.,* for treatment of specific aspects of the problem.
2. Dahlin, *op. cit.,* pp. 13 ff.; 25; Gatzke, *Germany's Drive,* p. 17.

3. Stresemann, "Nachlass," 3055/6839/127002 f.

4. Stresemann, *Deutsches Ringen und Deutsches Hoffen*, passim.

5. Stresemann, "Nachlass," 3055/6839/127331 f., 127345. Stresemann at first charged Foreign Office "weakness," later blamed the Chancellor for the ban: *ibid.*, 126993; *ibid.*, 3056/6843/127662.

6. *Ibid.*, 3055/6248/127331 f.: Stresemann also expressed awareness of the fact that the opposition was partly personal—some members of the Business Committee were not "overjoyed" at his re-election. See *ibid.*, 3052/6822/123529, 123753, and above, ch. i, n. 8, concerning his earlier career in the National Liberal Party.

7. *Ibid.*, 3064/6869/130189 ff.

8. *Ibid.* The Business Committee had acted in Bassermann's absence. An army reserve officer, he had elected to go on active duty. At a dinner in his honor on Dec. 14, 1914, he had declared that Germany would "know how to hold fast in the future the Belgian land conquered with so much blood": *ibid.*, 3054/6835/16264 f.; Grumbach, *op. cit.*, p. 71.

9. Such meetings had been initiated in August, 1914, by the Pan-German leader, Class, and Hugenberg of Krupp's: see Heinrich Class, *Wider den Strom* (Leipzig, 1932), pp. 319, 352 f.; Gatzke, *Germany's Drive*, pp. 38 f.

10. Stresemann, "Nachlass," 3055/6839/126925 ff. Stresemann regarded the War Committee highly: "There," he wrote, "do not sit dreamers or idealists but men of practical work who have spoken out for absolute annexation of all Belgium and the Baltic provinces in case the victory is such that Germany can stipulate these conditions." *Ibid.*, 127016 f.

11. *Ibid.* Siemens was one of the few industrialists who in June, 1915, signed a petition prepared chiefly by Theodor Wolff and Hans Delbrück which opposed annexations: Theodor Wolff, *Der Marsch durch Zwei Jahrzehnte* (Amsterdam, 1936), pp. 269 f.; Grumbach, *op. cit.*, pp. 409 ff.; A. Thimme, *Hans Delbrück als Kritiker der Wilhelminischen Epoche* (Düsseldorf, 1955), p. 121.

12. Stresemann, "Nachlass," 3055/6239/126925 ff., for this and the following.

13. The annexationist program of the War Committee was basically that detailed by Stresemann in his early speeches and pamphlet (see above, pp. 40 f.), except that no mention was made of colonial or extra-continental matters other than the demand that France lose her rights in Morocco: *ibid.*, 3055/6839/126969 ff.; *ibid.*, 3054/6835/126264 f. To one who later criticized Stresemann for voicing the war aims views of heavy industry, he replied that these were his war aims before he knew what those of heavy industry were. *Ibid.*, 3064/4680/130277.

14. *Ibid.*, 3055/6839/126996 f.

15. *Ibid.*, The Chancellor told the delegates he did not want to reopen the wounds of 1870 by taking any French territory; if found necessary to annex the Vosges fortress area he would give compensations to France from Southern Belgium.

16. *Norddeutsche Allgemeine Zeitung*, Oct. 13 and Nov. 25, 1914, cited in Gatzke, *Germany's Drive*, p. 10.

17. *Reichstag*, vol. 306 (Aug. 4, 1914), pp. 1 ff.; *U.A.*, 4. Reihe, IV, 251 f.

18. *U.A.*, 4. Reihe, VII (2), 308; Spahn of the Center Party was the spokesman for this demand; the Social Democrat Haase opposed annexations of any kind.

19. *U.A.*, 4. Reihe, VII (1), 3-13; Lutz, *Causes*, p. 189; F. Thimme, *Bethmann Hollwegs Kriegsreden*, pp. 14, 23; Haussmann, *op. cit.*, p. 14.

20. Stresemann, "Nachlass," 3054/6835/126264 f.

21. *U.A.*, 4. Reihe, VII (2), 308; Haussmann, *op. cit.*, p. 31.

22. Westarp, *op. cit.*, II, 46 ff., 52 f.; Scheidemann, *op. cit.*, I, 349 ff.; Bethmann-Hollweg, *op. cit.*, II, 34 ff.; Gatzke, *Germany's Drive*, pp. 14, 67.

23. Stresemann, "Nachlass," 3055/6842/127324.

24. *Ibid.*, 127325; *ibid.*, 3056/6843/127634; 127739.

25. *Ibid.*, 3055/6842/127491 ff.

26. *Ibid.*, 6839/126993 f.

27. *Ibid.*, 6842/127356 ff.

28. *Ibid.*, 127321 ff.
29. *Ibid.*, 127345; 127318; *ibid.*, 3054/6835/126257 f. Bassermann had written from Antwerp: "How could we, a people of the offensive, let ourselves be led . . . into this trench warfare so completely foreign to our nature? We cannot get through at all because line stands behind line. . . ."
30. *Ibid.*, 3055/6842/127318 f.
31. *Ibid.*, 3056/6843/127662, e.g., the Progressive von Payer had declared to Bassermann that he "by no means objected to annexations. . . ." *Ibid.*, 6843/127662 f. The Progressives did later join the annexationist majority: See below, p. 75.
32. Stresemann, "Nachlass," 3056/6843/127660 f. Apt had written one of the early annexationist pamphlets of the war: *Der Krieg und die Weltmachtstellung des Deutschen Reiches* (Leipzig, 1914). For the events referred to by Stresemann, see L. Bergsträsser, *op. cit.*, pp. 89 ff.
33. *Ibid.*, The issue of internal reform raised here became important later in the war. See below, pp. 75, 131 ff.
34. *Ibid.*, 3057/6847/*passim; ibid.*, 6848/*passim.* He still, on occasion, called for "the black, white, red flag . . . over the roofs of Calais": *ibid.*, 3065/6873/130912 f.
35. *Ibid.*, 3055/6842/127345 ff.
36. *Ibid.* Stresemann pointed out that he had just pressed for the proclamation of the German-American Economic Association, helped frame the recommendations of the War Committee, and had energetically called for the annexation of Belgium at an audience at the Chancellory.
37. Wertheimer, *op. cit.*, p. 82; Gatzke, *Germany's Drive*, p. 24.
38. Except for Class's "foolishness" of wanting to solve the Jewish question in conquered Poland by sending the Jews to Palestine: Stresemann "Nachlass," 3055/6842/127345 f. Class praised Stresemann for supporting a war aims program "in all essentials" the same as his own: *ibid.*, 127342, 127506.
39. *U.A.*, 4. Reihe, XII (1), 67. Bassermann also participated in these activities: Stresemann, "Nachlass," 3062/6850/128994.
40. Stresemann, "Nachlass," 3056/6843/127752. The document is also known as the "Petition of the Intellectuals." See also

Dahlin, *op. cit.*, pp. 42 f.; Gatzke, *Germany's Drive,* p. 118.
41. *Ibid.,* 3055/6841/127251 ff. The petition followed the general annexationist pattern but was even more extreme; it would divest France of her colonial holdings; it called for increased naval strength in the struggle against England by acquisition of naval stations and loosening England's hold on Egypt; it called for a large indemnity. See Grumbach, *op. cit.,* pp. 132-140.
42. Scheidemann, *op. cit.,* I, 283 f.; Gatzke, *Germany's Drive,* p. 122; D. Schäfer, *Aus Meinem Leben* (Berlin, 1926), pp. 171 ff.
43. Stresemann, "Nachlass," 3055/6842/127406 f., "at the request of influential persons." Since he uses this phrase in letters to Hugenberg and other members of the War Committee, it seems likely that this assignment came from the Foreign Office, as Stresemann had several conferences with Zimmermann, the Under State Secretary, at this time concerning Belgium: *ibid.,* 127313 f. A paper, "Belgien als deutsche Provinz und die deutsche Volkswirtschaft," (*ibid.,* 127402 ff.) was the probable result of this activity.
44. *Ibid.,* 127426 ff., 127434, 127498 ff. Although, according to the Ruhr magnate Emil Kirdorf, there was "not a deviating voice" as to the necessity of German control of Belgium, it is interesting to note that these influential industrialists offered reasons basically military and therefore outside their field of competence; there was in fact much disagreement as to the economic and political consequences of such action.
45. *Ibid.,* 3056/6845/128010-4; Görlitz, *op. cit.,* pp. 66 f. On the importance of this *Mittwochsgesellschaft* see Graf Harry Kessler, *Walter Rathenau, his Life and Work* (New York, 1930), pp. 230 f., cited in Gatzke, *Germany's Drive,* p. 137.
46. Stresemann, "Nachlass," 3055/6842/127445; 127509 f. The importance of Stresemann's activities, chiefly with the *Bund der Industriellen,* is shown in that one meeting was postponed because Stresemann, slightly injured in an automobile accident, was unable to attend. This accident also prevented Stresemann from making a trip to occupied Belgium to ob-

serve conditions there at first hand: *ibid.*, 127494; *ibid.*, 3054/6835/126251 ff.

47. *Ibid.*, 3056/6843/127604 f.; Gatzke, *Germany's Drive*, p. 43.

48. *Ibid.*, 3055/6842/127494 f.

49. *Ibid.*, 3054/6837/126542 ff.: The *Deutscher Bauernbund* had been fostered by the National Liberals in the pre-war period as a counter-balance to the Conservative dominated *Bund der Landwirte* (Agrarian League). The annexationist cause now brought together these groups as it did the associations of light and heavy industry (*Bund der Industriellen* and *Zentralverband Deutscher Industrieller*) which had also been in frequent conflict prior to the war.

50. Lutz, *Fall*, I, 305 ff.: While censorship prevented publication of the petition, the brief statement in the *Deutsche Tageszeitung* of March 11 indicated its annexationist tenor. The *Norddeutsche Allgemeine Zeitung* commented it was glad the associations were united but would prefer they "wait till victory before talking about the best peace treaty."

51. *Ibid.*, p. 311. Stresemann expected and had worked to get the *Hansa Bund* to join the *Bauernbund* in signing the annexationist petition: "Nachlass," 3055/6842/127497-7; he had closely associated with the group since his first election to the Reichstag and had had its support in his 1912 campaign. He was the League's economic adviser; a brother-in-law was one of its directors: *ibid.*, 3054/6836/126401 ff., 126456; 3054/6837/126542.

52. Stresemann, "Nachlass," 3056/6843/127565 f. See above, p. 54.

53. *Ibid.*, see also *U.A.*, 4. Reihe, VII (1), 133 ff.; Lutz, *Fall*, I, 256, 305 ff.; Grumbach, *op. cit.*, pp. 123-132.

54. *Ibid.*, 3056/6843/127604; 127662 ff. The National Liberal Hirsch, closely associated with Hugenberg and with heavy industry, guided the integration effort with Stresemann's aid.

55. *Ibid.* Stresemann's notes indicate the following as present: Hugenberg, Stinnes, Thyssen, Kirdorf (*Zentralverband Deutscher Industrieller*); Roesicke, Wangenheim (*Bund der Landwirte*); Böhme, deWente (*Deutscher Bauernbund*); Friedrichs, Stollwerck, Lehmann (*Bund der Industriellen*); Bas-

sermann (National Liberals); Heydebrand, Westarp (Conservatives); Camp (Free Conservatives); Gröber, Spahn (Center). Wangenheim also was high in the Conservative Party, while Stresemann represented both the *Bund der Industriellen* and National Liberals.

56. Westarp, *op. cit.,* II, 37, 46-52; Gatzke, *Germany's Drive,* pp. 14 f. The Chancellor had just told Scheidemann that he completely rejected annexationist schemes about Belgium: Scheidemann, *op. cit.,* I, 350 f.

57. For this and the following, Stresemann, "Nachlass," 3056/6843/127670.

58. Grumbach, *op. cit.,* pp. 123-132; Gatzke, *Germany's Drive,* p. 45.

59. Stresemann, "Nachlass," 3056/6843/127579 ff.; see also Dahlin, *op. cit.,* p. 43; Lutz, *Fall,* I, 312 ff.: the privately circulated petition was soon published by the Socialist *Berner Tageblatt,* the Vienna *Arbeiter-Zeitung,* and the French *Humanité.*

60. Lutz, *Fall,* I, 312 ff.; Dahlin, *op. cit.,* pp. 43 f.; Grumbach, *op. cit.,* pp. 375 ff., Gatzke, *Germany's Drive,* pp. 106 f.; Stresemann, "Nachlass," 3056/6843/127739.

61. For this and the following, Stresemann, "Nachlass," 3056/6843/127579 ff.

62. *Ibid.*

63. *Ibid.,* 127638 ff.

64. Grumbach, *op. cit.,* 6.

65. *Ibid.,* p. 69; *Reichstag,* vol. 306, pp. 172 f.; *U.A.,* 4. Reihe, XII (1), 67.

66. Grumbach, *op. cit.,* pp. 36, 73.

Chapter IV

1. Stresemann, "Nachlass," 3056/6843/127638 f.; *U.A.* 4. Reihe, vol. XII (1), 67; Grumbach, *op. cit.,* pp. 36 f.

2. Grumbach, *op. cit.,* pp. 36 f., 69, 70 f.

3. *Ibid.,* p. 73; see also Gatzke, *Germany's Drive,* p. 78.

4. Stresemann, "Nachlass," 3064/6869/130215 f.

5. *Ibid.*, 3057/6849/128666; 128700; Grumbach, *op. cit.,* p. 74; *New York Tribune,* delayed report from Zurich, Aug. 2, 1915.

6. *Ibid.*, 3064/6869/130215 ff.; *ibid.*, 3057/6849/128666 f.; *New York Tribune,* August 2, 1915. The meeting at Cologne took place on July 25, 1915.

7. *Ibid.*, 3064/6869/130215 ff.

8. Stresemann, "Nachlass," 3064/6869/130215 ff. According to Stresemann the rumor was being spread by Prince Hatzfeldt, a moderate, associated with Delbrück and Dernburg in the anti-annexationist petition of the *Bund Neues Vaterland.*

9. *Ibid.*, Through other sources the National Liberal leaders had learned that Stein of the *Frankfurter Zeitung* had conferred with the Chancellor and allegedly had reported that the proclamation would read: "We carry on no war of conquest and strive for no extension of our frontiers."

10. *Ibid.*, 130215-130225. Others invited included Friedberg, Vogel, Junck, Kahl, Schiffer, Krause, and Prince von Schönaich-Carolath. Stresemann believed the Chancellor was trying to split the National Liberal Party, regarding the divided nature of which see *U.A. 4. Reihe,* vol. VII (2) 300; Olden, *op. cit.,* p. 36; Eschenburg, *op. cit., passim,* esp. p. 10.

11. *Ibid.* Immediately following the meeting with the Chancellor, Friedberg, a member of the National Liberal Business Committee, had issued a statement in the *Nationalliberale Correspondenz* to the effect that the Party did not distrust the Chancellor, but was later forced to admit that this was a personal action and did not represent the National Liberal Party, which made the effect worse than ever.

12. *U.A.,* 4. Reihe, vol. XII (1), 67; Grumbach, *op. cit.,* 36 f.

13. Stresemann, "Nachlass," 3064/6869/130215-130225; *ibid.*, 3057/6849/128666 f. Stresemann maintained that the Chancellor's complaints against personal attacks were in reality complaints against the discussion of the war aims by the annexationists.

14. Grumbach, *op. cit.,* pp. 6 f.; Dahlin, *op. cit.,* p. 33.

15. *Ibid.* It was promulgated July 31, 1915.
16. Stresemann, "Nachlass," 3064/6869/130215-25. He suggests with mock magnanimity that the proclamation which Erzberger had "read with his own eyes" had been a weak draft which had not been shown to the Chancellor.
17. *Ibid.* In his exultation Stresemann apparently felt no need to consider soberly the perspicuous letter from Huldermann, Ballin's *Hapag* associate, criticizing the blind demands of the National Liberal proclamation for a "Greater Germany" at the expense of economic reconstruction, including a share of world markets, the real keys to Germany's strength and future: *ibid.*, 3057/6849/128735 ff.
18. The flood of annexationist pamphlets reached its crest in late 1915 and early 1916: Grumbach, *op. cit., passim.* Not only did National Liberals, Conservatives, and Centrists continue their agitation, but many Progressives moved over into the annexationist camp (*ibid.*, pp. 34-39; Hanssen, *op. cit.*, pp. 106 ff.); even individual Social Democrats found it possible to approve gains made in a defensive war and call for economic control of Belgium under a cloak of neutrality (Grumbach, *op. cit.*, pp. 260 ff).
19. Stresemann, "Nachlass," 3064/6869/130225.
20. Stresemann, "Nachlass," 3057/6849/128765 ff.
21. *Ibid.*, 128786 ff. A copy of the petition was sent by Stresemann to the Crown Prince: *Ibid.*, 128793.
22. Gatzke, *Germany's Drive,* p. 116.
23. Stresemann, "Nachlass," 3056/6846/128279 ff.
24. *Reichstag,* vol. 306 (Dec. 15, 1915), 430 ff.; Scheidemann, *op. cit.*, I, 379 f.; Grumbach, *op. cit.*, p. 433.
25. *Reichstag,* vol. 306 (Dec. 15, 1915), 433; Grumbach, *op. cit.*, p. 7.
26. Wolff, *Vollendete Tatsachen,* p. 86.
27. Stresemann, "Nachlass," 3056/6845/128096 f.
28. Zwoch, *op. cit.*, p. 18.
29. Stresemann, "Weltkrieg und öffentliche Meinung," *Reden und Schriften,* I, 81-104; *Reichstag,* vol. 306 (Jan. 18, 1916), 733-740.

30. Stresemann, "Nachlass," 3064/6870/130310; Hanssen, *op. cit.*, pp. 124 f.
31. Stresemann, *Reden und Schriften*, I, 89. Similarly, in May, he attacked the censorship on behalf of free discussion of war aims: *Reichstag*, vol. 307 (May 30, 1916), 1308 ff.
32. *Ibid.*, I, 100 ff.
33. *Ibid.*, p. 103. Stresemann's statement may be compared with that made by Dr. Ernst Hasse, founder of the Pan-German League, and also a National Liberal, to the then Chancellor Bülow, who records that when he pointed out to Hasse how difficult he was making it to create understanding between Germany and England because of his tactless press campaign, the Pan-German replied that it was his duty and right to express what the German people were feeling; it was Bülow's business to see to it that diplomatic relations with England were not prejudiced by anything he might say: *Memoirs of Prince von Bülow* (3 vols., Boston, 1930-1932), III, 353.
34. Stresemann, "Nachlass," 3063/6865/129534.
35. E.g., Stresemann's letter of July 8, 1915 ("Nachlass," 3056/6844/127808 f.) in answer to von Liebig on the interesting topic of a possible successor to Bethmann-Hollweg. Liebig's banned book, *Die Politik von Bethmann Hollwegs* (Munich, 1915), was circulated on thin paper as first-class matter to elude the censors: Gatzke, *Germany's Drive*, p. 127; Hanssen, *op. cit.*, p. 133.
36. W. Kapp, "Die nationalen Kreise und der Reichskanzler," (Königsberg), 1916, cited by Gatzke, *Germany's Drive*, p. 127.
37. "Junius Alter," *Das Deutsche Reich auf dem Wege zur geschichtlichen Episode* (Munich, 1919), first published in 1916. According to Hanssen, *op. cit.*, p. 144, the Chancellor accused Kapp of this attack which was in fact the work of a Pan-German editor, Franz Sontag. When circulating the brochure Stresemann commented that Bethmann, in denouncing the "slanders and defamations" in the Reichstag had "made so much advertising for the books attacking him that the demand cannot be met any more," "Nachlass," 3062/6851/129074; 129145.
38. Gatzke, *Germany's Drive*, p. 113.

39. *Reichstag,* vol. 307 (April 6, 1916), 858.
40. *Ibid.,* p. 851; Grumbach, *op. cit.,* p. 8.
41. *Reichstag,* vol. 307 (April 5-6, 1916), pp. 856 ff.; see also, Stresemann, "Nachlass," 3062/6850/128868 f.
42. *Ibid.,* pp. 885, 890; see also Grumbach, *op. cit.,* p. 114; Lutz, *Fall,* I, 235.
43. *Ibid.,* p. 866 ff.; Lutz, *Fall,* I, 338 f.
44. Westarp, *op. cit.,* II, 55.
45. Grumbach, *op. cit.,* p. 45.
46. L. Bergsträsser, *op. cit.,* pp. 180-188; Scheidemann, *op. cit.,* I, 351 ff.
47. Dahlin, *op. cit.,* pp. 66 ff.
48. *Ibid.,* p. 67; Hanssen, *op. cit.,* pp. 124 ff.
49. Stresemann, "Nachlass," 3062/6850/128899-904. In addition to Bassermann and Stresemann, Westarp and Erzberger represented their parties, while Stinnes, Hugenberg, Hirsch, and the Berlin banker Weber represented industry. Erzberger, the Center Deputy, was at this time an associate of the industrialist Thyssen and strongly annexationist.
50. *Ibid.* Stinnes warned that if the British held Calais there was danger that they would build a tunnel under the Channel which would make it bad for Germany in the event of another war.
51. *Ibid.* Stresemann's notes say, "Those who knew the people of the Rhineland and Westphalia best declared. . . ." The remarks, quoted above, which follow are similar to those spoken by Hugenberg at an earlier meeting. See above, pp. 53 f.
52. Stresemann, "Nachlass," 3062/6850/128904.
53. Grumbach, *op. cit.,* p. 37.
54. Stresemann, "Nachlass," 3062/6850/129024 ff.
55. *Ibid.,* 128964 f. Stresemann opposed the anti-Jesuit measure supported chiefly by Prussian Conservatives: "I am no friend of ultramontanism . . . ," he wrote, "but the experiences of this war convince me that it is impossible to retain this law which has no practical effect and is politically harmful." *Ibid.,* 3066/6879/131815; *ibid.,* 3061/6831/125694.

56. *Ibid.*, 3062/6850/129045.
57. *Ibid.*, 3065/6873/130801 f.
58. *Ibid.*, 130796; 130804 f. Stresemann also declined election to an organ of the Committee for the same reason. He disclosed to a friend (*ibid.*, 3062/6851/129223) that such service would require too close contact with Fuhrmann, a National Liberal from the Prussian Chamber of Deputies, and a personal enemy since Stresemann's first term in the Reichstag: see *ibid.*, 3052/6822/123753 ff. See above, ch. i, n. 8; ch. iii, n. 6.
59. *Ibid.*, 3065/6873/130894 f., 130875 f.
60. *Ibid.*, 3062/6850/128990; *ibid.*, 6851/129080 ff.; Dahlin, *op. cit.*, p. 84.
61. Stresemann, "Nachlass," 3062/6851/129081 f.
62. *Ibid.*, 3065/6873/130875 f.; 130884 f.
63. Bethmann-Hollweg, *op. cit.*, II, 18; Gatzke, *Germany's Drive*, pp. 10, 77.

Chapter V

1. Bethmann-Hollweg, *op. cit.*, II, 121; M. Erzberger, *Erlebnisse im Weltkrieg* (Stuttgart, 1920), pp. 208 f. There had in fact been no emphasis on submarine construction, and Germany possessed no more than twenty-five at the beginning of the war: Hanssen, *op. cit.*, p. 138; Erich Ludendorff, *Ludendorff's Own Story* (2 vols., New York, 1919), I, 254.
2. According to Tirpitz the February announcement "came as a complete surprise" to him: A. von Tirpitz, *My Memoirs* (2 vols., New York, 1919), II, 143 f.; see also Ludendorff, *op. cit.*; Erzberger, *op. cit.*, p. 212.
3. Bethmann-Hollweg, *op. cit.*, II, 114; Erzberger, *op. cit.*, p. 213, uses the expression "to force England to her knees"; see also Tirpitz, *op. cit.*, II, 348.
4. Tirpitz, *op. cit.*, II, 500.
5. The Supreme Command supported the Chancellor since it already despaired of ending the war successfully and felt Germany could not bear the addition of the United States to

her enemies with England undefeated or the German position otherwise guaranteed: see Bethmann-Hollweg, *op. cit.*,
II, 115 f.; Erich v. Falkenhayn, *Die Oberste Heeresleitung,
1914-1916* (Berlin, 1920), pp. 58 f.; *Official German Documents Relating to the War,* "The Reports of the First and
Second Subcommittees of the Committee Appointed by the
National Constituent Assembly to Inquire into the Responsibility for the War," trans. Carnegie Endowment (2 vols.,
New York, 1923), I, 131; II, 1116 (cited hereinafter as *O.G.D.*).

6. Gatzke, *Germany's Drive*, p. 80.
7. Stresemann, "Nachlass," 3056/6843/127588 ff.
8. Stresemann, "Flotte, Weltwirtschaft und Volk," speech of
   May 12, 1907, to the German Navy League in Cologne,
   Reden und Schriften, I, 61-71; "Nachlass," 3075/6883/132504
   f., reflects vigorous support of navy bill in 1908; see also,
   Olden, *op. cit.*, pp. 33 f.; Kaufmann, *op. cit.*, p. 23.
9. Stresemann, "Nachlass," 3052/6824/124185 ff.
10. *Ibid.*, 6822/123658; 123680; Olden, *op cit.*, pp. 35, 45 f.
11. Holborn, *The Political Collapse of Europe*, pp. 75 ff.; Rosen-
    berg, *op. cit.*, p. 143; Th. Wolff, *Vollendete Tatsachen*, pp.
    90 ff. In fairness to Tirpitz it must be pointed out that he
    claims to have urged the decisive use of the fleet early in the
    war but was opposed by William II, who cooled toward the
    Admiral from this time: Tirpitz, *op. cit.*, II, 74 ff.; he also
    states that in the pre-war period the U-boats were built as
    fast as technical problems could be solved: *ibid.*, II, 198.
12. Stresemann, *Deutsches Ringen und Deutsches Hoffen*, p. 8.
13. Stresemann, "Nachlass," 3057/6847/128453; see above, ch. i,
    n. 51.
14. Rosenberg, *op. cit.*, pp. 87, 137 f., 144.
15. Stresemann, "Nachlass," 3056/6843/127753.
16. *Ibid.*, 3057/6849/128765 ff.
17. *Ibid.*, 3056/6843/127729 ff.
18. Stresemann, "Nachlass," 3056/6843/127729 ff. This is in con-
    tradiction to Tirpitz's claim that he had suggested only a
    "blockade of the mouth of the Thames" rather than the
    declaration of a large "war zone" around the British Isles:

Tirpitz, *op. cit.,* II, 144 f. Moreover, in October Capelle told Stresemann that in February, 1915, there had not been enough submarines for unlimited war: Stresemann, "Nachlass," 3064/6871/130517 ff.

19. Stresemann, "Nachlass," 3056/6843/127729 ff.

20. Stresemann, "Nachlass," 3056/6843/127756 ff.; Erzberger, *op. cit.,* p. 210.

21. Stresemann, "Nachlass," 3057/6849/128765; *ibid.,* 128798; Erzberger, *op. cit.,* p. 211 f.

22. Stresemann, "Nachlass," 3057/6847/128453 f.; *ibid.,* 3056/6844/127778 ff.

23. Stresemann, "Nachlass," 3057/6849/128666 ff.; *ibid.,* 3064/6869/130215 ff.; *ibid.,* 3056/6844/127778 f.; Bülow, *op. cit.,* III, 291.

24. Stresemann, "Nachlass," 3057/6849/128786 ff.

25. *Ibid.,* 3056/6846/128194, 128242.

26. Bethmann-Hollweg, *op. cit.,* II, 119.

27. *Ibid.,* 114 ff.; Erzberger, *op. cit.,* p. 213; *O.G.D.,* I, 147; II, 1121; Falkenhayn, *op. cit.,* pp. 58 f., 182; Rosenberg, *op. cit.,* p. 95.

28. Erzberger, *op. cit.,* p. 210; Bethmann-Hollweg, *op. cit.,* II, 121.

29. Erzberger, *op. cit.,* p. 214. Erzberger noted on returning from abroad that Berlin was "a political madhouse; whoever opposed unrestricted U-boat war was branded as disloyal, antinationalist, or slacker." He added that when one asked what would happen when the United States entered the war "these sea-heroes of the study" either did not reply, said the answer would be found later, or that the U-boat would work too quickly for America to get into the war.

30. Bethmann-Hollweg, *op. cit.,* II, 121. In the Reichstag although the middle-class parties now formed a pro-annexationist majority they did not yet command a pro-submarine majority; the desire to preserve good relations with the neutrals, especially the United States, strengthened the Chancellor against Tirpitz: *U.A.,* 4. Reihe, VII (I), 3 ff.; Lutz, *Causes,* p. 190.

31. *Ibid.*, II, 122. The Chancellor attributed to the Admiralty the rumors that there were secret motives, e.g., that he was an Anglophile and therefore wanted to spare England, for his reluctance to prosecute the unlimited U-boat war. He felt military circles were not displeased at the Pan-German attacks against him: *ibid.*, 43.

32. Rosenberg, *op. cit.*, p. 95.

33. *Ibid.*, p. 113.

34. Stresemann, "Nachlass," 3064/6868/129960 f.; *ibid.*, 3056/6848/127729.

35. Hanssen, *op. cit.*, pp. 123 f.; Stresemann, "Nachlass," 3056/6846/128242. The British Q-boat *Baralong*, an auxiliary cruiser flying neutral colors, had sunk a surfaced German submarine which was lying alongside a British vessel it had captured.

36. *Reichstag*, vol. 306 (Jan. 18, 1916), 733 ff.; see also Stresemann, *Reden und Schriften*, I, 97.

37. *Ibid.*, vol. 307 (May 30, 1916), 1311.

38. Stresemann, "Nachlass," 3064/6870/130325.

39. *Ibid.*, 6871/130511, 130517. Stresemann's admiration endured. See his effusively sentimental note to Tirpitz in 1919 upon receipt of a copy of the latter's memoirs, personally inscribed: *ibid.*, 3088/6923/130002. His regard is emphasized by the fact that at this time (1919) he faced difficulties in organizing his new *Deutsche Volkspartei* because of his wartime stand on the submarine, for which he was now being severely criticized. Typical is a letter from a party associate in Wilhelmshaven reporting that the people there were saying, "That Stresemann and his U-boats! They are responsible for all our trouble!" He asked Stresemann for data to defeat this talk which was "a stone in the road for the party": *ibid.*, 3079/6920/137610 f.

40. *Reichstag*, vol. 307 (March 23, 1916), 810; see also *ibid.*, vol. 310 (Oct. 10, 1917), 3833.

41. Stresemann, "Nachlass," 3064/6871/130520 f. He declared at the Committee hearings that "the National Liberals were informed regarding the number of submarines even if the

public was not"; *ibid.,* 3062/6850/128868 f. In the spring of 1917 he was writing to his friends that he knew exactly how many submarines there were: 3066/6878/131711.

42. Erzberger, *op. cit.,* p. 210. Ironically, if one accepts as the "Tirpitz program" that described in his memoirs, Stresemann and the general public were far ahead of the Grand Admiral in their enthusiastic demands and expectations of the U-boat up to this time: Tirpitz, *op. cit.,* II, 137 ff.; 141 ff.; 147-152; 155 f.

43. Erzberger, *op. cit.,* p. 227; A. Thimme, "Gustav Stresemann, Legende und Wirklichkeit," *op. cit.,* p. 294.

44. Stresemann, "Nachlass," 3064/6871/130520 f.; Hanssen, *op. cit.,* p. 135.

45. *Ibid.,* 130571 f.; *ibid.,* 3062/6851/129084 f.

46. The Chancellor asserts that on March 1, 1916, Germany had 35 submarines ready for service: Bethmann-Hollweg, *op. cit.,* II, 117 ff. Erzberger claims there were "a few more than 50" at the beginning of the year, of which one-third were at a time operational: Erzberger, *op. cit.,* p. 212. Testifying before the Committee in March Admiral von Capelle stated that Germany had "20 modern submarines in operation against England and other small submarines in use off the Flemish coast." He added that Germany would have 54 new, modern craft by fall: Hanssen, *op. cit.,* p. 135 f. In June, 1916, the Admiral told Stresemann that Germany had "60 submarines, 40 big, 30 small [sic];" that within a year there would be a total of 111, including 52 large, the delivery rate being four per month: Stresemann, "Nachlass," 3062/6851/129086. It may be noted that the Admiral in giving his production estimate for the coming year did not take any possible losses into consideration.

47. According to various statements the number in 1916 ranged from five to twenty: Erzberger, *op. cit.,* p. 212; Bethmann-Hollweg, *op. cit.,* II, 117 ff.; Hanssen, *op. cit.,* 135 f. (statement of Capelle); Stresemann, "Nachlass," 3062/6851/129084 (statement of Zimmermann of the Foreign Office). The lower figure represents the number actually on mission, not those returning or in repair.

48. Stresemann, "Nachlass," 3063/6866/129731.

49. *Ibid.,* 3076/6900/135269.

50. Erzberger, *op. cit.,* pp. 209, 227 ff.

51. Stresemann, "Nachlass," 3068/6889/133460 ff.; see below, pp. 228 f.

52. Stresemann, "Nachlass," 3064/6869/130211; Hanssen, *op. cit.,* p. 135.

53. Stresemann, "Nachlass," 3064/6871/130571 ff.; Hanssen, *op. cit.,* p. 136; Tirpitz, *op. cit.,* II, 174 f.

54. Stresemann, "Nachlass," 3062/6850/128868 ff.; Hanssen, *op. cit.*

55. Stresemann, "Nachlass," 3062/6850/128868 f.; The Admiral described this as an "unfortunate phrase": *O.G.D.,* I, 605.

56. This conflicts with the annexationist demands for a Greater Germany based on "real guaranties" to come with victory rather than on "treaties which would not be honored."

57. Stresemann, "Nachlass," 3062/6850/128868 f.; *ibid.,* 3064/6871/130571 f.

58. *Ibid.; ibid.,* 3064/6869/130180 ff. The most prominent was Hugo Stinnes, a convinced annexationist. See above, p. 75.

59. *Ibid., ibid.,* 3064/6871/130559 f.; Hanssen, *op. cit.,* p. 135. The Chancellor had raised this question in his private talks with Stresemann: see above, p. 90.

60. Stresemann, "Nachlass," 3062/6850/128869 ff. He referred to the attitude of Congress, the coming elections, and the importance of the German-American votes.

61. *Ibid.*

62. Hanssen, *op. cit.,* pp. 138 f. He also rejected the demands of the Social Democrats that the Government desist on moral grounds from the unrestricted submarine warfare.

63. Stresemann, "Nachlass," 3062/6850/128868 ff.; *ibid.,* 3064/6870/130361 ff., 130373, 130571 ff.

64. *Ibid.,* 3064/6871/130578 ff.; *ibid.,* 3062/6850/128868 ff.; *U.A.,* 4. Reihe, VII (2), 307. The refusal of a vote of confidence of course had no influence on the Government's policy, for while the Committee hearings gave the party leaders a chance to air their views, the decision had already been taken in the dismissal of Tirpitz by the Emperor.

65. *Reichstag,* vol. 307 (April 6, 1916); *ibid.,* (May 30, 1916), 1311; Stresemann, "Nachlass," 3064/6871/130543.
66. Grumbach, *op. cit.,* pp. 36 f.
67. Hanssen, *op. cit.,* pp. 143 f.; Stresemann, *Reden und Schriften,* II, 349.
68. Stresemann, "Nachlass," 3063/6864/129275.
69. *Ibid.,* 3062/6851/129084.
70. *Ibid.,* 3065/6873/130860.
71. *Ibid.,* 3062/6851/129082.

Chapter VI

1. Bethmann-Hollweg, *op. cit.,* II, 126; *U.A.,* 4. Reihe, II, 142 f.; Lutz, *Causes,* p. 49 ff.
2. Rosenberg, *op. cit.,* pp. 123 ff.; *O.G.D.,* II, 978, 983.
3. Bethmann-Hollweg, *op. cit.,* II, 127; Rosenberg, *op. cit.,* p. 136; Ludendorff, *op. cit.,* I, 288, 364.
4. *O.G.D.,* I, 128, 130 ff.; II, 999 f.; Erzberger, *op. cit.,* pp. 218 f.; Haussmann, *op. cit.,* pp. 72 f.; Bethmann-Hollweg, *op cit.,* II, 128, 151 f.
5. Gatzke, *Germany's Drive,* p. 146.
6. *O.G.D.,* II, 983. When the Chancellor asked Bernstorff in Washington if "peace mediation by Wilson" would be "possible and successful" if Germany were to "guarantee Belgium's unconditional surrender," he added the warning: "Otherwise the unrestricted U-boat war will have to be carried on in dead earnest. . . ."
7. *Ibid.,* I, 131 f.; II, 1071, 1181, 1200.
8. *Ibid.,* I, 138; 149; II, 317 ff.; Bethmann-Hollweg, *op. cit.,* II, 135 ff.
9. Gatzke, *Germany's Drive,* p. 151; see also Lutz, *Fall,* I, 267.
10. *Reichstag,* vol. 310 (May 15, 1917), 3397.
11. Stresemann, "Nachlass," 3065/6873/130875 ff.
12. *Ibid.,* 130922 f.
13. Stresemann, "Nachlass," 3065/6873/130922 f.

14. *Ibid.*, 3063/6864/129298 ff.; see also *Reichstag*, vol. 308 (Oct. 26, 1916), 1822.
15. Olden, *op. cit.*, pp. 32, 36; Görlitz, *op. cit.*, p. 35; *U.A.*, 4. Reihe, VII (2), 300 f.
16. *U.A.*, 4. Reihe, VIII, 380 ff.; R. von Kühlmann, *Erinnerungen* (Heidelberg, 1948), p. 529.
17. Scheidemann, *op. cit.*, II, 36; see below, p. 141.
18. Stresemann, "Nachlass," 3054/6838/126715 ff.; *ibid.*, 3061/6833/125722 f.
19. See above, pp. 73, 82 ff. Stresemann displayed no enthusiasm for Falkenhayn despite early suggestions that he be Bethmann's successor.
20. Stresemann, "Nachlass," 3065/6843/127588; *ibid.*, 3065/6873/130875; 130884; 130993; *Reichstag*, vol. 307 (April 6, 1916), 866 f.
21. *Ibid.*, 3065/6873/130993: Stresemann was inclined to skepticism as to the real power of the High Command in political matters so long as von Jagow, who opposed extension of the submarine warfare, remained in the Foreign Office. Jagow left his post in November, 1916: Erzberger, *op. cit.*, p. 220.
22. *Ibid.*, 3065/6872/130605 f.
23. *Ibid.*, 130650.
24. *Ibid.*
25. *Ibid.*, 3063/6866/129778.
26. *Ibid.*, 3065/6872/130653; 130646; 130650.
27. Hanssen, *op. cit.*, p. 151.
28. Stresemann, "Nachlass," 3065/6872/130679.
29. *Ibid.*, 130653; 130683; 130689 f.. What the "other reasons, unsuitable for written statement" were, Stresemann does not say. One possibility is that he was aware, through Bassermann's contacts with Supreme Headquarters, of pending peace negotiations, which held the alternative of unrestricted submarine warfare; another is that he was aware that the Supreme Command was already exerting pressure against the Chancellor through other agencies, e.g., the Crown Prince: See Paul Herre, *Kronprinz Wilhelm, Seine Rolle in der Deutschen Politik* (Munich, 1954), pp. 76 ff.

30. *Ibid.,* 130683.

31. *Ibid.,* 130711 f.; *ibid.,* 3063/6866/129712.

32. Hanssen, *op. cit.,* p. 144.

33. Hanssen, *op. cit.,* pp. 145 ff., 153.

34. Erzberger had shifted from an annexationist position to a more moderate stand; Erzberger, *op. cit.,* p. 228; Gatzke, *Germany's Drive,* p. 166; see above, ch. iv, n. 49.

35. Hanssen, *op. cit.,* pp. 149 ff.; see below, pp. 141 ff.

36. Hanssen, *op. cit.,* pp. 154 f. On Gröber's annexationist views see Haussmann, *op. cit.,* p. 31; Gatzke, *Germany's Drive,* p. 145.

37. Rosenberg, *op. cit.,* pp. 146 f.; *U.A.,* 4. Reihe, VIII, 68.

38. *O.G.D.,* I, 132; II, 1071; Hanssen, *op. cit.,* p. 156; Erzberger, *op. cit.,* p. 220; Erich Ludendorff, *The General Staff and its Problems; the History of the Relations between the High Command and the German Imperial Government as Revealed by Official Documents* (New York, 1920), II, 285 ff. Henceforth cited as *Official Documents.*

39. Hanssen, *op. cit.,* pp. 151 ff.

40. Gatzke, *Germany's Drive,* p. 146.

41. Stresemann, "Nachlass," 3077/6909/135642 ff.

42. *Ibid.,* 3076/6900/135223; 6899/135017.

43. Dahlin, *op. cit.,* p. 11.

44. Stresemann, "Nachlass," 3063/6866/129731 ff.; 129778.

45. *Ibid.,* 3076/6900/135223.

46. *O.G.D.,* I, 798, II, 1211: Stresemann's volubility at this time as the sounding board of the Supreme Command is indicated by a letter written in January, 1917, by the Hamburg banker, Max Warburg. In the letter, introduced into post-war testimony by Helfferich, the banker pleaded that the German Government continue with peace negotiations with Wilson instead of resuming "the win-all, lose-all game" of unrestricted submarine warfare, declaring that ". . . the Stresemanns and others of that ilk are really of much less importance than the relations with America."

47. Stresemann, "Nachlass," 3076/6900/135255.

48. Stresemann, "Eine Atempause im Weltkriege," *Deutsche*

Stimmen, Jan. 10, 1917; "Nachlass," 3077/6909/135561-135577.

49. Stresemann, "Nachlass," 3077/6909/135532 f.; 135537 f.; 135578 f.; 135642 f.; *ibid.,* 3076/6900/135193 f.; 135199; 135202; 135215; 135223; 135261; 135269; *ibid.,* 3066/6876/131313 ff.
50. Stresemann, *Reden und Schriften,* II, 349.
51. Hanssen, *op. cit.,* p. 161; Erzberger, *op. cit.,* p. 220.
52. *Ibid.,* p. 164; *O.G.D.,* I, 645 f.; Stresemann, "Nachlass," 3065/6872/130605 f.; Erzberger, *op. cit.,* p. 221.
53. *U.A.,* 4. Reihe, VII (2), 307 f.
54. Hanssen, *op. cit.,* pp. 167 ff.
55. *Ibid.,* p. 165; Lutz, *Causes,* p. 190; Gatzke, *Germany's Drive,* pp. 166 f. While certain Socialist leaders opposed, the Center and Progressives accepted the new policy and National Liberals and Conservatives enthusiastically demanded it.
56. Stresemann, "Nachlass," 3076/6899/135035 ff.
57. *Ibid.;* see also *Reichstag,* vol. 309 (March 1, 1917), 2470 f.
58. Lutz, *Fall,* I, 267 f.
59. Gatzke, *Germany's Drive,* pp. 168 ff., gives details on Pan-German activities during this period.
60. Scheidemann, *op. cit.,* I, 283 f.
61. Stresemann, "Nachlass," 3076/6900/135175 f.; *ibid.,* 3066/6876/131315; 131326.
62. Gatzke, *Germany's Drive,* p. 168.
63. Stresemann, *Macht und Freiheit,* pp. 28 f.
64. *U.A.,* 4. Reihe, II, 142 ff.; Lutz, *Causes,* pp. 49 ff.
65. *Ibid.,* pp. 209 f.

Chapter VII

1. Stresemann, "Eine Atempause im Weltkriege," *Deutsche Stimmen,* Jan. 10, 1917, pp. 1-8; "Nachlass," 3077/6909/135661 ff.
2. Bülow, *op. cit.,* III, 171 f.

3. Olden, *op. cit.*, p. 33; Stresemann, "Nachlass," 3052/6822/ 123753; Stresemann, introduction to Th. Eschenberg, *op. cit.*, pp. viii ff.

4. "Stresemann, who knew half of Faust by heart, and Bülow used to let loose on each other their stocks of quotations during the beer evenings at the Chancellor's palace, where Bülow could declaim from memory pages from Horace, Camoëns, Villon, or Plato": Kürenberg, *op. cit.*, p. 160.

5. Stresemann, "Nachlass," 3061/6833/125783 f.; see below, pp. 141, 143.

6. *Ibid.,* 3076/6834/132710 ff.; *ibid.,* 6885/132907; *ibid.,* 3067/ 6886/132976 f.

7. *Ibid.,* 3076/6913/153332 ff.; *ibid.,* 3075/6884/132568 f.

8. *Ibid.,* 3094/7001/142056; *Ibid.,* 3905/7004/142643 ff.

9. Bülow, *op. cit.,* III, *passim,* esp. 23, 98, 133, 138.

10. *Ibid.* For Bassermann on Bethmann in the pre-war period, *ibid.,* pp. 100 f. For Stresemann's opinions see *Reden und Schriften,* I, 296 ff.

11. The farewell telegram of Bassermann and Stresemann and that sent in the name of the National Liberal Party best illustrate the regard for Bülow and his policies: Stresemann, "Nachlass," 3052/6822/123770.

12. *Ibid.,* 3054/6835/126108 ff.

13. Scheidemann, *op. cit.,* I, 189; Stresemann, "Nachlass," 3054/ 6838/126775.

14. *Ibid.,* 3061/6834/125870 f.; *ibid.,* 3054/6835/126237; see also Haussmann, *op. cit.,* pp. 15, 24, 40 ff.

15. See above, pp. 51 f.

16. Stresemann, "Nachlass," 3064/6839/130189; Stresemann, *Macht und Freiheit,* pp. 28 f.

17. Stresemann, *Reden und Schriften,* pp. 300 f.; see also Bülow, *op. cit.,* III, 186 f.

18. Stresemann, "Bethmann-Hollweg," *Deutsche Stimmen,* Aug. 24, 1919; Stresemann, *Von den Revolution bis zum Frieden von Versailles,* p. 204. See above, p. 22.

19. Stresemann, "Nachlass," 3064/6869/130251 ff.

20. Stresemann, "Eine Atempause im Weltkriege," *op. cit.,* p. 5.

21. Stresemann, "Nachlass," 3077/6909/135561 f.
22. *Ibid.*
23. *Reichstag,* vol. 309 (Mar. 1, 1917), 2470.
24. Stresemann, "Nachlass," 3065/6873/130884.
25. *Ibid.,* 3065/6872/130663; *ibid.,* 6873/130875.
26. *Ibid.,* 3056/6843/127707; 127713.
27. Stresemann, "Nachlass," 3056/6843/127707 f.
28. *Ibid.,* 127588 f.; 127742.
29. Lutz, *Causes,* pp. 196 ff.
30. Stresemann, "Nachlass," 3056/6843/127345.
31. E.g., Westenberger, a National Liberal newspaper editor who died early in the war, and Ballin and Huldermann of *Hapag,* who frequently differed with Stresemann: *ibid.,* 3055/6842/127321 f.; *ibid.,* 3056/6843/127601; *ibid.,* 3057/6849/128735 f.
32. *Ibid.,* 3055/6842/127345 f.; *ibid.,* 3056/6843/172695 f.; 127-588; 127742. Stresemann was surely aware of Erzberger's efforts in both Rumania and the Dual Monarchy: Erzberger, *op. cit.,* p. 110; Hanssen, *op. cit.,* pp. 111 ff.
33. *Ibid.,* 127713.
34. Bülow, *op. cit.,* pp. 233 ff., 245 f., 263; Erzberger, *op. cit.,* pp. 21 ff.
35. Stresemann, "Nachlass," 3056/6843/127707 ff.
36. *Ibid.,* 127742; Erzberger, *op. cit.,* pp. 40 f.
37. *Ibid.,* 127689.
38. *Ibid.,* 127588; 127662; 127707.
39. *Ibid.,* 3055/6842/127350; 127426 f.; *ibid.,* 3062/6850/128899.
40. *Ibid.,* 3076/6899/135064.
41. *Ibid.,* 3055/6842/127326 f.; *ibid.,* 3056/6843/127595.
42. Stresemann, "Nachlass," 3056/6843/127595; *ibid.,* 3054/6835/126264; *ibid.,* 3055/6839/126969.
43. *Ibid.,* 3056/6845/128043; *ibid.,* 3065/6873/130884 f.
44. *Ibid.,* 3066/6879/131702 f.
45. *Ibid.,* 3076/6898/1348888. He attributed the report to Graf Harry Kessler.
46. Bülow, *op. cit.,* III, 334 f.
47. Stresemann, "Nachlass," 3078/6913/136429.

48. Stresemann contrasted his views with those of the *Berliner Tageblatt,* the *Frankfurter Zeitung,* and the Socialist press, which stressed the war against Tsarist tyranny: *ibid.,* 3055/ 6839/126993. At the same time he distinguished between his purposes and those of Conservatives who hoped for peace and an alliance with Russia "as a bulwark against the democratization of Germany after the war": *ibid.,* 6842/ 127345 f.

49. Rosenberg, *op. cit.,* pp. 99 f.; *U.A.,* 4. Reihe, VII (1), 278.

50. The Progressives in 1915 favored the policy of weakening Russia through the creation of a Polish state: Hanssen, *op. cit.,* pp. 106 f. Hans Delbrück was perhaps the leading advocate of the Polish Proclamation which he hailed as an "act of political genius": A. Thimme, *Hans Delbrück als Kritiker der Wilhelminischen Epoche,* pp. 229 f. Stresemann wrote a scathing reply to Delbrück: "Nachlass," 3077/6909/ 135580 f.

51. Stresemann, "Nachlass," 3066/6879/131702; *ibid.,* 3065/ 6872/130771. See also Bülow, *op. cit.,* III, 273 ff., 278 ff.; Rosenberg, *op. cit.,* p. 139; Tirpitz, *op. cit.,* II, 37. In contrast Ludendorff states there was no real possibility of peace with Russia, despite the hopes expressed, since the military situation did not favor it: *Ludendorff's Own Story,* I, 476 f. This opinion is not unexpected since Ludendorff shared responsibility for creation of the Polish State (see below, pp. 118 f.); it also fits in with his view that Germany's major error was not in knocking Russia out of the war in 1915, prior to Hindenburg's assumption of the Supreme Command: Lutz, *Causes,* pp. 56 f.; *U.A.,* 4. Reihe, III, 37 f.

52. Stresemann, "Nachlass," 3065/6881/132144; 132154 ff.; *U.A.,* 4. Reihe, VII (2), 303 f.

53. *U.A.,* 4. Reihe, VII (2), 303 f.

54. Erzberger implies that the peace might have been made but for the attitude of Warburg, the German agent in Stockholm, the folly of hailing Stürmer in the German press as a friend of Germany, and finally the Proclamation itself: Erzberger, *op. cit.,* 231 ff. Hanssen suggests that Erzberger broke with

Bethmann because of the Chancellor's unwillingness to make an annexationless peace with Russia at this time: Hanssen, *op. cit.,* pp. 261 ff .

55. Ludendorff, *Official Documents,* II, 382; Rosenberg, *op. cit.,* p. 138.

56. Stresemann, "Nachlass," 3056/6846/128178.

57. Rosenberg, *op. cit.,* p. 138 f.; Bülow, *op. cit.,* III, 273 ff.; Ludendorff, *Official Documents,* II, 379: *Ludendorff's Own Story,* I, 476. The latter states that Bethmann had said in October, 1916, that there was no prospect of peace with Russia.

58. Lutz, *Causes,* pp. 279-282; Rosenberg, *op. cit.,* p. 139; Ludendorff, *Official Documents,* II, 384 f., *Ludendorff's Own Story,* I, 469 f.; 472 f. Stresemann was aware of the plans for Polish divisions as early as August, 1916: "Nachlass," 3065/6873/ 130860. The National Liberals opposed the Polish Proclamation despite the claim of military necessity: *ibid.,* 3065/ 6872/130771; *ibid.,* 3063/6865/129598.

59. *U.A.,* 4. Reihe, VII (2), 308; Gatzke, *Germany's Drive,* p. 140; Erzberger, *op. cit.,* pp. 231 ff.

60. Stresemann, "Nachlass," 3065/6872/130653 ff.

61. Stresemann, "Nachlass," 3066/6879/131788; *ibid.,* 6880/ 131914.

62. Scheidemann, *op. cit.,* I, 283 f.

63. Stresemann, "Nachlass," 3055/6839/126996; *ibid.,* 3056/6843/ 127565.

64. Stresemann, "Nachlass," 3075/6884/132568; *ibid.,* 3076/ 6898/134956 ff.

65. *Ibid.,* 3067/6887/133159 ff.

66. *Ibid.; U.A.,* 4. Reihe, VII (2), 308.

67. *Ibid.,* 3066/6880/131974 f. Stresemann also advocated the use of Parliamentary representatives, including Social Democrats, in order to facilitate the peace with Russia: *ibid.,* 3061/ 6833/125742 f.

68. *Ibid.,* 3078/6914/133721 f.; 136438; *ibid.,* 6915/136752.

69. *Reichstag,* vol. 311 (Mar. 19, 1918), 4453 ff.; Lutz, *Fall,* I, 766 f. The demands of the Supreme Command for annexa-

tion of Polish territory rested, ironically, on envisioned military maneuvers to take place there in the war which was to follow that which they were then fighting without having found a means to terminate successfully: Kühlmann, *op. cit.,* pp. 516 f.

70. Stresemann, "Nachlass," 3057/6849/128856.
71. *Ibid.,* 128765; 128786; *ibid.,* 3055/6842/127330; *ibid.,* 3056/6843/127595 ff.
72. Bethmann-Hollweg, *op. cit.,* II, 122. Despite the fact that he led the fight against the Chancellor and was instrumental in causing his fall, Stresemann never accused him of dishonorable motives: Stresemann, "Betrachtungen zum Weltkriege," *Von den Revolution bis zum Freiden von Versailles,* pp. 201-211, provides a post-war evaluation of the man and his policies.
73. Stresemann, "Nachlass," 3065/6873/130993.
74. Stresemann, "Nachlass," 3056/6846/128279 f.; *ibid.,* 3064/6871/130520 f.
75. *Ibid.,* 3063/6864/129298 ff.
76. Bretton, *op. cit.,* p. 5.
77. Stresemann, "Nachlass," 3077/6909/135193. The annexationists, particularly Bassermann and the National Liberals, received the announcement of the Peace Note from the Chancellor with little enthusiasm: Haussmann, *op. cit.,* pp. 78 ff.
78. *Ibid.,* 3063/6866/129778.
79. The Entente's reply touched off an explosive reaction among the annexationists: Gatzke, *Germany's Drive,* pp. 168 ff. "The outrageous refusal of the Allies has saved us from diplomatic defeat," confided the extremist Traub to Stresemann: "Nachlass," 3077/6909/135527.
80. Stresemann, "Nachlass," 3077/6909/135532; *ibid.,* 3076/6900/135199; 135223; 135255; 135261.
81. Stresemann, "Eine Atempause im Weltkriege," *Deutsche Stimmen,* Jan. 10, 1917, pp. 1 ff.
82. Stresemann, "Nachlass," 3077/6909/135537 f.
83. Gatzke, *Germany's Drive,* p. 165.
84. Erzberger, *op. cit.,* p. 231.

85. Stresemann, "Nachlass," 3055/6839/126874 f.; *ibid.*, 6840/127059; *ibid.*, 3056/6843/127595; *ibid.*, 3064/6868/129989.

86. *Reichstag,* vol. 309 (March 1, 1917), 2469 f.; *ibid.* (March 27, 1917), 2757 f.

87. *Ibid.*, vol. 307 (April 6, 1916), 866 f.; *ibid.* (May 30, 1916), p. 1311; Lutz, *Fall,* I, 336 ff.

88. Stresemann, "Wilsons Frieden," *Von der Revolution bis zum Frieden von Versailles,* pp. 166-171.

89. Stresemann, *Vermächtnis,* I, 371; Kaufmann, *op. cit.*, pp. 124 f.

90. Stresemann, "Nachlass," 3095/7004/142747.

91. Erzberger, *op. cit.*, pp. 229 ff.

92. Ludendorff, *Official Documents,* I, 337 f.

93. *Ibid.*, 275, 293; *Ludendorff's Own Story,* I, 364 f., II, 19.

94. Now *de facto* leader of the National Liberal Reichstag *Fraktion,* Stresemann became officially so on Bassermann's death in July, 1917. He was actually designated temporarily as second in the Party to Friedberg, out of deference to the older man, although considered as eventual successor as the Party leader: Stresemann, "Nachlass," 3075/6882/132209-13; *U.A.* 4. Reihe, VII (2), 300.

95. Stresemann, "Nachlass," 3061/6831/125668 ff.

96. *Reichstag,* vol. 309 (Mar. 1, 1917), pp. 2469 ff.

97. Stresemann, "Nachlass," 3078/6913/136419 f.

98. Reichstag, vol. 309 (Mar. 1, 1917), 2469 f.

99. Stresemann, "Nachlass," 3076/6869/134923.

100. *Ibid.*, 134880 f.; 134888 f.

101. Hanssen, *op. cit.*, p. 174.

102. Stresemann, "Nachlass," 3066/6879/131702 f. In July, 1917, Zimmermann exclaimed to Conrad Haussmann, "You know, this Stresemann . . . it is unheard of! He now attacks and in December he rejoiced over a torpedoing because it made the American war unavoidable!": Haussmann, *op. cit.*, pp. 125 f.

103. *Reichstag,* vol. 309 (Mar. 29, 1917), 2849; Stresemann, *Macht und Freiheit,* pp. 38 f.

104. Stresemann, "Nachlass," 3076/6898/134923 f.

105. *Reichstag,* vol. 309 (Mar. 29, 1917), 2849 f. Stresemann's triumphant speech came as the U-boat successes were nearing their height. In both February and March 500,000 tons of shipping were sunk, in April, more than 800,000 tons. In May, with the introduction of the convoy system and other anti-submarine techniques, there was a sudden drop in tonnage sunk and after a slight rise again in June the decline thereafter was, if gradual, almost constant.
106. Hanssen, *op. cit.,* p. 174.
107. Stresemann, "Nachlass," 3075/6881/132000.
108. *Ibid.,* 3066/6879/131754 ff.; Stresemann, *Macht und Freiheit,* pp. 65 f.

Chapter VIII

1. Lutz, *Fall,* I, 267.
2. Scheidemann, *op. cit.,* I, 337; Hanssen (op. cit., p. 181), reports the lugubrious joke current at Easter that Germany could not win the war—at least in the first generation!
3. Lutz, *Fall,* II, 411; Bergsträsser, *op. cit.,* p. 190.
4. *Ibid.,* I, 201 ff.
5. Bergsträsser, *op. cit.,* pp. 165 ff.; Eschenburg, *op. cit.,* pp. 135, 154; Heuss, *op. cit.,* pp. 250 f.; *U.A.,* 4. Reihe, VII (2), 300. Hopes had been raised by the appeals of the Emperor and Chancellor in August, 1914, and the reform issue had been debated in both 1915 and 1916; Gatzke, *Germany's Drive,* pp. 65 f.; Lutz, *Fall,* I, 201 ff.
6. Lutz, *Fall,* I, 213 ff.; *ibid.,* II, 419 f., 423.
7. *Reichstag,* vol. 310 (July 19, 1917), 3573 ff.; Lutz, *Fall,* II, 282 f.
8. Stresemann, "Nachlass," 3076/6898/134880.
9. *Ibid.,* 3061/6833/125722 f.; 125742; *ibid.,* 3066/6879/131714 ff.
10. *Ibid.,* 3066/6880/131891; *ibid.,* 3076/6898/135003.
11. *Ibid.,* 3061/6833/125707; *ibid.,* 3076/6898/134596 f.

12. Scheidemann, *op. cit.,* I, 337; Stresemann, "Nachlass," 3601/6833/125696 f.
13. Stresemann, "Nachlass," 3601/6833/125701 f.; Lutz, *Causes,* pp. 204 f.
14. *Ibid.,* 125696; see above, p. 109.
15. Stresemann, *Macht und Freiheit,* pp. 23-37.
16. Gatzke, *Germany's Drive,* p. 172.
17. Stresemann, "Nachlass," 3061/6833/125701 f.
18. *Reichstag,* vol. 309 (March 29, 1917), 2849-57.
19. *Ibid.;* see also Stresemann, "Neue Zeiten," *Macht und Freiheit,* pp. 38-58; Westarp, *op. cit.,* II, 235 f.
20. Stresemann, "Nachlass," 3061/6833/125701; Lutz, *Causes,* p. 220; Lutz, *Fall,* I, 251.
21. Lutz, *Causes,* pp. 196 f.; Wolff, *Vollendete Tatsachen,* pp. 163 f.
22. Stresemann, "Nachlass," 3066/6879/131776.
23. Görlitz, *op. cit.,* pp. 72 f., 95; Rheinbaben, *op. cit.,* pp. 115 f., 127, 130 f., 156.
24. Stresemann, "Nachlass," 3061/6833/125812 f.; 125707 f.; 125722 f.; 125742 f.; *ibid.,* 3066/6879/131714 ff. In the postwar era Stresemann refers to the "needs of unity and defense": *U.A.,* 4, Reihe, VII (2), 300.
25. *Ibid.,* 3061/6831/125480.
26. *Ibid.,* 3066/6879/131740 f.
27. *Ibid.,* 3075/6883/132445 f.; but see above, pp. 57 f.
28. *Ibid.,* 3066/6879/131714 f.
29. *Ibid.,* 3061/6833/125707 f.
30. *Ibid.,* 3066/6880/131891.
31. *Ibid.,* 3061/6833/125707; 125687 f.; 125783.
32. *Ibid.,* 125755 ff.
33. *Ibid.,* 125707; 125722; *ibid.,* 3076/6898/134956.
34. *Ibid.,* 3061/6833/125707; *ibid.,* 3066/6879/131714.
35. *Ibid.,* 3061/6833/125731; *ibid.,* 3066/6879/131713 f.
36. *U.A.,* 4. Reihe, VII (2), 302; Stresemann, *Von der Revolution bis zum Frieden von Versailles,* p. 78.
37. Stresemann, "Nachlass," 3061/6833/125722; *ibid.,* 125701 f.
38. *Ibid.,* 3066/6879/131727; *ibid.,* 6880/131860; Stresemann had

earlier reminded Bassermann of the difficulties which measures encounter in committee, *ibid.*, 3061/6833/125707 f. *See also* Lutz, *Causes,* p. 204.

39. *Ibid.*, 3061/6833/125707; *ibid.*, 3077/6912/136204.

40. *Ibid.*, 3076/1698/134956 f.

41. *Ibid.*, 3066/6879/131776.

42. *U.A.*, 4. Reihe, VIII, 184 ff. The electoral reform bill introduced into the Prussian Lower House in December, 1917, was blocked by the Conservatives supported by the Supreme Command, and remained unpassed when revolution brought the end to both Prussian monarchy and constitution: Bergsträsser, *op. cit.*, pp. 195 ff.

43. Stresemann, "Nachlass," 3078/6919/136853 ff.; Lutz, *Fall,* II, 425 f. Stresemann's letter to Ludendorff of April 29, 1918, urging equal suffrage, shows clearly that the domestic reform was entirely subordinate to the victory on annexationist lines: Ludendorff, *Official Documents,* II, 375 ff.

44. Craig cites Stresemann's acceptance of equal suffrage as an example of "the kind of courage that is needed to admit the inevitable": *op. cit.*, p. 71.

45. *U.A.*, 4. Reihe, VII (2), 302.

46. In addition to his speech of March 29, 1917 (above, pp. 133 ff.) see *Reichstag,* vol. 306 (Jan. 18, 1916), 733-740; *ibid.*, vol. 308 (Oct. 26, 1916), 1819-23.

47. *Reichstag,* vol. 308 (Oct. 26, 1919).

48. *U.A.*, 4. Reihe, VII (2), 301.

49. Olden, *op. cit.*, pp. 49 f.

50. Stresemann, "Nachlass," 3075/6883/132476-9; *ibid.*, 3067/6887/133182; *ibid.*, 3061/6833/125742 ff.

51. *Ibid.*, 3066/6879/131714 ff.; 131727 ff.

52. *Reichstag,* vol. 310 (May 3, 1917) 3398.

53. Gatzke, *Germany's Drive,* p. 185.

54. Westarp, *op. cit.*, II, 86 f.

55. Hanssen, *op. cit.*, pp. 124 ff., 192 f.

56. Stresemann, "Nachlass," 3066/6880/131974 f.

57. *Ibid.*, 3061/6833/125722 ff.

58. Haussmann, *op. cit.*, pp. 87-90; Scheidemann, *op. cit.*, I, 339;

Westarp, *op. cit.,* II, 170 f.; *Reichstag,* vol. 309 (Mar. 2, 1917), 2489. Stresemann was told by the Emperor's brother-in-law, the Duke of Schleswig-Holstein, that the Emperor had been "outraged" by the attempt to influence him: Stresemann, "Nachlass," 3076/6899/135079 f.; the Emperor's jealousy of Hindenburg was well-known; it was commonly accepted in Berlin that he had once exclaimed: "I do not want to ride victoriously through the Brandenburg Gate and hear all the people shout, 'Hoch, Hindenburg!' ": *ibid.,* 3056/6843/127742 f.

59. Stresemann, "Nachlass," 3076/6899/135079 f.; Olden, *op. cit.,* p. 50; Görlitz, *op. cit.,* p. 75. Haussmann implies that the only purpose of Stresemann's talk was as a cover for the conspiracy, but he does not name Stresemann as one of the conspirators: *op. cit.,* p. 87.

60. See Stresemann's letter to Berthold Körting, one of the Adlon group: "Nachlass," 3076/6908/135392 f. In 1916 Stresemann had also warned Körting against "blind adventures" against the Chancellor: see above, pp. 102 f.

61. Stresemann, "Nachlass," 3076/6899/135130 ff.; *Reichstag,* vol 309 (Mar. 2, 1917), 2518.

62. Stresemann, "Nachlass," 3061/6833/125783 ff.

63. *Ibid.,* 125812 ff. He also discussed with Ludendorff "the war aims in detail with complete agreement" on a broad, annexationist program.

64. Scheidemann, *op. cit.,* II, 36.

65. Stresemann, "Nachlass," 3066/6880/113922 f.; Westarp, *op. cit.,* II, 88.

66. Stresemann, "Nachlass," 3075/6881/132023 ff. Two weeks later Stresemann wrote effusively to Ludendorff concerning the serious situation he had just observed in Austria-Hungary, where people followed English propaganda—the Austrians opposed German war aims, and the Hungarians doubted the U-boat successes: "Your Excellency will forgive me if out of a seriously worried heart I . . . turn to your Excellency since I am of the firm conviction that the Supreme Command can best take the decisive steps needed here

so that we do not lose the regard of our allies in the unfortunate way we have lost that of the neutrals." *Ibid.*, 3075/6881/132049 ff.

67. Hanssen, *op. cit.*, p. 181.

68. Stresemann, "Nachlass," 3066/6880/131866; *ibid.*, 3075/6881/132017 ff. The Emperor, Ballin reported, was "not seriously oriented" at all in these matters. The industrialist Stollwerck had also replied pessimistically to Stresemann's joyous report on English tonnage losses: *ibid.*, 131988 f., 132102.

69. Erzberger, *op. cit.*, pp. 253 f.; Hanssen, *op. cit.*, pp. 196 f.; Friedrich von Payer, *Von Bethmann-Hollweg bis Ebert* (Frankfurt a. M., 1923), p. 29. The Center Deputy had raised the question of world tonnage in 1916: see above, pp. 103.

70. Erzberger, *op. cit.*, p. 255 f.; Hanssen, *op. cit.*, pp. 201-209. Erzberger's step toward the Peace Resolution reportedly was influenced by secret reports on Austria's condition given to him by Imperial circles in Vienna: Kühlmann, *op. cit.*, pp. 513 ff., 568. Stresemann had known in June that Erzberger would bring up the submarine issue, but the peace move apparently came as a shock: "Nachlass," 3061/6833/125821 ff.; Olden, *op. cit.*, p. 57.

71. Payer, *op. cit.*, pp. 29 f.

72. *Reichstag*, vol. 310 (July 19, 1917), 3573 ff.; Lutz, *Fall*, II, 282 f.

73. Payer, *op. cit.*, pp. 30 ff.; *see also* Ludendorff, *Official Documents*, II, 458 f.

74. Stresemann, "Nachlass," 3075/6881/132170.

75. *Ibid.*, 132157; Erzberger, *op. cit.*, p. 257; Westarp, *op. cit.*, II, 356; Payer, *op. cit.*, pp. 34 f.; Ludendorff, *Ludendorff's Own Story*, II, 57 f.

76. Stresemann, "Nachlass," 3075/6881/132157 ff. This document, which details his movements from the meeting with the military leaders on July 7 until his second visit to the Berlin Headquarters on July 12, described below, was written for the information of Bassermann, a few close friends, and the National Liberal archives. An article, "Gedanken

zur Krisis," which appeared in *Deutsche Stimmen* (XXIX, July 29, 1917, 413-432), containing "that which could be said for the public," is bare of mention of these activities of Stresemann. *See also* "Nachlass," 3077/6910/135750; *Macht und Freiheit,* pp. 60-81.

77. *Ibid.,* 132159 ff. The meeting of the military leaders with the Emperor took a "curious course," however. Told by Bethmann that no crisis existed and that he would have the support of the Reichstag leaders on Monday, the Emperor sent the two generals back to Kreuznach; *see also* Erzberger, *op. cit.,* p. 259; Payer, *op. cit.,* pp. 34 f.

78. *Ibid.,* Erzberger, *op. cit.,* p. 259. The Center Deputy does not mention Stresemann's presence at his meetings with Army representatives. The Chancellor's alleged cavalier attitude toward Erzberger and the parliamentary crisis, which he completely underestimated, was skillfully disclosed in order to get Erzberger's support against Bethmann. *See also* Ludwig Reiners, *In Europa gehen die Lichter aus* (Munich, 1954), pp. 302 ff.; C. Haussmann, "Herrn Stresemanns Zeugnis," *Berliner Tageblatt,* March 1, 1920 (contained also in the "Nachlass," 3091/6936/140279 ff.).

79. Stresemann, "Nachlass," 3075/6881/132161 ff.; Hanssen, *op. cit.,* pp. 216 ff.

80. *Ibid.;* Scheidemann, *op. cit.,* II, 34 f.; *U.A.,* 4. Reihe, VIII, 125-31.

81. Hanssen, *op. cit.,* p. 218; Payer, *op. cit.,* pp. 29 f.; Erzberger, *op. cit.,* p. 259; Westarp, *op. cit.,* II, pp. 72, 356; Haussmann, "Herrn Stresemanns Zeugnis," *op. cit.*

82. Hanssen, *op. cit.,* p. 217 f.; Haussmann, *Schlaglichter,* p. 102.

83. Stresemann, "Nachlass," 3075/6881/132162; He attempted to enlist Erzberger's support without immediate success; *see also* Erzberger, *op. cit.,* pp. 259 ff., and below, p. 211 f.

84. *Ibid.,* 132161; Hanssen, *op. cit.,* pp. 219 ff.

85. Ludendorff, *Official Documents,* II, 458 ff., indicates that Colonel von Haeften, who was keeping the Headquarters informed of happenings in Berlin, advised that a conflict appeared to be developing on this issue; *see also,* Hanssen,

op. cit., p. 218. Word that Bethmann had misinformed the Emperor as to the true nature of the July events also began to stir up resentment in the Center and Social Democratic Parties: Stresemann, "Nachlass," 3075/6881/132163; Erzberger, *op. cit.,* p. 259.

86. Erzberger, *op. cit.,* p. 258; *see also* Herre, *op. cit.,* pp. 87 ff.

87. Stresemann, "Nachlass," 3075/6881/132162; Hanssen, *op. cit.,* pp. 227 f.; Scheidemann, *op. cit.,* II, 34 ff.

88. Herre, *op. cit.,* pp. 86 ff.; *see also* Ludendorff, *Official Documents,* II, 458 f.

89. Stresemann states that the idea of the interviews originated with Bauer and Maltzahn: "Nachlass," 3075/6881/132162 f. Both the Prince and Maltzahn had conspired against Bethmann before: *ibid.,* 3055/6842/127430 f.; see above, ch. vi, n. 29.

90. Herre, *op. cit.,* p. 89; *see also* Hanssen, *op. cit.,* pp. 228-230.

91. *Ibid.,* pp. 89 ff.; Stresemann, "Nachlass," 3705/6881/132163 f.; Payer, *op. cit.,* pp. 30-34; Erzberger, *op. cit.,* p. 262; Ludendorff, *Official Documents,* II, 461.

92. Stresemann, "Nachlass," 3075/6881/132164; *see also* Payer, *op. cit.,* pp. 34 f.; Hanssen, *op. cit.,* p. 229; Erzberger, *op. cit.,* p. 262; Herre, *op. cit.,* p. 92.

93. *Ibid.,* 132166 f.; Hanssen, *op. cit.,* p. 230, states that Bethmann still hoped to get the support of the majority of the National Liberals, winning them away from Stresemann.

94. *Ibid.,* 132167: Stresemann clearly implies a connection between his visit to the Berlin Headquarters and the resignation requests later from Kreuznach. Ludendorff records a telephone call at 4:25 P.M. from the War Minister von Stein in Berlin asking for the "intervention of Main Headquarters": *Official Documents,* II, 462.

95. Ludendorff, *Official Documents,* II, 462 f.; Payer, *op. cit.,* p. 35.

96. Stresemann, "Nachlass," 3061/6833/125840 ff. The news came in almost too late for the dying Bassermann, whose interest in politics was almost extinguished. Stresemann's dispute with Conrad Haussmann over this incident shows the

pettiness of which Stresemann was occasionally guilty. He had telephoned Bassermann's wife triumphantly the day Bethmann resigned. Haussmann was quoted in the *Vossische Zeitung* as saying that Stresemann had telegraphed a triumphant message to Bassermann, "It is achieved" *(Es ist erreicht)*. Stresemann protested to the editor that he had "never sent a telegram in such poor taste," obtained letters from Bassermann's family that "no such telegram had ever been received," and with great indignation attacked Haussmann in the party press for making "false accusations": *ibid.,* 6832/125569-79; *ibid.,* 3075/6884/132621; *ibid.,* 3067/6885/ 132814-21.

Chapter IX

1. J. W. Wheeler-Bennett, *The Forgotten Peace: Brest-Litovsk, March, 1918* (New York, 1939).
2. Haussmann, "Herrn Stresemanns Zeugnis," *op. cit.*
3. Stresemann, "Nachlass," 3061/6833/125847; *ibid.,* 3067/6887/ 133189; *ibid.,* 3077/6910/135750; *ibid.,* 3068/6889/133591 f.; *U.A.,* 4. Reihe, VII (2), 304 f.; Scheidemann, *op. cit.,* II, 36.
4. Herre, *op. cit.,* p. 85; Erzberger, *op. cit.,* p. 259.
5. Herre, *op. cit.,* pp. 92, 94. The interviews alone were not fully convincing since the Progressive Payer had not agreed to, and neither the Socialist David nor Erzberger had unqualifiedly called for, a Chancellor change: Payer, *op. cit.,* pp. 32 f.; Ludendorff, *Official Documents,* II, 463-8. Herre also notes, pp. 90 ff., that the Bund Princes and the Ambassadors of the German allies, with whom the Crown Prince also talked later, had in general supported Bethmann.
6. Haussmann, "Herrn Stresemanns Zeugnis," *op. cit.;* Bethmann-Hollweg, *op. cit.,* II, 229, 235; Westarp, *op. cit.,* II, 360.
7. Lutz, *Causes,* p. 191.
8. Erzberger, *op. cit.,* pp. 251 f.; Gatzke, *Germany's Drive,* pp. 191 ff.; Stresemann, "Nachlass," 3075/6881/132157 ff. Rumors in Berlin at the time made Bülow the activator of Erzberger's move: *ibid.,* 132038 f.; Hanssen, *op. cit.,* p. 215 f.

Kurt Epstein's recent biography of Erzberger, confirms that
the Center Deputy's initial action in July was based primarily on motives entirely apart from the person of Bethmann-Hollweg: *Matthias Erzberger and the Dilemma of German Democracy* (Princeton, 1959), pp. 185-190. He points out
that Erzberger had clearly supported Bethmann as late as
April, 1917 (*ibid.*, p. 168), although failure of negotiations
with the Russians in Stockholm, which Erzberger blamed on
Bethmann's weakness in the face of Ludendorff, Stinnes, and
the annexationists, had inclined him to turn against the
Chancellor (*ibid.*, p. 181). Epstein's portrayal of the July crisis
substantiates the present account: Erzberger backed the National Liberals against Bethmann in return for their support of the Peace Resolution (*ibid.*, pp. 194 f.); his support
by the Center was conditional on similar action by the National Liberals (*ibid.*, p. 196). Epstein notes that if the Center
had adhered to Bethmann as did the Progressives and Social
Democrats, the Chancellor would have retained a majority
against which even Ludendorff admittedly would have hesi-
tated to provoke a conflict (*ibid.*, p. 199). The urging by
Stresemann and Bauer of Bülow's candidacy and their skill at
playing on Erzberger's vanity concerning Bethmann's devalu-
ation of the crisis and his prevention of a meeting with Ludendorff all had a bearing on turning Erzberger against Bethmann, whose position began to totter after Stresemann's
speech of July 9 (*ibid.*, pp. 195-199).

9. Gatzke, *Germany's Drive,* p. 193; Max von Baden, quoted in
   Herre, *op. cit.*, pp. 95 f.; Hanssen, *op. cit.*, p. 126.

10. Max von Baden, quoted in Herre, *op. cit.*, pp. 96 f.; Reiners,
    op. cit., pp. 226 ff.

11. Herre, *op. cit.*, p. 98; Hanssen, *op. cit.*, pp. 231-3: Although
    the Emperor had been unable to withstand the demand for
    one Chancellor's dismissal he could still oppose the sugges-
    tion concerning the naming of another—he rejected the nom-
    ination of Prince Bülow "with a harsh 'never!'"

12. Stresemann, "Nachlass," 3075/6881/132154 ff.; *ibid.*, 3067/
    6885/132770 f.; Payer, *op. cit.*, p. 34.

13. Michaelis had accepted the resolution with his famous phrase, "as I understand it"; *Reichstag,* vol. 310 (July 19, 1917), 3572; Hindenburg and Ludendorff in talking to the party leaders had accepted the Resolution but pronounced its tone as "weak": Payer, *op. cit.,* p. 35; in private they laughed at it as "naive and childish" and declared that they would make the peace that suited them: Hanssen, *op. cit.,* pp. 254 f.

14. Stresemann, "Nachlass," 3061/6833/125847 f.; *ibid.,* 3075/ 6882/132246 ff. *Reichstag,* vol. 310 (July 19, 1917), 3585; *U.A.,* 4. Reihe, VII (I), 6; *ibid.,* (2), 209; Lutz, *Causes,* p. 191.

15. Stresemann, "Nachlass," 3061/6833/125847 f.; Westarp, *op. cit.,* II, 472.

16. Bretton, *op. cit.,* p. 6. In post-war testimony Stresemann's words seem deliberately ambiguous: *U.A.,* 4. Reihe, VII (2), 311. However, in 1917 neither Westarp nor Scheidemann mistook the tactical purposes of his remarks in the Committee: Westarp, *op. cit.,* II, 341; Scheidemann, *op. cit.,* II, 34 ff.; Gatzke, *Germany's Drive,* p. 204.

17. *U.A.,* 4. Reihe, VII (2), 309.

18. Stresemann, "Gedanken zur Krisis," *op. cit.,* pp. 429 f.; see also, *Macht und Freiheit,* pp. 77 f.

19. Stresemann, "Nachlass," 3075/6882/132246 ff.

20. *Ibid.,* 3067/6886/133056 f., 132424 ff.; *ibid.,* 3075/6884/ 132687 f.; see also Gatzke, *Germany's Drive,* pp. 203 f. Stresemann's tactics were not unrecognized; Scheidemann wanted to exclude him from the Committee: Scheidemann, *op cit.,* II, 138, 141 ff.

21. Lutz, *Causes,* pp. 192 ff.; Ludendorff, *Official Documents,* II, 478-487; Kühlmann, *op. cit.,* pp. 477 ff.; Erzberger, *op. cit.,* 274 ff. Kühlmann replaced Zimmermann as a result of the latter's diplomatic errors in dealing with Norway: Gatzke, *Germany's Drive,* p. 222; Stresemann, "Nachlass," 3075/ 6881/132038 f. Stresemann wrote of Kühlmann at this time: "He is to me completely unknown, but I don't like him, which affects my entire personal attitude": *ibid.,* 6882/ 132315 ff.

22. Stresemann, "Nachlass," 3075/6882/132315 f.; see also

Scheidemann, *op. cit.,* II, 66 f.; Westarp, *op. cit.,* II, 535 ff.

23. *Ibid.,* 3067/6886/133056 ff.; 133109 ff.; Scheidemann, *op. cit.,* II, 76, 80; Kühlmann, *op. cit.,* pp. 458 ff.

24. *U.A.,* 4. Reihe, VII (2), 310 f., *Reichstag,* vol. 311 (Feb. 27, 1918), 4189-99.

25. Stresemann, "Nachlass," 3075/6882/132246 ff., 132315 ff.; *ibid.,* 3067/6886/133056 ff., 133109 ff.

26. *Ibid.,* 3075/6883/132383 ff.; *ibid.,* 6884/132687 f.; *ibid.,* 3067/6886/133141 f., 133047.

27. Lutz, *Causes,* p. 195 f.; Hanssen, *op. cit.,* p. 234, Gatzke, *Germany's Drive,* pp. 235 f.

28. Stresemann, "Nachlass," 3067/6885/132843 ff.; *ibid.,* 3075/6884/132710 ff.; Stresemann, "Die Herbstkrisis," *Macht und Freiheit,* pp. 130-155; Kühlmann, *op. cit.,* pp. 494 f.

29. *Ibid.,* 3067/6886/132976 f. He consoled himself that because of Hertling's advanced age the appointment would be only provisional. "If he should ever intrigue against the Supreme Command," wrote Stresemann to *Reichsrat* Buhl on November 5, "be convinced that I with the *Fraktion* shall stand on the side of the Supreme Command."

30. *Ibid.,* 133088, 133109 f., 132496; *ibid.,* 6888/133343 f., 133-355.

31. *Ibid.,* 3074/6886/133088, 133109 f.; *ibid.,* 6885/132143 ff.; Gatzke, *Germany's Drive,* pp. 239-242; Lutz, *Fall,* II, 351 f.

32. Hanssen, *op. cit.,* pp. 219 f.; see above, p. 144.

33. Lutz, *Fall,* I, 721.

34. Stresemann, "Nachlass," 3067/6886/133056 ff. He had never ceased his support of the unrestricted submarine warfare or to predict its successful outcome: "Gedanken zur Krisis," *op. cit.,* pp. 65-68; *Reichstag,* vol. 310 (October 10, 1917), 3830 ff.; *Macht und Freiheit,* pp. 105 ff.; *Berliner Tageblatt,* March 11, 1918, I, 2.

35. *Ibid.,* 6888/133343; *ibid.,* 3075/6884/132578 ff.

36. *Ibid.,* 3077/6888/133343 ff.: although "Bethmann's evil heritage" prevented satisfactory solution of the Polish question, the "main things" were achieved in the East. Even Lake Peipus, renounced in July, was now within reach: Westarp, *op. cit.,* II, 566.

37. *Reichstag,* vol. 311 (Feb. 20, 1918), 4018-4025; *ibid.,* (Feb. 22, 1918), 4086-4088.
38. *Ibid.,* (March 19, 1918), 4453-62; J. W. Wheeler-Bennett, *The Forgotten Peace: Brest-Litovsk, March 1918,* p. 305.
39. *Berliner Tageblatt,* Mar. 11, 1918, I, 2; Lutz, *Fall,* II, 351 f.
40. *Reichstag,* vol. 311 (March 19, 1918), 4453-62.
41. Gatzke, *Germany's Drive,* pp. 256 ff.
42. *Reichstag,* vol. 311 (Feb. 27, 1918), 4189-4199; *see also* "Zur politischen Lage," in *Macht und Freiheit,* pp. 179 ff.; Lutz, *Fall,* I, 385 ff.; see above, ch. ii, n. 37. Stresemann's solicitude for the Flemings must be considered in the light of his ideas for a "free Baltic" which would be organized in the interests of the German minority and where "no popular vote would be necessary" since the people "were not ready for parliamentary institutions": *Reichstag,* vol. 311 (March 19, 1918), 4453 ff.
43. Stresemann, "Nachlass," 3075/6884/132568 ff.
44. *Reichstag,* vol. 313 (June 24, 1918), 5611 f.; Kühlmann, *op. cit.,* pp. 572 ff.
45. *Ibid.* (June 25, 1918), 5658 ff.; Stresemann, "Nachlass," 3077/6911/135910; Hanssen, *op. cit.,* pp. 292 f.; Scheidemann, *op. cit.,* II, 141 f., 174. Stresemann had been unaware of Kühlmann's conversations with Colonel von Haeften concerning the necessity of a "peace offensive": *U.A.,* 4. Reihe, VII (2), 306; Kühlmann, *op. cit.,* pp. 572 ff. In his Reichstag speech Stresemann declared that his Party held as war aims only those objectives agreed upon by the Government and Supreme Command as essential for German security. He later could assert that this had represented a significant shift in war aims demands. Yet his statement, as ambiguous as any uttered by Bethmann-Hollweg, was in essence a restatement of support of the aims of the Supreme Command, which he knew included holding Belgium; furthermore the statement was made in an attack on the one man who seemed ready to face the realities of the situation: Stresemann, *Von der Revolution bis zum Frieden von Versailles,* pp. 6, 16; *Reichstag,* vol. 314 (Oct. 22, 1918), 6174; *U.A.* 4. Reihe, VII (2), 309.
46. *U.A.,* 4. Reihe, VII (2), 306, 310.

47. Stresemann, *Von der Revolution bis zum Frieden von Versailles,* p. 6.

48. Stresemann, "Nachlass," 3061/6831/125638 ff.; *U.A.* 4. Reihe, VII (2), 306.

49. *Ibid.,* 3077/6912/136261 ff.; Stresemann's views on treatment of Russia had changed since March; *Realpolitik* now called for supporting the Soviet regime, and in July he held many conversations with Joffe, Nadolny, and Krassin concerning economic agreements; *ibid.,* 3061/6831/125638 f.; *ibid.,* 3077/6912/136136, 136144-58; *ibid.,* 6911/135916.

50. *Ibid.,* 3077/6911/135910. On the same day he urged the National Liberal press to reply to attacks of the *Berliner Tageblatt* which had charged the Admiralty with "false prophesies" concerning the unrestricted submarine warfare. In outlining a reply Stresemann declared that had the U-boats been used in the spring of 1916, when there had been no defense against them, their effects would have been even greater. He denied that the submarine war had caused American entry into the war—this had come in order to save American loans to the Entente, a view he maintained in the post-war era: *ibid.,* 135887 f.; *ibid.,* 3144/7323/160745 ff.

51. *Ibid.,* 135709.

52. *Ibid.,* 6910/135771; *U.A.* 4. Reihe, III, 354; *ibid.,* VII (2), 311; Lutz, *Causes,* pp. 218 f.; Ludendorff, *Official Documents,* II, 337.

53. Hanssen, *op. cit.,* pp. 297 f., records that on Sept. 25 in the Finance Committee Stresemann appeared greatly depressed: "Dr. Stresemann . . . who always has been a good speaker was today physically and emotionally remarkably small and down in the dumps. Instead of a puffed-up turkey gobbler, he was a respectable little bantam. He could not command attention. During his speech members collected in groups and discussed the situation. . . ."

54. Lutz, *Causes,* p. 219; *U.A.,* 4. Reihe, VIII, 288.

55. *U.A.,* 4. Reihe, V, 46; *ibid.,* VII (2), 306, 311 f.

56. Stresemann, "Nachlass," 3077/6910/135771; 135784; 135834-59; *ibid.,* 3068/6889/13346 f.

57. Lutz, *Causes,* pp. 217-222; *U.A.,* 4. Reihe, I, 212; Stresemann, "Nachlass," 3068/6889/134460 ff. Stresemann assured Colonel Bauer that his criticisms of the Supreme Command had not referred to Hindenburg and Ludendorff but to the inept leadership of Falkenhayn who had failed to provide the needed munitions. "People are looking for a scapegoat and finding it in Ludendorff," he wrote, "but I shall not participate in this": "Nachlass," 3068/6889/133553 f. On Ludendorff's dismissal the Deputy wrote a glowing tribute in *Deutsche Stimmen,* Oct. 31, 1918; see also *Reden und Schriften,* I, 198-202. He remained in touch with Ludendorff in the early Weimar period: "Nachlass," 3089/6927/132246; *ibid.,* 3091/6933/139447; his relations with Bauer at the time of the Kapp *Putsch* in 1920 are of particular interest: *ibid.,* 3090/6932/139532 ff.; *ibid.,* 3094/7003/142847; *ibid.,* 3890/6927/138682.

58. Stresemann, "Nachlass," 3068/6889/134460 ff.; Lutz, *Causes,* p. 222. See also Stresemann's post-war testimony in *U.A.,* 4. Reihe, VII (2), 300-312; *see also Reichstag,* vol. 314 (Oct,. 22, 1918), 6174.

59. Stresemann, *Von der Revolution bis zum Frieden von Versailles,* p. 5.

60. Stresemann, "Nachlass," 3068/6889/133517; 133464 ff.; 133-563 ff.; 3077/6910/135831.

61. *Ibid.,* 3068/6889/135580 f. In 1927 Stresemann spoke of the possibility of a defense at the Meuse and the Rhine: *U.A.* 4. Reihe, VII (2), 306.

62. *U.A.,* 4. Reihe, I, 473.

63. Stresemann, "Nachlass," 3068/6889/133647 ff.

64. *Ibid.,* 133615 ff.

65. Hanssen, *op. cit.,* p. 336.

66. Stresemann, "Nachlass," 3068/6889/133615 ff.; *ibid.,* 3069/6896/134500 ff.

67. *Ibid.,* 3068/6889/133574 f.

68. *Ibid.,* 3069/6896/134500 ff. Stresemann believed that since the majority of the people wanted the monarchy the Social Democrats should set aside their "theoretical republicanism." He declared the Socialists would bear a "heavy guilt" for

unnecessarily bringing up the abdication demand at the moment of the armistice which would have quieted the population. The governmental crisis caused by the demand had only complicated armistice negotiations. Yet he sensed that keeping the Socialists in the government was necessary to prevent "Bolshevism in the capital and dissolution in the Reich."

CONCLUSION

1. Stresemann, "Nachlass," 3068/6889/133543.
2. *Ibid.*, 3095/7004/142747 ff.
3. Robert T. Clark, *Fall of the German Republic* (London, 1935), *passim; see also* Stern, *op. cit.*, pp. 24 f., but compare Craig, *op. cit.*, p. 82.
4. It has been suggested that he might have led a National Liberal-Center-Conservative coalition, still possible in 1916, which could have demanded and taken power if the will had existed: Rosenberg, *op. cit.*, p. 115.
5. Wheeler-Bennett, *The Nemesis of Power*, pp. 208 ff.
6. "The image is incomplete," wrote Jacques Bainville at the time of Stresemann's death. "It is as if Bismarck had died before Sadowa . . .": *op. cit.*, p. 146.

BIBLIOGRAPHY

PRIMARY SOURCES

Microfilm
Germany, Auswärtiges Amt, Politisches Archiv. *Nachlass des Reichsministers Dr. Gustav Stresemann,* National Archives, Washington, D. C.

Books and Pamphlets
Bethmann-Hollweg, Th. von. *Betrachtungen zum Weltkriege.* Vol. II. Berlin: Verlag Reimar Hobbing, 1921.
Bülow, Prince Bernhard von. *Memoirs of Prince von Bülow.* Vol. III. Translated by F. A. Voigt and Geoffrey Dunlop. Boston: Little Brown and Co., 1931.
Class, Heinrich. *Wider den Strom.* Leipzig: K. F. Koehler, 1932.
D'Abernon, Viscount Edgar. *Lord D'Abernon's Diary.* Vols. I & II. London: Hodder & Stoughton, Ltd., 1929-30.
Erzberger, M. *Erlebnisse im Weltkrieg.* Stuttgart: Deutsche Verlags-Anstalt, 1920.
Germany, Reichstag. *Das Werk des Untersuchungsausschusses der Verfassunggebenden Deutschen Nationalversammlung und des Deutschen Reichstags, 1925-1929: Die Ursachen des Deutschen Zusammenbruchs in Jahr 1918.* 4. Reihe. 12 vols. Berlin: Deutsche Verlagsgesellschaft fuer Politik und Geschichte, G.m.b.H., 1929.
Germany, Reichstag. *Verhandlungen des Reichstags, Stenographische Berichte,* Vols. 227-425. Berlin: Reichsdruckerei, 1907-1929.
Grumbach, S. *Das Annexationistische Deutschland.* Lausanne: Verlag Payot & Co., 1917.
Hanssen, Hans Peter. *Diary of a Dying Empire.* Translated by Oscar Winther. Edited by R. H. Lutz *et al.* Bloomington: University of Indiana Press, 1955.
Haussmann, Conrad. *Schlaglichter.* Frankfurt a. M.: Frankfurter Societaetsdruckerei, 1924.

Kühlmann, Richard von. *Erinnerungen.* Heidelberg: Verlag Lambert Schneider, 1948.

Ludendorff, E. *The General Staff and its Problems; the History of the Relations between the High Command and the Imperial Government as Revealed by Official Documents.* Translated by F. A. Holt. 2 vols. New York: E. P. Dutton & Co., Inc., 1920.

————. *Ludendorff's Own Story.* 2 vols. New York: Harper and Brothers, 1919.

Lutz, R. H. (ed.). *The Causes of the German Collapse in 1918.* Stanford: Stanford University Press, 1934.

————. *Fall of the German Empire.* 2 vols. Stanford: Stanford University Press, 1932.

Official German Documents Relating to the World War. "The Reports of the First and Second Subcommittees Appointed by the National Constituent Assembly to Inquire into the Responsibility for the War." Translated by Carnegie Endowment. 2 vols. New York: Oxford University Press, 1923.

Payer, Friedrich von. *Von Bethmann-Hollweg bis Ebert.* Frankfurt a. M.; Frankfurter Societaetsdruckerei, 1923.

Rich, Norman and Fisher, M. H. (eds.). *The Holstein Papers.* 2 vols. Cambridge: Cambridge University Press, 1955.

Schäfer, D. *Aus Meinem Leben.* Berlin: K. F. Koehler, 1926.

Scheidemann, Philipp. *Memoiren eines Sozialdemokraten.* 2 vols. Dresden: Carl Reissner Verlag, 1928.

Statistisches Jahrbuch fuer das Deutsches Reich. Berlin: Reichsdruckerei, 1914.

Stresemann, Gustav. *Deutsches Ringen und Deutsches Hoffen.* Berlin: Reichsverlag Hermann Kalkoff, 1914.

————. *Das Deutsche Wirtschaftsleben im Kriege.* Leipzig: S. Hirzel, 1915.

————. *Englands Wirtschaftskrieg gegen Deutschland.* Stuttgart: Deutsche Verlagsanstalt, 1916.

————. *Die Entwicklung des Berliner Flaschenbiergeschaefts.* Berlin: Funcke, 1900.

————. *Industrie und Krieg.* Berlin: Selbstverlag des Bundes der Industriellen, 1916.

————. *Macht und Freiheit*. Halle: Carl Marhold, 1918.

————. *Michael Horch, Der Seewind Pfeift: Kriegsbetracht-ungen*. Berlin: Hermann Kalkoff, 1916.

————. *Reden und Schriften: Politik, Geschichte, Literatur, 1897-1926*. 2 vols. Dresden: Carl Reissner Verlag, 1926.

————. *Vermaechtnis. Der Nachlass in drei Baenden*. Edited by Henry Bernhard. 3 vols. Berlin: Verlag Ullstein, 1932.

————. *Von der Revolution bis zum Frieden von Versailles: Reden und Aufsätze*. Berlin: Staatspolitischer Verlag, G.m.b.H., 1926.

————. *Warum Müssen Wir Durchhalten?* Berlin: Kriegs-presse Amt, 1917.

Sutton, Eric (ed. and trans.). *Gustav Stresemann: His Diaries, Letters, and Papers*. 3 vols. New York: The Macmillan Co., 1935-40.

Thimme, F. (ed.). *Bethmann-Hollwegs Kriegsreden*. Stuttgart: Deutsche Verlags-Anstalt, 1919.

Tirpitz, A. von. *My Memoirs*. 2 vols. New York: Dodd, Mead & Co., 1919.

Westarp, K. *Konservative Politik im Letzten Jahrzehnt des Kai-serreiches*. Vol. II. Berlin: Deutsche Verlagsgesellschaft, 1933.

Wolff Theodor. *Der Marsch durch Zwei Jahrzehnte*. Amsterdam: Allert de Lange, 1936.

————. *Vollendete Tatsachen*. Berlin: Kronen-Verlag, G.m.b.H., 1918.

Zwoch, Gerhard. *Gustav-Stresemann-Bibliographie*. Düsseldorf: Droste Verlag, 1953.

Articles
Stresemann, Gustav. "Eine Atempause im Weltkriege," *Deutsche Stimmen*, January 10, 1917.

SECONDARY SOURCES

Unpublished Material
Edwards, Marvin L. "Gustav Stresemann: A Study in Appraisal,

1923-1948," Unpublished Master's Essay, Department of History, Columbia University, 1952.

————. "Index to Stresemann Nachlass Microfilm Collection." Unpublished. Columbia University Libraries, New York.

Warren, Donald, Jr. "Gustav Stresemann as Organizer of German Business Interests, 1901-1914," Unpublished Ph.D. Dissertation, Columbia University, 1959.

Books and Pamphlets

Bainville, Jacques. *L'Allemagne*. 2 vols. Paris: Librairie Plon, 1939.

Bauer, Heinrich. *Stresemann: Ein Deutscher Staatsmann*. Berlin: G. Stilke, 1930.

Bergsträsser, Ludwig. *Geschichte der Politischen Parteien in Deutschland*. 7th ed., Munich: Isar Verlag Dr. Günter Olzog, 1952.

Bevan, Edwyn. *German War Aims*. New York: Harper and Brothers, 1918.

Brandenburg, Erich. *Von Bismarck zum Weltkriege*. Berlin: Deutsche Verlagsgesellschaft fuer Politik und Geschichte, G.m.b.H., 1924.

Bretton, Henry L. *Stresemann and the Revision of Versailles*. Stanford: Stanford University Press, 1953.

Clark, Robert T. *Fall of the German Republic*. London: Geo. Allen & Unwin, Ltd., 1935.

Clough, S. B. *A History of the Flemish Movement in Belgium*. New York: R. R. Smith, Inc., 1930.

Craig, Gordon A. *From Bismarck to Adenauer: Aspects of German Statecraft*. Baltimore: The John Hopkins Press, 1958.

Craig, Gordon A. and Gilbert, Felix (eds.). *The Diplomats, 1919-1939*. Princeton: Princeton University Press, 1953.

Cruttwell, C. R. M. *History of the Great War, 1914-1918*. New York: Oxford University Press, 1934.

Dahlin, Ebba. *French and German Public Opinion on Declared War Aims, 1914-1918*. Stanford: Stanford University Press, 1933.

Epstein, Klaus. *Matthias Erzberger and the Dilemma of German Democracy.* Princeton: Princeton University Press, 1959.

Eschenburg, Th. *Das Kaiserreich am Scheideweg.* Berlin: Verlag fuer Kulturpolitik, 1929.

Falkenhayn, Erich von. *Die Oberste Heeresleitung, 1914-1916.* Berlin: Mittler, 1920.

Gatzke, Hans W. *Germany's Drive to the West (Drang nach Westen).* Baltimore: The Johns Hopkins Press, 1950.

————. *Stresemann and the Rearmament of Germany.* Baltimore: The Johns Hopkins Press, 1954.

Görlitz, Walter. *Gustav Stresemann.* Heidelberg: Ähren-Verlag, 1947.

Herre, Paul. *Kronprinz Wilhelm, Seine Rolle in der Deutschen Politik.* Munich: Verlag C. H. Beck, 1954.

Heuss, Theodor. *Friedrich Naumann, der Mann, das Werk, die Zeit.* Stuttgart: 2nd ed. Rainer Wunderlich Verlag Hermann Leins, 1949.

Hirth, Friedrich. *Stresemann.* Paris: Les Editions des Portiques, 1930.

Holborn, Hajo. *The Political Collapse of Europe.* New York: Alfred A. Knopf, 1951.

Jäckh, Ernst. *The New Germany.* London: Oxford University Press, 1927.

Kaufmann, Walter H. *Monarchism in the Weimar Republic.* New York: Bookman Associates, 1953.

Kürenberg, Joachim von. *The Kaiser, a Life of Wilhelm II, Last Emperor of Germany.* Translated by H. T. Russell and Herta Hagen. New York: Simon & Schuster, 1955.

Liddell Hart, B. H. *A History of the World War, 1914-1918.* Boston: Little, Brown & Co., 1934.

Löwenstein, Hubertus zu. *Tragedy of a Nation.* New York: The MacMillan Co., 1934.

————. *Stresemann, das Deutsche Schicksal in Spiegel Seines Lebens.* Frankfurt a. M.: Verlag Heinrich Scheffler, 1952.

Meyer, Henry Cord. *Mitteleuropa in German Thought and Action 1815-1945.* The Hague: Martinus Nijhoff, 1955.

Naumann, Friedrich. *Central Europe.* Translated by Christabel M. Meredith. New York: Alfred A. Knopf, 1917.

Nippold, Otfried. *The Awakening of the German People.* New York: George H. Doran Co., 1918.

Olden, Rudolf. *Stresemann.* Translated by R. T. Clark. New York: E. P. Dutton & Co., Inc., 1930.

Reiners, Ludwig. *In Europa Gehen die Lichter Aus.* Munich: Verlag C. H. Beck, 1954.

Rheinbaben, Rochus, Baron von. *Stresemann, der Mensch und der Staatsmann.* Dresden: Verlag Carl Reissner, 1928.

Rosenberg, Arthur. *The Birth of The German Republic 1871 1918.* New York: Oxford University Press, 1931.

Shuster, George N. and Bergstraesser, Arnold. *Germany, A Short History.* New York: W. W. Norton & Co., Inc., 1944.

Stern-Rubarth, Edgar. *Three Men Tried . . . Austen Chamberlain, Stresemann, Briand, and Their Fight for a New Europe.* London: Duckworth, 1939.

Taylor, A. J. P. *The Course of German History.* New York: Coward-McCann, Inc., 1946.

Tetens, T. H. *Germany Plots with the Kremlin.* New York: Henry Schuman, 1953.

Thimme, Annelise. *Gustav Stresemann; eine politische Biographie zur Geschichte der Weimarer Republik.* Hanover: O. Goedel, 1957.

Vallentin, Antonina, *Stresemann; vom Werden einer Staatsidee.* Leipzig: P. List, 1930.

Vansittart, Robert, Lord. *Lessons of My Life.* New York: Alfred A. Knopf, 1943.

Wertheimer, Mildred J. *The Pan-German League, 1890-1914.* New York: Privately printed, 1924.

Wheeler-Bennett, J. W. *The Forgotten Peace, Brest-Litovsk, March, 1918.* New York: Wm. Morrow & Co., 1939.

————. *The Nemesis of Power. The German Army in Politics, 1918-1945.* New York: St. Martin's Press, 1954.

Articles

"Adenauer und Stresemann," *Das Ganze Deutschland, Wochen-*

zeitung Fuer Politik, Kultur, Wirtschaft. Jg. 1, Nr. 10 (1949), 1.

Boas, George. "Stresemann—Object Lesson in Post-War Leadership," *Public Opinion Quarterly,* VIII (1944), No. 2, 232-243.

Bernus, Pierre. *Journal des Debats,* XXXIX, Pt. 1 (March 4, 1932), 337-338; (May 6, 1932), 694-697; (May 13, 1932), 751-753; (May 20, 1932), 781-783; (May 27, 1932), 817-818; XXXX, Pt. 1 (January 20, 1933), 103-106; (January 27, 1933), 144-145.

Economist (London), XVII (1949), 1113.

Gatzke, Hans W. "The Stresemann Papers," *Journal of Modern History,* XXVI, No. 1 (March, 1954), 49-59.

Gauvain, Auguste. *Journal des Debats,* XXXV, Pt. 1 (May 11, 1928), 768-769; (May 18, 1928), 807-808.

Haussmann, Conrad. "Herrn Stresemanns Zeugnis," *Berliner Tageblatt,* March 1, 1920.

Hearnshaw, F. J. C. *The National Review* (London), CV (November, 1935), 678-680; CX (February, 1938), 254-266; (June, 1940), 755.

Hirsch, Felix. "The Portent of Stresemann," *Commonweal,* XXXI (Summer, 1945), 486-489.

Muret, Maurice. "M. Stresemann, Homme de Lettres," *Journal des Debats,* XXXIV, Pt. 1 (October 14, 1927), 646.

Poincaré, Raymond. *L'Illustration,* No. 4655 (May 21, 1932), 90.

Schömann, Millian. "Les Jugements de Stresemann sur Napoléon," Revue d'Allemagne, VI (June 15, 1932), 493-502.

Stern, Fritz. "Adenauer and a Crisis in Weimar Democracy," *Political Science Quarterly,* LXXIII, No. 1 (March, 1958), 1-27.

Thimme, A. "Gustav Stresemann, Legende und Wirklichkeit," *Historische Zeitschrift,* Heft 181/2 (April, 1956), 287-338.

INDEX

Adenauer, K., 12
Adlon conference, 140-141
Admiralty. See Navy; Submarine warfare.
Agrarian League, 60, 61 n
Alldeutsche Blätter, 77
Alldeutscher Verband. See Pan-German League.
Allied blockade, 44 n, 81, 95, 96, 131
Allies. See Entente.
Alsace-Lorraine, 20, 30, 53, 100
Andrassy, Count J., 118
Anti-Semitism, 58 n
Antwerp, 41, 53, 75
Apt, M., 57
Arabic, 69, 82, 86-87
Arbeiter-Zeitung (Vienna), 63 n
Army, German, 19, 20, 24, 31, 35, 47-48, 112, 147, 153-159; and domestic controls, 100-101, 134 (*see also* "State of Siege"); military needs and war aims, 36, 39-41, 53-54, 76-77, 120 n. *See also* Marne; Rumania; Supreme Command; Verdun.
Army League, 38
Asia Minor, 44
Aurich, 21, 26, 51-52
Auskunftsstelle Vereinigter Verbände, 58-59
Austria-Hungary, 19, 31, 114-115, 118, 140, 141 n, 142 n, 159. *See also* Francis Ferdinand; *Mitteleuropa.*

Baden, Prince Max von. See Max, Prince von Baden.
Balkans, 44, 70
Ballin, A., 27, 42 n, 44 n, 112,

115 n, 125, 142, 155, 163
Baltic, German war aims in, 36, 40, 42-44, 53 n, 54, 118-120, 140, 153-154, 162. *See also* Russia.
Baltic Germans, 36 n, 43, 72, 120, 162
Baralong affair, 89
Bassermann, E., 29 n, 57, 59, 118, 121 n, 132-133, 136, 137 n; and Bethmann-Hollweg, 67-68, 75 n, 102, 111, 146, 163; and Bülow, 110, 111 n; and domestic reform, 100, 135, 138-139; illness and death, 124, 146 n; National Liberal leader, 20, 38, 68, 72, 166-167 (*see also* National Liberal Party); and submarine warfare, 86, 90-92, 101-104, 107; and war aims, 52, 55, 61 n, 66-68, 75 n
Bassermann, Mrs. J., 146 n, 156
Bauer, Col. M., 141-145, 148 n, 155, 156, 158 n
Bavaria, 65-67, 135
Belgium, and German war aims, 36, 40-42, 52n, 53-62, 69-77, 82, 98 n, 109, 150-155; and peace issue, 70-71, 75-76, 122, 151-152, 155, 159; and war origins, 20, 23, 54-55, 112-113. *See also* Flemish question.
Belgrade, 30, 31
Benedict XV, Pope, 151. *See also* Papal Peace Note.
Berchtold, Count L. von, 31 n
Berlin, in East-West struggle, 11
Berlin, Treaty of, 166
Berlin-Bagdad Railroad, 44
Berliner Lokalanzeiger, 22
Berliner Tageblatt, 55-57, 66-67, 118 n, 156 n